About the author

Stephen Chan is professor of international relations and was the foundation dean of law and social sciences in the School of Oriental and African Studies, University of London. He began life as the son of Chinese refugees in New Zealand, studied classics, came to the UK and then spent several years in Africa as an international civil servant. He has held visiting positions in many universities and has lectured on five continents. In his academic writings he attempts to find the fusion he believes has been important in his life. His previous books include *The Zen of International Relations*, *Robert Mugabe: A Life of Power and Violence*, *Out of Evil* and *Grasping Africa*.

Praise for this book

'International-relations scholar Chan has written a beautifully digressive plea for pluralism. The book's wide-angle viewpoint takes in André Malraux's imagining of a Chinese assassin, the Finnish construction of a national myth, contemporary African novels, Sufism and Zoroastrianism, the archangel Gabriel distracted from his "cosmic satnav" by a beautiful woman, Hans Küng's parliament of the world's religions, and the videogame *Assassin's Creed*, read (rightly) as a critique of Dick Cheney.'
Guardian

'A long and rather splendid dinner with Stephen Chan: a ten-course tasting menu from a three-star Michelin restaurant specialising in global cultural history ... I left the restaurant with a sound appreciation of the limits of my own knowledge, and a sense of how superficial are my pretensions to cosmopolitanism. So I'll be coming back for more.'
Independent

'Fascinating and energetic ... the field of international relations is given an overdue shake-up by an author unusually conversant with a wide range of literature, as well as videogames and martial arts.'
Guardian

'This is a gloriously ambitious book. No one has done anything like it. The great scholar Stephen Chan sought to write an intellectual essay which would read like a magical realist novel and succeeds. The project has produced a book light in touch but displaying extraordinary erudition, which unveils the riches and illuminating perspectives of other cultures and shows us that there are other ways of creating a better world. Forget Francis Fukuyama and Samuel Huntington. Stephen Chan is the public intellectual with his finger on the global pulse.'
Baroness Helena Kennedy

'Stephen Chan was advised not to write this book. The reader would be advised to read it and even to read it again. It is a novel of true philosophy, it is philosophy through a novel, it is impressive and fascinating. This important book is like a circle crossed by woven threads, it is a window to the world as much as a mirror to the self. Profound and refreshing.'
Tariq Ramadan

'A strikingly original disquisition on international politics, deploying all the cultural, aesthetic and technological resources of our age to revisit the most important questions of human coexistence. Chan has had the courage to subvert standard scholarly approaches to show that the very framework within which academics operate is itself an impediment to the leap of imagination required to meet the demands of our sublimely chaotic world. *The End of Certainty* is a tough-minded but elegantly written plea for a new way of thinking politically that is rooted in our common history.'
Patrick Chabal, King's College London

The end of certainty

Towards a new internationalism

STEPHEN CHAN

Zed Books
London & New York

The End of Certainty: Towards a New Internationalism
was first published in 2009 by Zed Books Ltd,
7 Cynthia Street, London N1 9JF, UK and Room 400,
175 Fifth Avenue, New York, NY 10010, USA

www.zedbooks.co.uk

Paperback edition with new Afterword published in 2010

Copyright © Stephen Chan 2009, 2010

The right of Stephen Chan to be identified as the author
of this work has been asserted by him in accordance with
the Copyright, Designs and Patents Act, 1988

Designed and typeset in ITC Bodoni Twelve
by illuminati, Grosmont, www.illuminatibooks.co.uk
Cover designed by Rogue Four Design
Index by John Barker
Printed and bound in the UK by the MPG Books Group

Distributed in the USA exclusively by Palgrave Macmillan, a division
of St Martin's Press LLC, 175 Fifth Avenue, New York, NY 10010, USA

All rights reserved. No part of this publication may be
reproduced, stored in a retrieval system or transmitted in any
form or by any means, electronic, mechanical, photocopying or
otherwise, without the prior permission of Zed Books Ltd.

A catalogue record for this book is available from the British Library
Library of Congress Cataloging in Publication Data available

ISBN 978 1 84813 402 7 Pb

Contents

Preface

I am advised not to write this book. Firstly, because there is no tradition of the intellectually formed and philosophically informed essay in Britain that, nevertheless, aspires to be accessible to a wide reading public. There are the US models of writers such as Edward Said and Susan Sontag, and of course the French models ranging from the dashing extremes of André Malraux and Bernard-Henri Lévy to the brooding intensities of Sartre. I am advised I shall be accused of putting on airs. London is not New York or Paris, the Thames is not the Hudson or the Seine. The British digression into thought is via historical works – empirical, narrative, with foundations, girders and roofbeams to anchor any speculation. There is no Left Bank, there is the *politesse* of Bloomsbury.

And that is the second body of advice. I am advised not to write this book because it will do me no good in my professional career as an academic. Whether I work in a Bloomsbury institution or not – but particularly if I do – the nation's officialised and centralised measures, adjudications and financing of research,

upon which universities depend, have crafted thought into carefully policed technical parameters. This is not a book that can
be entered in any Research Assessment Exercise, or be assessed
by any governmental 'bibliometric' scheme, and my reputation
will fall.

I wish to write this book, however, precisely because there is
an intellectual vacuum in British political and social life. Three
decades of dogged soundbite phraseologies of both Thatcherism
and Blairism have made debate a contest between assertions of
certainty, and these certainties are about the best form of coercion to apply in any international moral impasse. Intellectuals
sign petitions, perhaps march in the streets, attempt their own
soundbites when broadcasting, but confine their extended energies to debate and discourse among themselves. This discourse
borrows from continental thought – the British being still not
very good at original philosophy – and is, because continental
thinkers have said it is, meant to be emancipating. By itself, it
emancipates no one. The French tradition was one of thought
coupled with action – even if the two were not always properly related. The German tradition remembers the concentration camps
and was meant to make philosophy too critical, and too complex,
ever to be appropriated by dictators again. What has happened
is that it is now too complex to be spoken in public by anyone.
The illusion of emancipation exists in small classrooms.

Outside the classrooms of Bloomsbury a world burns with
slaughters and starvations and serious illnesses. No word is
enough for those who die in such fires. And no book, whether
technical or not, is enough. This book is an unashamed, perhaps
overweening, effort to inaugurate a new anglophone tradition:
to speak about complex things, with imagination, in public; to
let imagination carry some of the complexity; and to discharge
an intellectual's public role – to say 'this is how the world is,

this is not how the world should be, this is how to think about the world as we wish it to be, this is how to turn that wish into action, this is how not to despair when action fails, this is how to try again, this is how to defy the rulers, this is how to make the rulers themselves think.'

The book is constructed like a meandering novel. Characters and points of thought disappear, reappear and are developed in unusual ways. I asked, 'What would a magical realist novel look like as an intellectual essay?' Even so, it became necessary to lighten such an approach, to vary it. There are three parts to this book. The first six chapters are where key themes and thoughts are introduced and discussed, and weave in and out, and much play is made upon the imagination of readers; this is particularly the case in the first two chapters. The second part comprises three chapters and, without losing the ethos of the book, provides a more sustained look at its subject matter. The third part, a long concluding chapter, seeks to render all the woven threads into a rainbow scarf that can be worn, with sober dark coats if necessary, to ward off the winters of our troubled world.

I apologise to those readers who may find this approach initially annoying or unsettling. I do hope they can persevere to the end, treating the book with the same patience as a novel. In anglophone literature there are few examples of such an approach. The closest there is in any sustained European tradition – even if it is a minority aspect of a larger tradition – is in francophone work. Hélène Cixous's apparently stream-of-consciousness but carefully plotted meditation on the life of Jacques Derrida is a case in point.[1] But *my* point is that, in the literatures of many

---

1. Hélène Cixous, *Portrait of Jacques Derrida as a Young Jewish Saint*, New York: Columbia University Press, 2001.

of the cultures we misunderstand, this approach to reasoning is much more common and mainstream. I have tried to convey the method in English.

I make acknowledgements at the end of the book. I am of course grateful to many people, including many kind (and not so kind) sceptics who made me go away and rethink my work. What is here contains, I am confident, many spectacular faults. They are mine alone.

This book also concludes my part of a very long conversation with my brothers and sisters. It has gone on exactly 38 years. It is unlikely to satisfy all members of my family – and it may fail to satisfy many readers at all – but it was written in a spirit of seeking a way forward to a new and better world.

Pimlico, London, March 2008

A story introduces it

This story was told me in Asmara in February 1993, on the eve of the independence of Eritrea. I was sequestered in a government hotel, surrounded by UN election monitors – many of whom had never ventured far from Manhattan. They were a third-string team. The first string was monitoring a fraught election in Cambodia. There was no hot water and the team complained bitterly. Every morning, however, before the team awoke, an antique truck with a makeshift tank would arrive in the hotel car park; the driver would lift a hidden flagstone and pump water into the hotel reservoir. We had the only running water in town, but the monitors never did realise this. In Cambodia meanwhile, much of the election monitoring was being done by young volunteers. It was these who suffered the most casualties and deaths while deployed in the rural areas. In the capital, the first string enjoyed, I am told, hot water.

This is not the story. This is to say how one approaches stories. It depends upon one's vantage point – sleepily complaining in a hotel or under fire. The following story may be approached as

a romance, as an act of chivalry, as an act of undisciplined sol-
diery, as a quaint episode amidst the barbarism of war. Perhaps
it is being read in a warm bath. This is the story.

In mountainous terrain, an Eritrean detachment found itself
ambushed one night by Ethiopian soldiers. Trained and officered
by Soviet personnel, the Ethiopians had become a formidable
force. The Eritreans, comprising both male and female combat-
ants, fired back, but all knew they were probably destined shortly
to die. One of the male fighters lay beside a female fighter, both
firing into the darkness. Neither knew the other's feelings, but
each had been admiring the other, and quietly falling in love
for some time. Now, they turned to each other, their eyes met,
and they knew that each was cherished. They had barely time
to smile at this recognition when an Ethiopian bullet killed the
female fighter. Beside himself with the suddenness of both love's
requital and death, the remaining fighter stood up and ferociously charged the Ethiopian lines. The Ethiopians could not
believe the madness of this lone act and momentarily recoiled,
before shooting him down. But the mad attack had bought just
enough time and distraction for his comrades to retreat. This
is the story as it was told to me by one of those who survived
that night.

What does the story mean? It is indeed a story of love, but
it was not a peaceful love, not a pacifist or Christian love. It
is a story of bravery, but it was not a self-conscious bravery. It
is a story of war, but war is not meant to contain romance and
sentimentality. It is a story of ambush and survival, but many
who were not in the forefront of the story died that night without
commemoration. It is a story of ideologies clashing in the field,
but many who fought and died on that field were conscripts who
also wanted to love and survive. It is a story from the Eritrean
fight for freedom, but that freedom has now been betrayed.

These are not unusual conjunctures. Why raise them from a war that was largely unknown, even though it lasted thirty years, in a country that is also largely unknown? The Eritrean cause was not, in fairness, completely ignored. New Zealanders are revered in Eritrea, partly because of a New Zealand (turned Australian) eye surgeon and his field support for the fighters, partly because during the 1984 famine a New Zealand ship managed to land a cargo of food relief for the Eritreans, despite Ethiopian warnings and threats. But, whether unknown or known partly, Eritrea knows us. In a way, the demeanour of the liberation struggle reflected the demeanour of the metropolitan 1960s, and the image Western protesters had of what a liberation struggle should be. The early efforts at feminism in the West meant also that, for the first time in an African war, female soldiers fought on an equal footing with their male counterparts. Popular musical culture in the west meant that the young Eritrean fighters grew their hair like Jimi Hendrix and, in the mountains using field generators, electrified their zithers to create what is now a national music that sounds directly derived from the distorted and sliding guitar chords of 'All Along the Watchtower'. These are conjunctures that suggest, in one story, exotica (when we hear it for the first time) and familiarity (when they tell it to a Western audience). But the familiarity has to be explained to us. Sometimes a conjuncture is not immediately a conjuncture. This book derives from that basic point.

The book derives from a second basic point. On that same trip to Eritrea, not far from the bombed-out ruins of Massawa – by the Red Sea, ships laden with Toyotas already beginning to arrive at the hastily refurbished dock – I visited an execution ground used by the Ethiopian dictator Mengistu. A green sheet-metal wall had been roughly thrown around it. Untying one knotted rope allowed access. Inside, stacked more or less in ammunition crates, some very much less, were the bleached remains of 600 Ethiopian officers who had rebelled against the tyrant. Not all the remains had been sufficiently eaten away to be bleached. Perhaps a certain jadedness either disfigures, or preserves, the emotions. I am told my first thoughts could not be typical. 'I hope they died bravely, with some dignity' was what I thought. And, even if bravery is not universal, the grieving of their families would be. The second point is that, within or without our various conjunctures, grief unites the human species and, as I hope to demonstrate, so does a capacity for compassion.

And to conclude with something more familiar: swimming in the Red Sea, I met a young Eritrean; he was in Massawa to mourn his brother who had died in the battle for the city. We talked about the terrible famine just nine years earlier in 1984. When he heard where I lived, he said, 'I am told that there was a singer then who tried to help us.' I do not wish to say in this book that we, in the West, have forgotten compassion. Not always, but often, we misdirect it, having allowed it to well up amidst our own misunderstandings. Bob Geldof did not misunderstand at least the idea of hunger. Did we, however, misunderstand the nature of relief required, and send only food?

I

A failed species?

When a Jehovah's Witness knocks on your door he will wish to speak, and will begin by citing the terrors of the world: war, famine, disease – the harbingers of death – all the riders and wild horses of the Apocalypse. And you will be torn by annoyance at the gross renditions of his account, knowing he is leading to an offer of gross redemption, and admiration for the fact that, perhaps on a cold winter's day, he is standing there and putting in the freezing hours to trudge his sermon door to door – the draught horse of the Apocalypse and the salvation to come. And you listen out of courtesy and respect: for you know these Witnesses blazed a civil rights record for free speech and worship in the United States, were thrown into concentration camps in Nazi Germany, and were the subject of pogroms from Stalin's Russia to Banda's Malawi; and you know that, amidst the white settler states of Africa which lorded it over the population, the authorities greatly resented the Witness missionaries with their 'egalitarian heritage and oppositional

ethics'.[1] But, finally, courtesy's five minutes elapse, you close
your door and pour coffee for one person, and you think that
the world's problems are terrifying but not simple, nothing that
the flourish of a few scriptures can diagnose or answer.

For even the rider of the black horse of the Apocalypse carried
scales to measure hunger. What the Witness at your door does
not do is measure causes, distribution, types of consequence
and types of suffering. In particular, he or she does not measure
the distribution of recent wars and hunger: why it is that famine
seems to stalk Africa in particular, while the industrialised world
is curiously entitled to food; why it is that wars seem now to take
place on the borderlands of the industrialised world, and that
world wears the diamonds and burns the oil that come from the
borderlands but, otherwise, cares little for all their other wars.
Why it is that, even within those borderlands, the distribution
of suffering is class-related and age-related and, more often than
not, also gender-related – so that the young, female poor are
the first to grow poorer. And why it is that, so far as the rider of
the pale horse of disease unto death is concerned, AIDS should
ravage the borderlands while those minority sufferers in the
metropole have access to pharmaceuticals that stall and contain
the sickness. The Witness does not cite the harmful (and sometimes positive) effect of multinationals, and nor does he mention
the resistance of antiglobalist protesters. The witness does not
mention resistance at all, and certainly has not even imagined
a resistance to war and suffering within the very borderlands he
dismisses as fodder for the fulfilment of prophecy. And the Witness, consumed by the scriptures he carries, and the pre-thinking
they have contributed to his own thought, imagines not at all
the myths, spiritual impulses, songs, literature and philosophy

---

1. Gerald Horne, *From the Barrel of a Gun: The United States and the War against Zimbabwe, 1965–1980*, Chapel Hill: University of North Carolina Press, 2001, p. 97.

that have, themselves together, imagined into existence whole nations, whole movements and great systems of thought – and which allow us to contrive a hope that, somehow, we might finally imagine one world (if only we might overcome the nationalisms, ideologies and philosophies that divide us).

It was the imagination of ourselves into nations, however, that was a great hallmark of the twentieth century. More states became independent then than at any other time. Nor was this confined to the Third World. Europe has been imagining and re-imagining itself constantly: now one Germany, then two, then one again; various configurations of the Balkan states; one Czechoslovakia, then divided into two; struggle over what might be called Ireland and, within Britain itself, end-of-century devolutions to Scotland and Wales. The United Kingdom examples apart, what has been happening in Europe has been, first, the imagination of nations and, then, the political organisation of them into states – often with great struggle. But it was the imagination that came first – sometimes led by devious rulers and ruling parties; sometimes spontaneous – more often than not imbued with visions and constructs of antiquities, heritage and lineage, and the nobilities said to reside in them all.

One example may, in particular, be seen as writ large, although at first sight it is inconspicuous – and this is the example of Finland. It became officially independent only at the end of 1917, after a modern history of Swedish and then Russian domination. It spent years within the Soviet shadow, without ever being absorbed into the Soviet Union. Indeed, one of the enduring images of the early Second World War is the utterly heroic and completely hopeless charge of mounted Finnish cavalry units against Stalin's tanks. Sabres drawn, urging their horses on in the winter snow, they all surely knew that this was a stupid – if romantic – way to die. For a hundred years before independence, Finland had been emerging from Swedish cultural influence. The sense of nationhood the cavalrymen died for was only one generation older than themselves in its construct, and its construct – although romantic – was deliberately artificial. Not the ingredients of the construct, but its methods. As the great Finnish diplomat Max Jakobson put it: 'A nation is made not born. Nationhood is a frame of mind. A tribe, or an ethnic identity, is transformed into a nation by the development of a consciousness of a shared past and a common destiny. Such a consciousness can only be created by the historians and poets, artists and composers.'[2] In Finland's case the work of the poets and composers, in constructing artefacts to induce or consolidate 'a frame of mind', was highly visible and audible. In 1835, Elias Lonrot, a district health officer with a scholarly interest in folk song, published *The Kalevala*, which was described as a set of old Karelian poems about the ancient times of the Finnish people. Lonrot had simply collected, then anthologised, a great many folk songs and poems – but he anthologised them in a narrative sequence; and he constructed bridging passages. The result was not a disparate collection but an epic poem, and it was almost immediately adopted as *the* epic poem of the nascent Finnish nation. It is an immense poem, and its construct deliberately sets out to rival Homer, and to establish a mythic sense of long-standing Finnish cosmology. The heroes liberate the sun, moon and stars. The same heroes are also forever taking saunas and, literally clean-limbed, are given to duels where their swords remain scabbarded, and they sing each other into the swamplands of what they call 'the nation growing'.

It was the composer Jean Sibelius, born thirty years after Lonrot published *The Kalevala*, who ensured the world knew

---

2. Max Jakobson, *Finland: Myth and Reality*, Helsinki: Otava, 1987, p. 21.

about the themes at least of the new epic. Tone poems, such as *The Swan of Tuonela*, refer directly to Lonrot's poem; and his best-known work, *Finlandia*, aspires to be a musical history of the enslavement, then liberation, of the Finnish people. The long after-effects of *Finlandia* could not have been anticipated by Sibelius but, ten years after his death, in 1967, the doomed soldiers of the new nationalism of Biafra – under African skies and not charging across snow – marched to defeat in time with their new national anthem, drawn from *Finlandia*.

The Finnish example is very neat but, even in Finland, it was never as easy as partial hindsight suggests. 'What' is imagined, 'how' it is imagined, and 'why', inaugurate a tripartite series of investigations. Not every nation has a convenient Lonrot, and, since he came at an appropriate moment, there is a fourth investigation called 'when'. Timing is everything, nationalism not being a simple aggregate. But, in so far as all these are investigations of the imagination, and should take into account clashes of imagination, it might be fair to suggest that what Jakobson neglected to say was something to do with the successful politicisation of an imagined community – and that politically realised community either supressed others, or suppressed (or subsumed) the imagination of others. The latter can take much time. In Finland, it took decades after 1917 before – *The Kalevala* apart – there was a national literature written in Finnish rather than Swedish. Even a dictator in a ruthless hurry must allow some time for an organic process to mulch itself into soil for 'the nation growing'; and he has to use pre-existing fragments at least of cultural identity, writing or composing them into a plausible and persuasive epic.

This is why the experiments in African nation-building, conducted by Kaunda in Zambia and Nyerere in Tanzania, still seem remarkable. In Zambia, there are some seventy-two languages and seventy-two ways to articulate a sense of self and community. For years, Zambian radio would repeat the mantra, 'One Zambia, One Nation', while Kaunda sought to fashion a political philosophy that overcame linguistic and spiritual differences by the simple assertion of English and Christianity, and that purported to fuse together every worthwhile ethnic value. It was an African humanism driven by a Christian cement – for what was worthwhile was whatever accorded with the gospel creed and, to an extent, the democratic socialism of English thinkers such as Harold Laski. In what became Tanzania, in its early days as Tanganyika, Nyerere propagated a philosophy of *ujamaa*, a self-reliance said to reside also in African history. It involved massive dislocations in what had become African in his country, disrupting patterns of settlement and relocating them into *ujamaa* villages, where the new philosophy could be scientifically put into organised operation. It was a disastrous effort at social engineering, but Nyerere's people, though not believing their leader's vision, went along with it. When Nyerere appeared before them on the hustings, speaking of his vision and asserting that it was historically and culturally African, he was seldom challenged, 'because he speaks in a language – literally and figuratively – known to his audience, he is easy to accept partially: he can be both agreed with and ignored.'[3] Neither *ujamaa* nor his translations of Shakespeare into Swahili have survived this very gentle man. There had better be a fifth investigation for students of nationalism and its cultural imagination: what element of urgency is required to drive the process forward? Must there be a sense of threat or danger? Must there be, as some have suggested, an industrial or technological base which can facilitate the sense of community

3. Henry Bienen, *Tanzania: Party Transformation and Economic Development*, Princeton: Princeton University Press, 1967, p. 252.

by providing the artefacts that imagination decrees a nation's culture should need?

To an extent, these are second-order questions. Danger and technology, by themselves, do not imagine a nation. They may hasten and facilitate, provide the means to consolidate what has been imagined, but they are not themselves imagination or culture, memory or rememory. Imagination takes not so much memory, but rememory, forward. It imagines a foundation past into the future. The past must be related to the future and cannot be accurate and dispassionate history. Getting the fit right is a fortuitous and timely moment. The fit has to be politicised, in order to attract support – or suppress dissent – and then it must be operationalised. Here, technological instruments may be important – but Gandhi's insistent symbol of himself at an antique spinning wheel (this wheel containing also an inner symbol of life cycles and incarnations, the past always becoming future) suggested not. But the fit cannot be gerrymandered. What Nyerere and Kaunda, but particularly Kaunda, did was to amalgamate a Christian romanticism (all men could be righteous as they moved to modernity) with a partially sacralised version of history (traditional African values could carry the mandate of modernity – elevating a partly mythical version of these values, and elevating also its capacity to fit modern development) and an internationalised secular romanticism (the social welfare state was possible, and human engineering was both its animation and constantly improved product). His Zambian electorate, like that in Tanzania, never did find it persuasive. Zambians became the fellow travellers, not the citizens of the new nationalism. The first-order question has to be: how much romanticism, and how much bone-hard rationality, must go into the mix of imagination? If the mix is not right, the fit cannot be persuasive and cannot be operationalised. To a very large extent, this question of how to mix romanticism and rationality has haunted the great nationalisms of the world for over 200 years. And, yes, at a certain point, the response to danger carries it forward; but danger must have something to carry forward.

The years of eighteenth-century Enlightenment – when philosophy and the drive to republicanism seemed to coincide, and those republics were meant to be repositories of rights for individual citizens, and those rights had a philosophical foundation – have continued to mark Western thought and action. The older Greek idea that what was right followed what was natural, and the Renaissance idea that what was right had a centre in human agency and urgency, were now followed by the Enlightenment idea that what was right followed what was moral – and what was moral was both universal and equitable. The increasing interest and skill in science, alongside philosophy, suggested that man was both humane and rational; that thought was logical; and that thoughtful government should also be orderly, logical, and non-arbitrary and, because also moral, it had to be fair. The hierarchies of monarchy, aristocracy and church were supplanted or ceased to be first-principle means of government. This is to put it in terms that flatter the Enlightenment, since they are terms that are the Enlightenment's own. There was, however, a concurrent body of thought and action, usually described as Romanticism, personified by dashing poets, heroic but irrational revolutionaries, and which was certainly apparent in the new classical music of composers like Beethoven (even though it was a later generation of music that came to be classified, in the accepted typologies, as romantic).

In a way, Enlightenment philosophy contained within it a romantic streak, so that logical thought and romantic thought were not so much concurrent as interlinked and symbiotic. Kant's sense of a universal morality as a given condition, Hegel's sense of a motivating spirit of history, provided what were essentially illogical and unscientific foundations for complex and logical philosophical systems. And the entire idealism and logical purity of Enlightenment was counterpoised by Byron's and Goethe's renditions of the Faust story – the scientist who wanted it all; selling his soul that was, after all, merely antique; but mixing the very human attributes of desire, the will towards possession and power, nobility and imperfection, with the drive for knowledge. This much is not a remarkable observation. Even Bertrand Russell included a chapter on Byron, alongside more systematic thinkers, in his *History of Western Philosophy.* What is not often remarked, by contrast, is the systematic (if not always internally logical) construction of an apparatus of narrative symbols that sought to displace Christian symbolism and iconography with its own pictorial and suggestive power. The place of Masonic thought and symbols is curiously invisible in the histories of republican revolutions – even though starkly visible on US dollar bills. The pyramid and the eye seem design curiosities now but they were, at the time of the American Revolution, the signs of an underground effort to supplant established religion – tarbrushed with conservatism and allegiance to the old order – with a secular system, in that it was not traditionally 'religious', but which offered all the same an alternative spiritual history of the world since Christ, and how that history had roots in the very first empire of signs, monuments, and ceremonies at the interface of earth and the universe, in Egypt.

It is as if the new American nationalism had to be furbished with something discernibly ancient – and it is the element of discernibility that was lacking in the Zambian and Tanzanian efforts. It was not that they had no technological base; they had no sets of focus for imagination, and imagination's pathway into thought. The philosophies of Kaunda and Nyerere were didactic and pedagogical – not given to the glimpse of epiphany that they were right because a thickly condensed romanticism *carried* them into rightness.

This is, of course, to labour an essentially modest example. The US was not set ablaze by Masonic symbols. Many of the founding fathers were, however. Moreover, the confidentiality of the Lodge made the brotherhoods ideal communities in which plotting and organisation could take place. And the whole idea of a 'new world' demanded also an alternative, if not immediately new, mythology of spiritual power. The symbol, in short, must be powerful enough to carry people into risk and commitment, even if only the ringleaders. This is certainly what happened in Nazi Germany, as the Third Reich re-created a German national-ism, but here symbols inspired and carried great multitudes. Here, the intensity of symbols and their cemented alliance with other emblems of the nation – so that each cross-referenced, interpreted and reinforced the other – were of vast importance. Thus, the visual use of the cross brought into Nazi modernity the historical romances of the Teutonic Knights, and the use of the swastika – the cross which sought to link each arm with the next, the continuing cross – evoked a prehistorical anchor to the Nazi nation, earlier and more arcane than any possessed by its rivals. The appropriation of philosophy – so that Hegel's spirit of history moved to a Nazi apotheosis, if not consummation, and did so by means of Nietzsche's will to power, flavoured by Goethe's literary nobility, and amplified by Wagner's orchestrations of gods and thunder, all funnelled through to the great Nuremburg rally, where spectacle, symbol, ritual visual performance, and the weight of one uniform series of shouted chants – resounded convincingly of a nation to which technology and military might merely gave means for expansion; of asserting not so much a na-tionalism, but that nationalism's security and primacy over other nationalisms, and even the internationalism of the prevailing world order. We shall not see such fusion, on such a grand scale, again. But the impulse towards a fusion of rational and planned, with a selected hoard of romances, was apparent throughout the twentieth century. Kaunda and Nyerere did not have sufficient believable romance in their philosophies, but others did.

When the Red Army marched triumphantly into the Square of Heavenly Peace, Mao stood on a podium high above the parade. Who could believe the peasant soldiers could now march in such drilled formation? In front of Mao was a web microphone. Into it he sang, or chanted, the antique poem of liberation – like a shaman calling to ancestral spirits that it had been done as they would have wished. It sounded very like the folk songs Lonrot recorded for *The Kalevala*, almost supernatural in their singing from the earth – something Sibelius never quite replicated in his tone poems.[4] The fusions of Marxist and Chinese thought during Mao's reign are well known – at least in outline – but the ceremonial importance of Mao's dirge-like chant above the square is not. The Red Army often recruited its peasant soldiers through a calculated use of Mao's favourite historical novel, *The Water Margin*. Written in the thirteenth century, it is a novel of rebellion and revolution against the established and corrupt order. Each of 108 outlawed heroes, drawn from all walks of life – from generals and judges to peasants and fishermen – fought alongside each other as equals. This was not only striking to a Chinese audience, it was to its early Western translator, Pearl Buck, who named her version *All Men Are Brothers*. But it was these brothers who, by their equal commitment to justice, despite being outlawed by a vengeful regime, gained the mandate of heaven. In the final chapter, their leader asks, 'who would

---

4. I am grateful to Professor Vilho Harle for sharing archive recordings of these folk songs with me.

believe, my brothers, that I, a humble clerk, should be born under a star of heaven?' Each of the heroes was mandated by a star. The soldiers of the Red Army made much of the red stars on their caps, and their recruiting cadres made the direct link between the novel's uprising and their own. In that novel, the most abject peasant could find an archetype who, all the same, rose up. To rise, when heaven willed it – at the moment of heaven's allowance – and to fight under a star is the stuff of romance. But, before he settled down to the early brutalities of rule, Mao stood above the square and, through the old web microphone, claimed the mandate of heaven.

The novel had a more curious impact in the Japan of the nineteenth century. It gave rise to an industry of paintings and posters, depicting the 108 heroes: long of hair, perfect of physique – their clothes always being torn off by enemies they were sure to overcome – and their backs covered in tattoos. Because the 108 were outlaws, outsiders, they became in Japan the archetype for the Yakuza, the alternative society made criminal. It was not an ingredient in a cultural nationalism that was inventing and re-inventing its samurai ethos, but an antidote to that nationalism; but even an outlaw culture needs its symbols, and the marked and indelibly inked body is an inerasable symbol.

The declaration of symbols is, in this case, evident enough. That the inspiration should have come from China to a very different Japan is the matter for comment. The relationship, given the history of the two countries, is deeply ambivalent. Forms and levels of ambivalence are, however, part of the equation – and especially so when nationalism must encounter internationalism. It is still the case, as the postcolonial world is reforged into something passably autochthonous, that the presentation of a national must be fitted with the trappings of what has been dominant international learning. Thus the translator of the great

Persian text, Ferdowsi's eleventh-century *The Epic of the Kings*, labours in his introduction to draw parallels between the heroic character Rostam and Achilles; Key Kavus and Agamemnon; Giv and Ajax – not stopping until all the major figures in the *Iliad* are mated. He does, however, also draw a parallel between the 'fragile social order' of Ancient Greek times and the 'tension and strife' of the Persian epic, but then, almost casually, injects the judgement that 'Ferdowsi has endowed his cosmos with a higher morality and thus the lapses of his heroes are more grave and aweful [*sic*].'[5] Although *The Epic of the Kings* was an effort to write back to a recently lost Zoroastrianism, the sense of higher morality, even in the succeeding Islamic years, was never lost in Persian literature. Sufi epics, such as 'Attar's thirteenth-century *The Speech of the Birds*, speak of the debate between Greek thought – 'the thought of Alexander' – and the higher morality of divine revelation. In both cases, Zoroastrian and Islamic, the national is counterpoised with the international, but within an ambivalence that allows the national to emerge superior.

The national is here both insecure and a construction of security. Although it should be pointed out that Ferdowsi is concerned not so much with Greek thought – unlike his later translator – as with recounting events and wars involving, among others, wars between the Persians and the Roman armies of the Caesars. This recalled the era from Pompey, through the next two hundred years, as the two great empires sought to establish fitting borders. *The Epic of the Kings* gives a view of this conflict that is non-Roman. It also gives a view that is strikingly cosmopolitan: in one chapter alone, Persian ruler, Roman Caesar, the Khan of China, four Greek philosophers, a Christian city and a debate on Hinduism (not to mention a

---

5. Ferdowsi, *Shahnameh: The Epic of the Kings*, Tehran: Yassavoli, 2001, p. xiii.

Roman princess and forty Greek eunuchs 'who captivated the heart') make an appearance. But the highlight is when a Zoro-astrian philosopher lectures the Roman Caesar on Christianity, and his intellectual merits are rewarded by Roman approval; and Roman military support for his Zoroastrian king. In this chapter, on one of only two occasions in the entire epic, an angel comes to intervene in the affairs of men, blessing in effect the righteous and philosophically attended king. There is here a confidence that the national, the Persian, is greater than the international – because it is able to encompass all that is inter-national, both in the original terms of its thought and in the national capacity to gloss and interpret international thought and to give then a national thoughtfulness that is superior. In all epics, from all cultures, this is rare; and, although Persia became Islamic, this sense of the cosmopolitan continued to inform it until more recent times, when the international once again rendered the national insecure.

Even the Iranian Revolution, when it adopted a national con-stitution in 1979, far from enshrining a purely Islamic document for what was meant to be an Islamic revolution, constructed an Islamic document that was full of secular exceptional provision – precisely so that Iran could still function within a species of modernity. This has, of course, rendered the constitution suf-ficiently ambivalent, at least in parts, for the political struggle between conservative clerics and reformers to be anchored upon it. Command its interpretation, and both law and the precedent for further legislation are commanded. Amassing a vast body of petty legislation – for example, laws on motor traffic, which have no possible emanation from the Quran or sharia – provides an entry point for juristic debate. Of greater consequence, however, is the Islamic precept of emergency. 'Emergencies make it permissible to do what is forbidden', provided there is no original desire to perform the forbidden. The juristic debate would thus permit at least the contention that 'emergency' would include conditions of compulsion, distress and disadvantage.[6] Since these may be subjectively felt, the element of an individual right is instantly introduced. This does not, in itself, provide an automatic avenue for Western notions of individualism and rights. There are centuries of Islamic philosophical debate as to the nature of human standing within the universe, and to what extent humanity in general, or any human, can be autonomous. God may be the 'necessary existent', and all humans may be merely 'contingently existent' – that is, existing necessarily and dependently on God; but God wishes our welfare and, thus, does not desire our wilful self-harm; God recognises our existence is contingent on more than Him alone, and Himself awards the right to self-protection in the face of oppressive circumstance. However, and the extent of this is what has been for centuries debated, God wishes us also to advance towards Him – that is, attain some progressive measure of self-perfection.

This is the Sufi and, to an extent, Ismaili position – so that the eleventh-century Ismaili philosopher Nasir Khusraw saw self-perfection as self-realisation, which could be willed as a self-requirement. Moreover, in going beyond the position of God as 'Necessary Existent', Khusraw formulated the view of God as 'First', meaning both prior and all-encompassing. However, this 'Firstness' 'is the Intellect and nothing is hidden from it',[7] providing for Khusraw, particularly in the inflections of his poetry, an avenue for the self-exercise of the intellect within humans – on the basis that it aspired towards union with the 'First'.

---

6. Asghar Schirazi, *The Constitution of Iran: Politics in the Islamic Republic*, London: I.B. Tauris, 1998, pp. 173 and 202, nn. 1, 2.

7. Nasir Khusraw, *Knowledge and Liberation: A Treatise on Philosophical Theology*, London: I.B. Tauris, 1999, p. 92.

Khusraw was much persecuted in his lifetime, and his constant self-vindication was simply that he was using his intellect.

> Better it is to sleep with noble intellect in a burning furnace
> Than to accompany low-born fools in royal tents.[8]

Having said that, there is no doubt that the debate in today's Iran owes also, but not entirely, to western thought. Khusraw himself established his positions in debate with Aristotelians and Platonists. Avicenna, famed as a thinker who fused Islamic with Aristotelian thought, was a contemporary. The question is to do not only with the proportions of the influences that might be mixed together, but the methodologies of mixing; and the securities or insecurities that the mixing (or effort to ban mixing) might entail.

Declaring the barricades to mixing

The insecurities of mixing are crystallised in those fleeting moments of history when a triumph has occurred, a revolution has been won, and the thought that underpins triumph needs to be safeguarded, preserved for posterity and made hegemonic for the foreseeable future. The revolution will eat its children if they question the stability and jurisdiction of that instance of thought made flesh. Some have seen that of the Iranian Revolution; but, as noted above, the 1979 constitution had itself to be, even if contingently, mixed. The more insidious example is that moment of global hegemony which seemed to say 'enough mix already; this far and no further; the description of Western values is now triumphant, should be concretised, have barricades built around it, and those barricades should move strategically outwards

---

8. From his long poem, *Divan*, cited at length in Alice C. Hunsberger, *Nasir Khusraw: The Ruby of Badakhshan*, London: I.B. Tauris, 2000, p. 254.

– bringing more world into the domain of one mode of thought on all values.' This is, of course, to put it very broadly; however, this is what was said – with more nuance but not more precision – by thinkers who arose in the wake of 1989, the fall of the Berlin Wall, and the Western victory in the first Gulf War.

Francis Fukuyama's 1989 article became almost a leitmotif of the US triumphalism of the period. Borrowing from Hegel's image of the spirit of history moving to its moment of self-perfection and self-consummation, he declared the 'end of history'; history could get no better; the triumph of liberalism was what history had sought and it would seek no more. It was a brief article and a brief argument, but was enormously influential. It clothed triumphalism with, if not thought, then with the image of thought – or at least with an image of history. If this was insidious, Fukuyama's book-length follow-up evoked the image of something sinister.[9] Perhaps the 'last man of history', the creature of liberalism, would not be able to sustain his triumph. Mixing images drawn from Nietzsche with those from Hegel, the 'last men' might become 'men without chests', having desire and reason, but lacking *thymos*, the craving and demand for recognition; in short, too comfortable to sustain through action their own thought. By contrast, there was the danger of a new breed of 'first men', anxious to restart history on their own terms. These would be deprived and uncomfortable men; they would not have desire and reason, but be consumed by *thymos* alone. Without desire and reason they would be 'bestial', slaves who would rise against their masters. Above all, they should not be allowed to restart history.

The images used here, although poetic and rhetorical, were powerful. Above all, they suggested the appropriation

---

9. Francis Fukuyama, 'The End of History?', *The National Interest* 16, Summer 1989; Francis Fukuyama, *The End of History and the Last Man*, London: Penguin, 1992.

by liberalism, by the West, of all civilised desire and reason. Thought did not ride with the 'first men'. What rode with them seemed like the horsemen of an apocalypse.

It is the notion that the horsemen could be fenced off from the plains and pastures of the West that lay at the heart of Samuel Huntington's appeal. If Fukuyama was taken into the celebration of the first Gulf War, Huntington's thought lay close to the origins of the second, particularly in so far as a link was made between the 'war on terror' and the war on Iraq. In any case, the two wars were against men who were sinister, and men who died and killed without thought – and who were against the civilised thought and values, the reason, of the West. Huntington's work on the 'clash of civilizations' was exactly that something should be fenced off.[10] The war on terror also chose to take the fight to those who, in a 'bestial' manner, had leapt the fence and had, themselves, attacked the homeland of thought and values. And, although Huntington protested he had never himself proposed a moratorium on the mixing of cultural and differently civilised values, the descendant Bush administration seemed to freeze in time all that the US had become – so that it would not be made into anything else – and this frozen moment of pure thought and value would be defended with renewed *thymos*. This freezing of a moment into purity is hardly new and, to be fair, has been conducted with far greater vehemence by others. As noted above, the Nazi use of Hegel and Nietzsche set into motion extremes and purities that have not been attempted since – except perhaps in Cambodia and the restarting of history from Year Zero by the Khmer Rouge. The war on terrorism, starting from Ground Zero,

10. Samuel P. Huntington, 'The Clash of Civilizations?', *Foreign Affairs*, Summer 1993; Samuel P. Huntington, *The Clash of Civilizations and the Remaking of World Order*, New York: Simon & Schuster, 1996.

is an unfortunate duplication of terminology; but, even if the extremes are less, the global effect is set to be momentous.

Who starts what and why, and who resists whom, what and why, becomes an endless dialectical maze of accusations and interrogations. How things are started and resisted form the more interesting questions, and are the questions asked less frequently than the making of accusations. The temptation is to say that the respective sides 'orientalise' or 'occidentalise' the other, misunderstanding what the other truly means – or could have truly meant if only it had been given an earlier chance. This may be true, but it removes or reduces a responsibility for self-scrutiny. Each might also 'orientalise' or 'occidentalise' itself, reducing its history and thought to a pure (and simplified) forward bastion of consolidated strength – anything qualifying and questioning that consolidation jettisoned, made suspect, unofficialised.

This is what Edward Said had in mind when lecturing on Freud's deduction that Moses had been Egyptian and, even more, that the Judaic monotheism owed to the Egyptian cult established by the heresy of Akhenaten, the pharaoh who turned against the traditional cosmology of his kingdom at about the time that many calculate the Israelites left Egypt.[11] In his late-twentieth-century opera named after Akhenaten, Philip Glass celebrated the fragile beauty of this original monotheism. The appropriation of one god, and one originary prophet, ensures a foundation for official difference between Jews and Arabs – despite the genetic Semitism they have in common (and despite the later, curiously similar, monotheism of Islam adopted by the Arabs). It is the claim to Moses that prevents the Jews from being 'Arabised' in their geneaology, despite much miscegenation even

---

11. Edward W. Said, *Freud and the Non-European*, London: Verso and Freud Museum, 2003.

in the Old Testament stories (Joseph marries an Egyptian; Boaz marries a Moabite; Solomon marries, among many other exotic women, a Shulammite; Esther becomes the Queen to the Persian emperor Ahasuerus – this last suggesting an even more cosmopolitan intercourse than the broadly but merely Semitic).

The 'orientalisation' of self is seen, controversially but spectacularly, in the case of Japan. The suppression of the old samurai powers by the shogunate of 1600–1868 saw the codification of what it meant to be the acceptably 'new' samurai. What was 'new' and acceptable was dressed in the clothes of the old; but, now, a complete fidelity to the state was written into the meaning of being samurai. Manuals of correct behaviour, such as the *Hagakure* and *Budo Shoshin Shu*, prescribed not only state loyalty, unquestioning unto death, but the complete aesthetic nature of every fragment of samurai behaviour. Curious fusions could be allowed: for instance, tea could be drunk from modern cups, but had to be poured from a pot that was unvarnished and shaped in the old style – that is, the source had always to appear old. What was officially declared old became the true licence for behaviour. The true origin of licence – or the lack of it – was the state. Thus, samurai were encouraged to wear a little make-up, in order to look good if, that day, they were required to die on behalf of the state. The colour of make-up was within derogated licence; the matter of living or dying was not. Huge protocols of dressing emerged, so that the *hakama*, the culottes worn by men, was secured in place by an elaborate series of ribbons tied in knots. Each knot had to be exact, and each ribbon kept flat. Although only part of what resulted was visible, those ribbons and knots beneath the outer material of the *hakama* had also to be perfectly, and ritualistically, tied. All personal as well as public performance became ritualised in an array of *kata* or prearranged patterns. Desirably (but here some leniency was allowed) even sleeping with a high-class geisha had to follow a ritual sequence of excitement. One had better not overflow one's cups before the moment to do so had been permitted.

The post-shogunate era, when the emperor was restored but the embrace of technological modernity meant that the samurai as military guardians were now useless, did not mean the latter's obsolescence. The very fact that, with their now codified and consolidated lore and laws, they could not progress, meant they were available as a stable historical image that could be fused to the actuality of modern life – to give the Western apparatus of technology a domestication and cultural licence. Indeed, as modernity intensified and Japan was plunged into an international economy that became increasingly competitive, a recourse to 'cultural essentialism', to the colonisation of self by the image of the samurai as invincible and stoic warrior – loyal as prescribed by the shogunate, but a warrior unequalled by those of any other culture – allowed Japan to 'recognise and locate itself in relation to the other' – that is, in relation to and in contrast with the West.[12]

Having said that, there is much sociological debate as to exactly the constitution of invention/self-conception, and its work of contrast. Are there two cultures in Japan, with the Japanese appropriating from one or the other as if ordering from a menu? Does one stand in relation to the other as an isolated entity, as an antagonist, or does each inform the other so that culture becomes a fusion? The German sociologist (working out of Australia, but not speaking Japanese) Arnason argued that Japan contains not one culture at all, but two. Both are

---

12. Hiroshi Yoshioka, 'Samurai and Self-colonization in Japan', in Jan Nederveen Pieterse and Bhikhu Parekh, eds, *The Decolonization of Imagination*, London: Zed Books, 1995, p. 104.

adapted and adopted, and both are now inherently 'Japanese'.[13] The problem with any of these views is that the processes of mixing and matching, the arbitration of what is mixed, the politics of prioritisation, are left vague. And even the most pro-nounced fusion retains something that is at least imagistic, and that elevates the eternal samurai above all else. One of the most popular *manga* or comic-book series in Japan is called *Bastard* almost as an effrontery to any 'normal' value. It chronicles the fortunes of a group of young heroes and heroines who defend a cosmic outpost from the forces of evil. At first sight the series conforms to a sword-and-sorcery genre. However, each signifi-cant character is him- or herself a significant fusion. Some have Caucasian features and blond hair. One seems hermaphrodite, or at least without male genitals. They all command vast technology in their struggle, as do the monsters against whom they battle. It is, however, the invisible energy that each contains that is always more decisive than that of any machine. These warriors contain the *ki* or power carried along the meridians beloved of Chinese acupuncture and Japanese shiatsu – and which do not, in the Western anatomical universe, exist. Finally, what distinguishes these warriors (with their flowing robes and swords, but in their vehicles of a most advanced modernity), and saves the cosmos, is Japanese. What is hegemonic in a fusion here commands a point of cultural essentialism.

It is this hegemony that is in fact the point. The English footballer David Beckham was once described as a black man (although he is white) because he dressed in the style of black men in hip-hop videos. Black music in general may have infused popular culture – and an endless list is possible, to do with race, gay taste, anything minoritarian inflecting the mainstream

---

13. Johan P. Arnason, *Social Theory and Japanese Experience: The Dual Civilization*, London: Kegan Paul, 1997.

– but when Tony Blair supports George Bush in a 'war on evil', the values opposed are non-Western, and the values championed are moral, universal, accommodating of pluralism, but Western. Indeed, the more accommodating of pluralism these values can be described as being, the more universal they can seem within a Western agenda. The point is that it is not, for instance, a Buddhist pluralism which makes room for the West; or, even more, an Islamic pluralism (which was certainly not unheard-of within the history of the Ottoman Empire) which makes this room. That which accommodates provides the structure of the accommodation. The fittings and decor change; the core infrastructure and superstructure of the house improve and remain. And the owners of the house take great care constantly to reinvent the house identifiably as itself, with heritage and conservation orders over all key drawing rooms. This house may have oriental chambers (encouraged into a chinoiserie), but occidentalises itself.

So that resistance and dissidence within must also partake in the project of reinforcing and reifying the structure of the house. The champions of hip-hop, whether or not they sprang from a ghetto culture, need the multinational record and media companies (and swell their profits), and commodify their own images with designer labels that say they have 'made it' within the house. They are generating noise, but they are knocking nothing down. In the fusion of ghetto lawlessness and Versace sunglasses/Mercedes limousines/gold chains from Gaultier, it is not the ghetto that the artist formerly known as Puff Daddy represents; which is precisely why David Beckham feels comfort-able in saying that Puff Daddy has the best dress style in the world – and this style is now 'black', black being as ever the new chic. So if, alongside Schubert, Puff Daddy occasionally blared from the Bang & Olufson of Condoleezza Rice, Bush's black secretary of state, it is not hard to discern who is in fact at the point of hegemony and what that point stands for.

There are, as ever, points of resistance. The dropout demeanour of the hippy era has now been supplemented by a harder anti-globalisation within the alternative communities. Rootless though urban, against regimentation but fiercely disciplined and brave in their protests, unreliable but formidably organised in putting thousands upon the streets, against capitalism but making use of its artefacts and communication systems, lawless but loyal to one another, tolerant of their softer and woollier allies but dismissive of those without their hard edge, something is happening that at least seeks to challenge the leaders of the world in their summits of curious isolation and facades of moral language. But these are alternative communities, plural, and there is no coherent philosophical point of departure for them. Anarchists and libertines march alongside the 'Straight Edge', an underground radical puritanism which neither drinks nor is promiscuous but indulges all the same in a thunderous rock music – which it distributes hand-to-hand on its own labels, alongside its own books, printed on its own presses, without ISBN numbers and concerned with the social theory of angst and rebellion. Pierced, tattooed, deafened and alarmingly well-read, they may also be teetotal, vegetarian, chaste and fiercely secure in the cause they espouse: part Leveller, part Christian moral outrage, part anti-globalist and anti-capitalist – part, indeed, of all the other parts in the emerging federation of the Western pockets of protest. And that is the problem: they are pockets, and the pockets have pockets, and the virtue of pluralism means, finally, that one day – if they seem to become too powerful – the world leaders in their summits, dachas, air-conditioned suites, will tear gas, then divide and rule. And it is not as if the reading and literary heroes of the federation of pockets is unknown to those in the suits and the suites. French foreign minister, later prime minister, Dominique de Villepin, may have made one of the great UN speeches in 2003, against going to war with Iraq, and his own heroes may be Rimbaud and Artaud – depraved outsiders longing to unleash a whirlwind upon the world – about whom he wrote an 824-page book,[14] but the French foreign policy he supervised, and the mixed history it represents, and the Gallic ambition it presupposes, have much to answer for. Villepin may have wished to break through all that, but he remained the romantic dandy prisoner of it all. The point is that both the indignant French protester on the streets of Paris and the ministers who call upon the club-wielding policeman to reshape his head will know and admire Rimbaud. The French philosopher – at least television and celebrity magazines make him seem so – Bernard-Henri Lévy transacts, dashingly, both groups. Flitting from street action to audiences with ministers, from the rebel warlords of Afghanistan to the predecessors and successors of Dominique de Villepin, from ridiculously crafted photo opportunities during the siege of Sarajevo to his Moorish castle-refuge in Morocco, does he take the protester's hopeless dream of Rimbaud running the nation to the minister, or the minister's hopeless dream of France as a Rimbaud among nations – dethroning the logic and power of America, at least over Iraq and Iran – to the street? And yet, for a brief moment, a bad philosopher transacts a thought linked both to power and to its overthrow. In that brief moment, the point of hegemony is, even if for nanoseconds, blurred. What is it that all this can mean?

---

14. Dominique de Villepin, *Éloge des Voleurs de Feu*, Paris: Gallimard, 2003.

2

Fusion, frenzy and madness

Bernard-Henri Lévy, for all his championing of international causes – and the virtues of a secular or non-dogmatic Islam, something that is complex and able to grapple with the fluidities of modernity, even possibly postmodernity – remains heart-on-sleeve Jewish.[1] This is also a secular Jewishness, although sometimes in his controversial career as an activist–philosopher – nothing more than the archetypical *homme engagé* pioneered by Malraux and lionised as an ideal in postwar France – he must have felt like the biblical scapegoat, appointed in his namesake book of Leviticus to bear collective sins in a wilderness of exile. We could make fun of Bernard-Henri Lévy as goat. His early career as womaniser suggested a cheery exile. We could hold imaginary conversations with him – and this would serve him right, since a prime device in his writing is the concoction of conversations, either of himself with a great thinker of the past,

---

1. See Lévy's self-views as Jewish in Joan Juliet Buck, 'France's Prophet Provocateur', *Vanity Fair*, January 2004. Lévy's first book, *La Barbarie à Visage Humain*, was established on the Holocaust.

or of that great thinker conversing with his or her friends. It is as if all thought could be captured in a play, with Bernard-Henri Lévy as the playwright – not creating dialogue as such, but capturing the dialogue as it might have been. It is himself not just as *interlocuteur*, but the king of interlocution. It is his imagination of meaning that transmits an insight, and this is to an extent totalitarian since it is not reason that holds pride of place; the origin of the insight is not something that can be reasonably debated since it was never exactly reasonable. The fictional dialogue functions, effectively, as a metaphor. It is an illumination of what a meaning could be – in Lévy's sense, what it should be. It is a literary device and not properly and systematically philosophical.

The device of someone pretending to speak for, or as, someone else: perhaps this is why Lévy, an admirer and biographer of Sartre,[2] should seem preoccupied by the role in Sartre's life of Benny Lévy. This earlier Lévy features, complete with imaginary conversations, in Bernard-Henri's film and 1991 book on the modern French philosophers,[3] and in his later biography of Sartre. Benny Lévy, who died in 2003, was a (somewhat withdrawn, leading from the back) student leader of the 1968 uprisings in France. He was a Cairo-born Jew who, early in his student career in Paris, detected the end of the European Communist project and embraced Maoism. In 1974 Lévy became Sartre's secretary and, since Sartre was old and partially blind by this time, he effectively became the interlocutor between Sartre and the world. It was he who read to Sartre, he who suggested to Sartre how he should respond to new issues, and sometimes it

2. Bernard-Henri Lévy, *Sartre: The Philosopher of the 20th Century*, Cambridge: Polity Press, 2003.
3. Bernard-Henri Lévy, *Adventures on the Freedom Road: The French Intellectuals in the 20th Century*, London: Harvill, 1995, pp. 352-4.

was thought that it was he who actually spoke in Sartre's voice – the quotation attributed to Sartre by newspapers would have been penned by Lévy, and was perhaps more Lévy than Sartre himself. The brash young Maoist, purveyor of the non-European brand of communism, infiltrated the persona of the grand old man of European idealism and despair. In his last years Sartre seemed to abandon pessimism, and Sartre the activist flowered. Some of this was certainly apparent long before Lévy became his secretary, but from Lévy's time a certain form of internationalism infused the pronouncements of the wizened man.

Benny Lévy, as Maoist, was drawn to notions of popular struggle. Bernard-Henri has Benny, in one of the contrived conversations, trying to persuade Sartre to write a popular novel. Sartre was to inspire the masses. We might forgive Bernard-Henri's inflection of a raised eyebrow here (even if it was raised against his own imagined conversation), as the thought of Sartre as popular author is impossible. But Benny Lévy was also becoming increasingly drawn to Jewish theology. He began to think of a positive Jewish religion. This was itself a near-impossible project: to disentangle Jewishness as it had been created by centuries of persecution, and hence the views of others, and to posit it afresh. Never mind that the founding laws of Leviticus were devised precisely to shake off the 'Egyptianness' of the raw young Jewish nation. To be Jewish was to be recognisably in contradistinction to all else. Benny Lévy died before he could make great progress on his project. His legacy, perhaps, was his sponsorship of Emmanuel Levinas, whose philosophical luminosity might have been what Lévy sought to find in his own identity.

For Sartre, what all this meant was a certain confusion. Edward Said, who died shortly before Benny Lévy, recalled a 1979 visit to Paris. It was to attend a seminar on peace and the

Middle East – held in the apartment of Michel Foucault. *Tout Paris*, or at least philosophical Paris, was there – the event having been organised by Sartre and Simone de Beauvoir. But Said became increasingly affronted by the extreme ignorance of the Arab world demonstrated by the organisers, de Beauvoir in particular. Finally, exasperated, he demanded that Sartre himself should clarify his views to the seminar. Said's account, in a 1993 interview, is solemnly hilarious: 'So Sartre goes off into a corner with one of his little henchmen and eventually the henchman comes back and says...' The next day, when Sartre himself spoke, Said became even more disappointed than before. Not a word on the Palestinians. 'It came from some sort of philo-Judaism and some sense of wanting to make restitution for the European holocaust.'[4] One of the 'little henchmen' was almost certainly Benny Lévy – and this hiding behind another, behind Sartre, is obviously greatly offensive to Bernard-Henri. Even so, in both Lévys the need to address the European holocaust was inescapable. What was also inescapable for both is the project of seeking to understand the non-European world on European terms – greatly sympathetic terms in the case of Bernard-Henri, but European terms nevertheless. I shall elaborate on the extents and limits of such sympathy below. For Benny Lévy, the philo-Judaism was – let us not forget that Sartre influenced him too – precisely a European-influenced Judaism. The Hegelian idealism of Sartre is not unrelated to the spiritual world of Levinas – a spiritual world condensed to the articulation of a recognisably European philosophical discourse. As for the Maoism, well, that faded as all of 1968 faded; but, even here, the Maoist idea of popular armed struggle – which was in the air around Sartre before Lévy ever came to his side – and

---

4. Zoë Heller, 'Radical Chic', *The Independent on Sunday*, 7 February 1993.

the idea of peasant armed struggle in the lands of non-Europe, were transmuted into two things. First, it became for Sartre, introducing Fanon, a question of interiorised violence exploding into an exterior world.[5] The moment of catharsis as a revolutionary act was, essentially, a Sartrean moment for psychological exposition – and the psychological tools are European. Second, the whole tenor of Sartre's introduction of Fanon's work is of the African rebel, or revolutionary, as peasant. These are not, in themselves, difficulties, but they subsumed in a very short space of time a huge tract of possible ways of thinking about African uprisings. I shall return again, below, to this; but what it did was to establish a philosophical corroboration of what I take to be a very conservative American political scientific conclusion of 1968, in what was seen as a landmark work by Zolberg, that the African condition was implicitly violent.[6] The short extension of that was that the African condition was also simple – untutored, peasant. This is not the impression one has when reading Fanon himself;[7] although as a Western-trained psychiatrist he was also influenced by the dichotomy between interior and exterior, so the Sartrean moment of catharsis which brings one out into the other is understandable, but not as a total account. Sartre's introduction to Fanon was an electrifying statement in its time – Maoist with European methodology – but has not been long helpful in a terrifyingly complex world. How, then, are we to approach this complex and terrifying world?

Let us take one of Bernard-Henri Lévy's heroes, the archetypical *homme engagé*, André Malraux. The young student dropout, freebooter, looter of oriental antiquities, and exaggerator of the

5. Jean-Paul Sartre, 'Preface' to Frantz Fanon, *The Wretched of the Earth*, London: Penguin, 1967.

6. Aristide Zolberg, 'The Structure of Political Conflict in the New States of Africa', *American Political Science Review* 62, 1968.

7. Frantz Fanon, *Black Skin, White Masks*, London: Pluto, 1986.

political significance of his own life, probably had no right to
become a great man (even Levinas wrote a book about him) – but
he did, both because of a conspicuous heroism (which he lost no
opportunity to make more conspicuous) and a genuinely capa-
cious empathy that infuses his non-European characters. One
of his early novels, *La condition humaine*, translated as *Storm
in Shanghai* and later, more fittingly, as *Man's Fate* or *Man's
Estate*,[8] was published when he was only 32. It is set in China,
and concerns the ill-fated Communist uprising in Shanghai in
1927. Despite an international cast, befitting the international
solidarity of the proletariat (or at least its vanguard activists
– that is, its Party agents), Malraux's rendition of his oriental
characters is frankly amazing for one who was so young. One
of the final scenes, in which a terrible execution hangs near
the multinational band of fighters – Chinese, half-Japanese,
Russian – is extremely moving. They are all condemned, but
death will be by being thrown alive into a locomotive furnace.
It will be terrible. They have enough cyanide for two, and those
who take it will have a merciful death. The gallantry of the
cyanide's distribution, and the complete absence of personal
origin, is a sadly under-remarked passage in twentieth-century
literature. It is the Russian who goes alive to the furnace, but
any nationality represented in the book had that capacity – to
choose that sort of death. Malraux was young, almost certainly
romantic, when he wrote it; but the sense of an equality among
cultures of origin, and of the need for a miscegenation of equal
(and, if not equal, equalised) cultures, stayed with him. In one
of his last works, a famously infamous autobiography, in which
he essentially conversed as real author with a fictionalised self,
he seemed to accuse the West of narrowness, of being dedicated

8. André Malraux, *Man's Estate*, London: Penguin, 1961.

to its own conceit. What Malraux loved about the Hindu city of Benares was its university among 'sacred trees, rooms in English Gothic style, professors in yellow robes'.[9] In short, the university – as a true university should be, in dedication to a universe of knowledge – was a mixture of many things; and no one thing took precedence over another. These days, it is easy to say such words, perhaps to try to write such things. These are days of a declared multiculturalism, and the nominal weight of this word, 'multiculturalism', is better than no weight at all. In Malraux's day, the equality of Chinese and European was not assumed. Jonathan Spence has written eloquently of the various phases of reception the broad idea of being 'Chinese' underwent.[10] Only a minority of them were positive, or even open-minded. And Lily Ling has written about the pervasiveness, in the second half of the twentieth century, of the Fu Manchu stereotype.[11] It is very hard to find, in Malraux's era, comparable examples of literary work in which a Chinese heroic figure, or figures, could emerge. Pearl Buck's retelling of *The Water Margin* story of the 108 fighters, retitled *All Men are Brothers*, is a rare exception; as are the works of Han Suyin, who, after all, was herself Chinese. She was also beautiful enough for publicity's work, wrote on romantic and almost sentimental themes, was a medical doctor, and settled in Switzerland. With all of this, she was partialised – that is, not fully Chinese, or able to be stereotyped as Chinese; and Pearl Buck was American, though having lived years in China. The fully Chinese book that became popular in the West had to be pre-dated by Chinese films. It was not literature that allowed the Chinese hero, but something as downmarket, as fundamentally

9. André Malraux, *Anti-Memoirs*, New York: Henry Holt, 1967, p. 181.
10. Jonathan Spence, *The Chan's Great Continent: China in Western Minds*, New York: Norton, 1998.
11. L.H.M. Ling, *Conquest Desire: Postcolonial Learning Between Asia and the West*, New York: St Martin's Press, 2001.

trashy, as the kung fu movie. Almost all Asia understood this, when, in an early film called *Fist of Fury*, Bruce Lee kicked down the sign by the Shanghai park that read 'No Dogs or Chinamen', audiences from Taiwan to Singapore leapt to their feet to applaud. Malraux, if one is to believe his autobiography, even had a Chinese tank-driver in World War II France. In any case, he was ahead of his time. But, if Malraux could write with an uncontrived empathy about oriental characters, could anyone then do the same about African? Could they write about Fanon's African – or even Sartre's? Bear in mind that, shortly after the time of Sartre's writing on Fanon, the chaos and bloodbath that was the newly independent Congo saturated Western perceptions. Zolberg's dire rendition of Africa seemed evidenced by events all could see. No African Bruce Lee emerged and, right up to the twenty-first century, no great Western novel has portrayed a central and heroic protagonist as African. Even Romain Gary's novel set in Africa, *The Roots of Heaven*, which has been unjustly ignored by English audiences, has a white man as its hero. So when Bernard-Henri Lévy confesses that if he had 'Malraux's courage, the freedom of Romain Gary, and the resonance of Sartre, then [he] would have won', he is unwittingly making a statement that is full of absences.[12]

It was left to Africans to declare Africa and a sense of African-ness. Here I refer to the work of Léopold Senghor of Senegal (and, probably equally, of France), and Aimé Césaire of Martinique. That they established their sense of 'negritude' in Paris was determining in much the same way as Marcus Garvey had foundations in Harlem. They were part of a ferment of intellectual activity in the Paris of the 1930s and the years after World War II – heavily influenced by the great French poets such as Baudelaire and

---

12. Joan Juliet Buck, 'France's Prophet Provocateur', p. 93.

Rimbaud. These were, as the new millennium began, the same poets – the stealers of fire – admired by Dominique de Villepin. There was indeed something Promethean about what Senghor and Césaire attempted. Strangely, perhaps ironically given the rift between de Villepin's foreign policy and that of the USA over the second Gulf War, it is in the USA that – perhaps largely unacknowledged – their influence most strongly lingers. Ali Mazrui, at least, has pointed out the twin thrusts of US 'Black Studies' or 'Afro-American Studies' – neither of these thrusts being particularly grounded in intimate knowledge of Africa itself. One is the objection to having been written out of, or underwritten within, white scholarship. The other has been 'influenced by negritude with its emphasis on black cultural distinctiveness rather than black intellectual competitiveness'.[13] This is an explosive but not crude observation, and I shall explain below what Mazrui meant. If, before then, we look at some of the 'Afro-American Studies' texts, then we see not only a declared Afrocentrism (which may be fair enough given the complaints against Eurocentrism in majority scholarship), but an Afro-generalism. What is the Africa that is at the centre? Many of the texts are litanies of random examples from various (and quite different) cultures. A cosmology from Mali might be described in the same terms as an artistic predeliction for sculpture from Benin; a poem translated from Swahili in the same terms as the technique for 'finger piano' in Southern Africa. The linkage is essentially one of a certain African creativity, and intuitive earth-relatedness that has animist qualities, and a sense of self-agency which is not (cf. the West and the Aristotelian legacy[14]) bounded by Euro-rationalism. An

---

13. Ali Mazrui, *Cultural Forces in World Politics*, London: James Currey, 1990, p. 134.

14. Marimba Ani, *Yurugu: An African-Centred Critique of European Cultural Thought and Behavior*, Trenton: Africa World Press, 1994, pp. 88–90.

African, as opposed to black American scholar, Kwame Gyekye, has indicated forcefully – and as generously as possible – what can and cannot be generalised about Africa, and African philosophy in particular. He concludes a startling book with the injunction that it is not too late for 'African philosophers' to start from where one 'should have started', which are the 'intellectual foundations of African culture and experience', and this start has to involve the knowledge of African languages, 'which fact is essential for investigating the philosophy of a people'.[15] That, at a stroke, disqualifies entire 'Black Studies' faculties from claiming to speak expertly on and for Africa. Gyekye's book is an example of what he meant should be practised more widely: a properly philosophical investigation of one people's conceptual system, based on their language, and carefully analysing its range of ontological possibilities and epistemological foundations. This is necessary for Mazrui's work of 'intellectual competitiveness' – not that one tries to outrace another, but that there is no debate if in fact debate is avoided. The privileging of intuition above rationality is an escape clause – unless intuition and its range of works can first be demonstrated and not asserted.

Yet it was Senghor and Césaire who seemed to celebrate the absence of all that Europe held rationally dear and had, by rational means, created. Césaire's poem is such a celebration:

> Hooray for those who never invented anything
> Who never explored anything
> Who never discovered anything!
> Hooray for joy, hooray for love
> Hooray for the pain of incarnate tears.
> My negritude is no tower and no cathedral
> It drives into the red flesh of the soil.

15. Kwame Gyekye, *An Essay on African Philosophical Thought: The Akan Conceptual Scheme*, Cambridge: Cambridge University Press, 1987, p. 212.

In part of course Césaire is writing a contradistinction: joy, pain and love are greater than cathedrals and towers. The lack of invention and curiosity is also of course an overstatement. But it is a statement all the same that invention, exploration and discovery have been overvalued. Earth-linkedness becomes the greatest value, and the implication here is of a fixedness, a timelessness, a lack of movingness. On this basis Césaire sought, all the same, a place for the black man at the 'rendezvous of victory'. Senghor's description of negritude seemed to say the same things:

> Negritude is the whole complex of civilised values – cultural, economic, social and political – which characterize the black people or, more precisely, the Negro-African world. All these values are essentially informed by intuitive reason... The sense of communion, the gift of myth-making, the gift of rhythym, such are the essential elements of negritude, which you will find indelibly stamped on all the works and activities of the black man.[16]

This has given rise to a great many protests from black Africans. Wole Soyinka famously lampooned the concept of negritude by positing a tigritude for tigers. African university senior common rooms have all witnessed the exaggerated 'ain't got rhythm, ain't got music' mini-burlesques over morning coffee that satirically refute Senghor. And, indeed, to seem to locate an entire complex of civilised values in communion, myth and rhythm seems more like a narrow anthropology than a manifesto of equality – and negritude was always intended as a manifesto that declared the black man equal to the white, but on the grounds of a different complex of values, endeavours and accomplishments.

---

16. These renditions of both Césaire and Senghor are from Gerald Moore, cited in Mazrui, *Cultural Forces in World Politics*, pp. 134-5.

There was, however, much more to Senghor than the lampoons in African universities – where the frequent alternatives to intuition were neo-Marxist formulas of exquisite exactitude, in rational sequence projecting the progress of an African class struggle in countries where a Leninist class structure had not yet formed; there being more to myth-making perhaps than even Senghor suspected. Having said that, Mazrui is quite right in distinguishing forms of negritude. Literary negritude might have articulated the possibility of an alternative black approach to values and accomplishment, but there was also the implicit negritude of Julius Nyerere's and Kenneth Kaunda's political programmes towards an idealised African community. What is at stake here, in Mazrui's words, is a 'methodological romanticism'.[17] It is clearly romanticism, but the term 'methodological' might bear further comment. In terms of nation and culture-building, Nyerere's and Kaunda's methodologies were clearly unsuccessful. In terms of literary methodology, Senghor's work is much more complex than the shallow word 'intuition' would suggest. Ebou Dibba has pointed out that Senghor was (in the manner of a French grammarian) fond of labelling his literary techniques.[18] Thus readers would find a hypallage (the transposition of natural relationships in a sentence), a hendiadys (the linking of words sequentially, using 'and', to express a complex idea), an asyndeton (the omission of a conjunction, such as 'and'), and so on, all to establish what Senghor called an 'asymmetric symmetry'. These are literary devices, if not literary conceits. However, in so far as these devices reflected African oral story-telling, which is what Senghor often sought to replicate in his own poems, they suggest far more artifice

---

17. Ibid., p. 135.
18. Ebou Dibba, 'Léopold Senghor – A Taga', *West Africa*, 18–24 November 1996, p. 1790.

in constructing a world view than 'authentic' and natural red flesh of soil might allow. The emergence of the African person of negritude, both authentic and intuitive on the one hand, and complexly articulated on the other, was always going to present both the person and negritude as asymmetrical. But this is exactly the imbalance, the possibility of a not fully compensated flaw, that allows tragedy, drama, endeavour and heroism in the struggle both against self and against all external odds. Certainly this was so in Greek and Shakespearean drama – and it has been so in recent African political history. And in literary expression. There is hardly a single unflawed hero in any of the long pioneering titles of the Heinemann series of African novels. No one has symmetry. Everyone has been acted upon by events to the extent that his or her actions in reply are more contingent than those of any other emerging literature. This is a huge general statement. But it would have been impossible, for instance, to generate a 'magical realism' in African literature in the same way as it has been generated in Latin America. The lightness, the rising above tragedy to some sort of surrealism, metaphysical farce – and the advent of the hero of no conse-quence, who neither makes nor receives impact, but who drifts in the surreal landscape, all the same somehow as a moral figure – did not come early to African literature. The recent, almost indecent industry that has come to celebrate posthumously the work of the Zimbabwean novelist Dambudzo Marechera does so precisely because – finally, no frills attached – he represents a psychologically dysfunctional author who is also the main character in all his writings.[19] Here is naked asymmetry. Here is madness. And this is precisely what Sartre sought to say when introducing Fanon. The African had arrived at a psychological

---

19. Dambudzo Marechera, *The House of Hunger*, Oxford: Heinemann, 1978.

moment, and this was the moment of rebellion. The throwing of the bomb against any target, rationally chosen or not, innocent, guilty, symbolic, random, was it. The throwing of the bomb was the act of rebellion. It was an abjection from the system of years of oppression. The pent-up was thrown out. It didn't have to make sense – that is, have strategy or policy. Sartre's was, in effect, a violently political and dirty negritude, and this said as much about the consuming psychoses of French intellectual life as it did about Africa.

The need almost to sanctify killing and criminality was apparent in Sartre's rendering of Genet – or Saint Genet as he was labelled. Here was an early philosophical celebration of transgression: the man who commits outrages against society was also, in Genet's case, the man who wrote of being a transvestite prostitute having his mouth penetrated by a man crouching above his face, who was in turn having his anus penetrated by a man above him. What is abjected into society is first absorbed into self: self-abnegation became a prerequisite for abjection. Filth and horror came into the world by first being stored and fermented within. Although Julia Kristeva is the one who most clearly articulated the term 'abjection', citing Céline's descriptions of the bowels of corpses leaking on the battlefields of the Great War,[20] the idea that the body and soul contained much suffering that had been impelled into them was the hallmark of the century of Freud and his interiorities, his division of the mind with opaque barriers between ego and id, consciousness and unconsciousness, and the sense that one part could only ever be understood in so far as it extruded into the other sufficiently to be, under psychoanalysis, or within the therapy of creative writing, articulated.

20. Julia Kristeva, *Powers of Horror: An Essay on Abjection*, New York: Columbia University Press, 1982, ch. 6.

Sartre and all of psychoanalytic France that followed were, it seems, determined clinically to re-create the impulsion inwards, as a first understanding of what was to be abjected outwards. For the African peasant native it was simple, uncomplex enough. He threw the bomb because of the indignities and subhumanising creativity of colonialism. This was, in the way Sartre said it, itself a racism. Because, for the European on the other hand, particularly in metropolitan France, in Paris, the race was on to discover – and experience – all manner of complex impulsions inwards. It was not for nothing that Foucault, when he visited California, discovered what for him were the joys of being fist-fucked.[21] The San Francisco bathhouses, with the use of the term 'bath', suggest a cleanliness. Having someone penetrate your anus with his fist and forearm, perhaps wearing a latex glove or not (probably not in Foucault's case, as he may well have contracted HIV in this era), and, on a successful day, getting it in up to the elbow, is a sort of a triumph of desire over anatomy. It is also incredibly dirty, and the shit in the lower system gets packed tight deeper back into the body's cavity where, now, a fist also fills it. The gay poet Greg Woods wrote that the body becomes a glove for the fist-fucker.[22] One's whole self is worn on another's hand, and this hand can literally rip out one's interior. For Foucault, the sense of being invaded, of having what should normally come out packed in, was abetted by his liking of the fact that this sexual act was also, for him, non-orgasmic. Nothing was ejaculated; that part was restrained by metal rings; the entirety of the act was the infusion into self of the huge apparatus of another's arm, which was then held in place for as long as possible. Some bathhouses staged competitions as to how far, in a line-up with spectators cheering, any one in a row of persons could be penetrated.

---

21. David Macey, *The Lives of Michel Foucault*, London: Random House, 1995.
22. Greg Woods, *May I Say Nothing*, Manchester: Carcanet, 1998.

Deleuze has written of the complex detail of certain fantasies
from this kind of subculture. The careful, and painful, stitching
together of the anus and insertion of pins into the buttocks, the
cheeks of which were also stitched together, prevented fist or
penis from entering – but it also prevented shit from escaping.
It had to be contained inside. If the urethra was also sealed over
or stitched shut, then nothing could get out and the body would
have to luxuriate in its own internal decomposition. It became a
sealed site of decay, and the stitching and pins would be, for the
hours of enactment, the external signs that abjection was, from
this site, impossible. Deleuze said this was no longer fantasy,
but a programme. He suggested that there was a certain abstract
ethics in becoming a 'body without organs'.[23] Georges Bataille
wrote that the mouth spews forth such cancerous words that the
most beautiful sight is a mouth that is shut.[24] That is one thing,
perhaps. The storing in of foul words, like the stitching in of
decomposition, did not however mean a body without organs. It
only meant a body with the organs of abjection sealed. It is almost
as if the absorption and retention of nausea was an ethical act:
the desire to store within oneself that which would otherwise
pollute the world. Only that it polluted oneself instead, so that the
Freudian and neo-Freudian philosophers and psychoanalysts of
Paris wrote endlessly about *jouissance*, the play and pleasure by
which one performed good in the world – not necessarily for the
sake of goodness, but so that one would not be discovered to be
the cesspool that one had realised oneself to be and, in extreme
cases, had rehearsed oneself as being; so that the programmatic
symbols would be regular reminders. In that case, the throwing

23. Gilles Deleuze and Félix Guattari, *A Thousand Plateaus: Capitalism and Schizophrenia*, London: Continuum, 2003, p. 151.
24. Georges Bataille, *Visions of Excess*, Minneapolis: University of Minnesota Press, 1985, pp. 59-60.

of the bomb would not be the ultimate abjection, but the planting of a bomb deep within would be – so that, in being blown apart, all corruption would also be blown asunder.

The dark existentialism and dark absurdity that followed the naive but cleaner absurdity of Camus rendered much of late-twentieth-century Paris a cheerless place. It talked of transgression, of crossing borders – a metaphor perhaps for seeping across the ideologies of tyranny and restraint – but one can transgress in the privacy of one's own city forever, hundreds of philosophers being tied down, stitched and pinned, and tyranny will be not a whit worse off. We may certainly be a malodorous species, but all this is a long way from Malraux and a more romantic heroism. At least it was less self-absorbed and more empathetic. In so far as Bernard-Henri Lévy uses Malraux as a sort of pre-televisable model, then we are making progress. And, even if we do not permit Bernard-Henri Lévy to be a model, then we need at least to find some way to view the Others, the 'simple peasants' of the world, who do throw abjection into our faces with their bombs – or with the jet airliners they have hijacked to fly into our greatest buildings, our citadels. Somehow, an 'engaged transgression' must cross not external object with the depths of one's internal body, but cross borders and cultures. Half a century has been self-engaged in Paris, and we are still no closer to seeing any alternative, certainly no more complex alternative, to Senghor's African; to the 'mad Mullahs' of Iran; to the 'fundamentalist' suicide bombers of Palestine. And just in case they might successfully abject into us, it is ours that must be the greater weapons of mass destruction, theirs must be restrained and diminished, as we roll across their ancient deserts.

What the Parisian fixation – and it should be said that it merely philosophises a Western metropolitan habit, albeit an extreme version – has done, however, is to portray sexual self-brutality as a metaphor for international brutality against others, only the others do not choose it. In this sense at least the interior and the exterior match: the commonality is the era of brutality. It is an era of abjection, but it is not an era of abnegation. No one sacrifices him- or herself to prevent abjection hurled against another. Bernard-Henri Lévy in Sarajevo, admittedly at the height of its bombing, pretending to take cover while under fire (while others, out of camera-shot, languidly draw on a cigarette and stand at ease), is a simulation of the abnegating personality. He might be within risk, but he sacrifices nothing. So the era of the philosophers is not simply one of abjection – even rehearsed, symbolic, programmatic abjection or the turning inwards of what should be abjected – but one in which the recognition of abjection could not be turned into sacrifice, into abnegation. Where, in the German philosopher Gadamer's terms is the point of *sacrificium*?[25] Being sewn shut only to be unsewn by previous arrangement hours later, to have a fist claw at one's bowels only to unclaw is not a sacrifice. But others sacrifice themselves in the Middle East and against the World Trade Center. We have no understanding of their abnegation.

What do we have? If we have a mixture of fear and loathing, a loathing of our abjection and inability to abject, and a fear of genuine abnegation before the world at large, then it may be that this combination was most accurately caught in twentieth-century music. The indecision, ambivalence – with real courage seeking to outflank real fear – and prototypical discord of music was prefigured by Shostakovich. Was he defying Stalin? Kowtowing to Stalin? Mixing, ingeniously and artistically, both? He seemed at the least a long way from Wagner, with his – depending on your point of view – grand vision, bombast,

25. Hans-Georg Gadamer, *Philosophical Hermeneutics*, Berkeley: University of California Press, 1976.

heroic humanism, and sheer calculation of portentousness. At least he was confident. That was the strength of his music that appealed to the Nazis – although whether Wagner should be seen only as the posthumous dupe of fascism is another question.[26] But the chaos of the early and middle twentieth century was caught in, of course, Stravinsky's work: not so much the clichéd drumbeats of *The Rite of Spring*, but the 1961–66 works starting with *The Flood* and ending with the *Requiem Canticles*, a series of melodramas that appear at first positive, but that are pessimistic in the extreme, mindful of death and inflected with an arch cynicism. By this time melody had given way to tonal experiments, and the discord of the heart was portrayed in the discord of the music. In a sense this reached an apogee in Luigi Nono's 1960 opera *Intolleranza*, with its heartfelt denunciation of oppression. Here, even Sartre has a voice-over part in Scene V: 'At no time has the wish to be free been more urgent or stronger. At no time has oppression been more violent or better armed.' It soon got more violent and better armed. And, although Nono sought to see humanity emerging from the discord of oppression, the musical discord of his opera is all-consuming. Not much by way of hope emerges. Thirty-five years later the pop singer turned experimental musician Scott Walker released a critically acclaimed but never subsequently heard album entitled *Tilt* in which, without acknowledgement, he emulated Nono's themes of torture and some of his musical devices to construct bleakness. It is a 'pop' masterpiece, itself now unacknowledged, and showed how humanity still wilts with despair before oppression. But, if there was a very great musical composition that portrayed chaos and repression, sacrifice and hope, then it was Poulenc's 1957 opera *Dialogues des Carmélites*, which used many of the same

---

26. See the discussion on Wagner in Daniel Barenboim and Edward Said, *Explorations in Music and Society*, London: Bloomsbury, 2002, pp. 169–84.

compositional devices that Stravinsky was felt to have pioneered. Poulenc's opera was subtitled *La Peur*, the fear. Indeed, the fear of discovery and execution that afflicted an outlawed order of nuns during the atheistic phase of the French Revolution is terrifyingly wrought. Finally, the nuns are captured and taken to the guillotine. The opera ends with the nuns, in chorus, singing 'Salve Regina'; one by one, the chorus is diminished as the swish and thud of the guillotine is heard above the singing. Finally, only one voice is left. It belongs to a girl who could have escaped but chose to die with her sisters. She sings alone until, for her too, the guillotine thuds down. Here, almost alone in music at the time of Sartre, was the amazing human spirit. And it was religious – as if portending that, by century's end, we should all know that the fundamentally religious know how to throw themselves at death.

Throw themselves madly, mindlessly? There was an answer to this in Paris, in a rare highlight in the disquisitions on *jouissance* and the maledictions of the interior. This can be gleaned in the treatments by Lacan and Anouilh of Sophocles' ancient Greek play *Antigone*.

Antigone

Sophocles, acclaimed as one of the three great Greek dramatists, wrote three plays set in Thebes, each concerned in part with the nature of kingship, in part also with the caprices of fate and heaven and, above all, with the human interface of state and heaven. The Theban plays were written at different times in his life, and their central characters are Oedipus (reintroduced to a twentieth-century audience by Freud as the primal exemplar of being inhabited by a certain complex) and his daughter Antigone. In the play named after her, Oedipus has died and she has emerged from his life of public shame, only to be caught up in a struggle between her two brothers for supremacy in Thebes. Leading rival armies, the two brothers fight and kill each other. Creon, the regent, orders that the brother who had led an army of foreigners against Thebes should remain unburied, and his body left to rot. Antigone, mortified by this insult to family, decorum and religious law, disobeys Creon and symbolically buries her brother. She is arrested and brought to trial. Creon's son Haemon is her fiancé. The trial and the exchanges between Antigone and Creon are a great debate on whether state justice or spiritual law is higher. Many have seen Antigone as a Kantian figure, obeying Kant's 'categorical imperative' by appealing to a moral and spiritual code over and above the state's. The French psychoanalyst and philosopher Lacan presented a very different Antigone (in part to establish an attack on Kant), and made much of Antigone's frenzied drive into madness.

This much is the summary. Let us now explore what is at stake here. The problem with much of the sense of moral self, moral purpose, moral mission, and moral vindication – all mainstay assumptions in our lives of place and interaction – is that this sense cannot be taken for granted. The ghost in the entire machine of the twentieth century was the *mad* self, and this mad self had its own subjectivity. What else was Freud articulating? Not just that madness made our daily lives abnormal, but that the madness had its own patterns, responded to its own drives and triggers, had its own history and sexuality. Without this double subjectivity – our own conscious subjectivity and the subjectivity of our madness – psychoanalysis would not have had its advent. Now the Western problem is not this. It is that the madness is seen almost entirely in negative terms. It is an internal identity that is made up of impulses of guilt and shame; it has certain malevolences towards the structure and power relationships of family; and, in the Hegelian extension outwards from the family, to civil society and even the state itself. The internal identity, in its interaction with the external, makes of the external identity a perpetual malcontent – a malcontent with itself and all around it. This inherently unreconciled and unsatisfied – unconsummated – self is able to establish a stasis between its malcontent and its aspiration to be social, to do good to others. Lacan called this a form of *jouissance*, a pleasure in which guilt also is hidden behind the public veil of good as something performative; good is performed as a camouflage of that which makes one feel guilty or shameful. It is not good for goodness's sake. Now, having said that, Lacan differentiates the case of Antigone. For him, she is possessed of *ate*, the good impulse that is prepared to prosecute itself with a fervour that enacts madness, and does not pause even when transgressing the laws of the state.[27] This is not Kant's 'categorical imperative', where the linkage is with a greater moral force outside the self, but a linkage with an inner force that cannot be resisted. Antigone sweeps *jouissance* aside, and is prepared to die for it. At least she will die a whole person.

She will also die, by her own choice, triumphant above the caprice of fate that had undone her father. When he marries Jocasta, Oedipus does not know she is his mother, that he has killed his father to inherit this bride. Nor does she, but when he begins to intuit the truth, that he is living in incest, she remonstrates with him:

> Fear? What has a man to do with fear?
> Chance rules our lives, and the future is all unknown.
> Best live as best we may, from day to day.
> Nor need this mother-marrying frighten you;

27. Jacques Lacan, *The Ethics of Psychoanalysis 1959–1960*, London: Routledge, 1992, p. 263.

Many a man has dreamt as much. Such things
Must be forgotten, if life is to be endured.[28]

The key words here are 'chance rules our lives'. Oedipus is the
arch sufferer at the hands of fortune, of heaven, of the gods.
It did not matter how good a king he tried to be. He was led
into a trick, a trap. The gods led him to marry his mother. The
Greek universe had a curious amorality about it. The gods were
supernatural beings who did not have to obey any natural laws
of good or justice. Martha Nussbaum has written a masterwork
about the strategic, often malicious, place of luck, fortune, fate
and the gods in the Greek view of agency – and the limits they
placed upon agency.[29] In the two earlier Theban plays, *Oedipus
the King* and *Oedipus at Colonus*, Antigone is just an extension
of Oedipus, the dutiful daughter leading around the self-deposed
king who had blinded himself when he discovered the shameful
reality of his marriage. In the play bearing her own name, however, she takes upon herself all the reprobation of the state and, in
her frenzied good – so determined, frenzied, to commit the good
of decent burial – has triumphed over the caprice of the gods.
Her frenzy is too strong even for them. For, as Bernard Williams
has pointed out, in the Greece of her day, neither Antigone nor
Oedipus could possibly have been regarded as moral. Theirs had
been a public shame. Whether Oedipus suffered from a private
complex or not, his marriage and the discovery of its truth were
public; and Antigone was the offspring of a union that was a
public excoriation.[30] It was not only the gods who denied her a
free subjectivity; her society also denied it. Antigone triumphed

28. Sophocles, *Oedipus the King*, in *The Three Theban Plays*, trans. E.F. Watling,
Harmondsworth: Penguin, 1974, p. 52.
29. Martha Nussbaum, *The Fragility of Goodness*, Cambridge: Cambridge University
Press, 1986.
30. Bernard Williams, *Shame and Necessity*, Berkeley: University of California
Press, 1993.

over heaven and earth with her frenzy and mad determination to commit an act of good. It simultaneously killed her and freed her, and offered an indictment of all those around and above her.

Lacan was, in his work, attacking Kant and his presumption of a universal moral symmetry. Lacan's Antigone is not symmetrical with anything in the external world. Even so, Lacan still had to treat her as a character in Sophocles' play. In this play she is able to debate, to defend herself, to be coherent. Lacan did not rewrite the play, but another French thinker did. Antigone is almost incoherent in Jean Anouilh's rewriting. This is no longer Sophocles and Athens. This is now wartime France and the pressing demands to collaborate with the Germans, or die. In this sort of situation, the balancing of dangers, the cautions and precautions, the constant calculations before taking a small risk – the retention of self as safe – all become everyday. Not so for Antigone. She is prepared to abject her whole self into defiance. There is, however, a basic distinction to be made between Anouilh's Antigone and Lacan's. Anouilh's is not mad – that is, she is not propelled from within. Nor is she Kantian. She is not animated by a correspondence with an ethical universe. She is simply, overridingly disgusted by the universe in which she lives:

> You disgust me, all of you, you
> and your happiness! And your life, that
> has to be loved at any price. You're like dogs
> fawning on everyone they come across. With
> just a little hope left every day – if you don't
> expect too much. But I want everything now!
> And to the full! Or else I decline the offer, lock,
> stock and barrel! I don't want to be sensible,
> and satisfied with a scrap – if I behave myself!
> I want to be sure of having everything, now,
> This very day, and it has to be as wonderful as it

was when I was little. Otherwise I prefer
to die.[31]

Of course Anouilh has taken the cadence from that of a spoilt
teenager. In a way, as *demandeur mal*, this Antigone was a
precursor of Jim Morrison and the Doors, with their famous line,
'We want the world, and we want it now.' However, she was also
precursor to those who protested the world system at Seattle,
Prague, Genoa, a half dozen other places, demanding very ethi-
cally that the world in its entirety should change. Now.

Anouilh's play, which appeared in 1944, was an indictment
of wartime collaboration. Antigone parallels Joan of Arc – also
able to be described as mad, hearing voices, possessed, but
articulating and leading the mission of freedom. In Anouilh's
play the Regent of Thebes, Creon, is a reasonable and rational
man – as, indeed, he is in Sophocles' original, communitarian, placing the needs of the commonwealth above individual
needs – and he tries to persuade Antigone to be reasonable, to
'understand'.

> ANTIGONE　　I don't want to understand. It's
> alright with you. Me? I'm in the path to
> understand something quite different. I'm in the
> path that says 'no', to say 'no' to you
> and to die.[32]

Why say 'no'? Why choose self-sacrifice by saying 'no'? The
answer lies in Creon's saying 'yes'; and nowhere is this more
starkly highlighted than in Antigone's fiancé and Creon's son
Haemon's stripping bare the moral foundations of his father's
rationality:

---

31. Jean Anouilh, *Antigone*, trans. Barbara Bray, in *Anouilh Plays: One*, London:
Methuen, 1991, p. 123.

32. Jean Anouilh, *Antigone*, quoted in S. Benyon John, *Anouilh: L'Alouette and
Pauvre Bitos*, London: Grant & Cutler, 1984, p. 14 (my translation).

HAEMON   Do you think I can go on living without her?
Do you think I'm going to accept that life
you talk about? Every day, morn till night,
without her? All your bustle and blather, all
your emptiness... without her?

That great strength and courage... that giant god
who used to gather me up in his arms and save
me from ghosts – was that you? The thrilling
smell, the delicious bread in the lamplight, the
evenings when you used to take me into your study
and show me your books – was that really you,
do you think?

And all that trouble, that pride, those books –
were they only leading to this? To becoming
a man, as you call it – a man who's supposed
to consider himself lucky just to be alive?

Oh, Father, it isn't true, it isn't you, it isn't
happening! We're not both driven into a corner
where we can only say yes![33]

Anouilh was writing, in the first instance, of those who said
'yes' during the war – that is 'yes' to the Germans and their
demands for collaboration. But all his plays are about saying 'yes'
or 'no'. Some are simply horrific depictions. In *Pauvre Bitos*, Act
Two opens with an account of executions, splitting skulls, and
two executioners being concerned about being drenched in blood
– not morally concerned, but concerned about the difficulties
of doing the laundry.

CHARLES   Your wife must have said a thing or
two when you got home!

JOSEPH   She knew you couldn't keep clean
killing all day.[34]

---

33. Anouilh, *Antigone*, trans. Barbara Bray, pp. 127–8.
34. Anouilh, *Pauvre Bitos*, trans. Lucienne Hill, in *Anouilh Plays: One*, p. 370.

These plays are saying two things: the first, simply, is that the precondition to the possibility of good is the ability to say 'no' – even when it is not sensible, rational, or discursively facilitated to say 'no'. The second is that this moral refusal – this intuitive, subjective, ontological *knowledge* of the rightness of refusal; this will to die on behalf of this intuition – is also a precondition to the possibility of society. Although Anouilh's plays are set within state debates – *Pauvre Bitos* is set in Robespierre's revolutionary France – they are centrally concerned with the moral volition and willingness of individuals and their societies. They are in short to do with the moral composition of what we now casually call civil society. They are about the possibility of binding a people to a belief, a cause, a justice. This is some distance from Lacan's statement only of *ate*. Sometimes there may be more than frenzy and madness to what looks like a mad act.

But the intuition of what is right does not stand alone, foundationless. Anouilh's Antigone stands on the memory of a free nation, and that freedom and nation were complexly developed to enable the memory of being able to say 'no'. We shall return to all this in the next chapter.

After Antigone

The problem with much recent French work is the sense of its own enclosure. It discusses frenzy with the same composure as a talk about wine. It talks about madness as if from (the psychiatrist's side of) a chair, taking notes, chewing the end of a pencil, the patient neatly arranged on a designer couch, hands folded across the abdomen, looking abstractedly ahead or above, prompted only by the psychiatrist to continue a probe into abstractions, by clinical sessions to give rational articulation to memories, impulsions, to become naked, to abject politely and cleanly, and all abjection melts into air. It can all be done wearing Yves Saint Laurent. It was probably done *by* Yves Saint Laurent. And even Bernard-Henri Lévy's imaginary conversations, are these not also the stage-set probings of the analyst? Is this not a complex form of voyeurism, with the voyeur as prompter? One can lay bare a society's century-long psychosis in this manner, and it will fuel a fifty-minute university lecture one day – the lecturer looking up distractedly at fifty students taking notes and calmly chewing pencils – and what has sometimes been called the 'Deleuzean century' will be distilled into syllabus, programme and shorthand. Afterwards in the seminar (in those British universities that can still afford seminars), the lazier students, who have neither gone to the library nor even bothered to surf the web for him, will ask, 'how exactly do you spell "Deleuze" again?', and not linger over the moral consequences of a body without organs.

An egg is its own enclosure. It has no orifices, nothing can get in or out. It is smooth and has no edges. If it is a porcelain egg or a stone egg – perhaps carved and smoothed by some roadside African hawker – it cannot be shattered. It cannot be accused of anything. This egg is moral by virtue of being incapable of immorality and, in its formlessness – its Zen-like curvature so close to circularity – it is a statement of the abstract. Codes and ideologies cannot impact upon it. Yet, in Zen, and in Deleuze's knowledge and use of oriental motifs, the egg accuses the world by the sheer fact of its perfection. The egg is a standard that anything with an edge cannot reach. The ideal body without organs is like this, and has little to do with the cheap jibes I have thrown its way earlier. I admit this. But I am also saying that the programmatic *simulation* of the body without organs is, at best, the rehearsal of a metaphor; at worst it is flagellation for the sake or sense of self – having nothing to do with medieval visions of salvation or a modern statement of critique. It is self-absorbed and, in that sense, is certainly like an egg. The body without organs may or may not be, or momentarily feel, perfect, but the body without organs is vain. It is, even with the wish for a new ethics on the part of Deleuze, an impossible vision by which to enter a disgusting world. In this world, what and how one abjects, and for what reason other than the self one undertakes abnegation, these are important things. The mental life that accompanies and links both will not, in an al-Qaeda training camp, be the same as that which seeks an exposition of itself on a Parisian psychiatrist's couch. The egg-like circle that infuses a Zen master's art or meditation is something done, not only as something abstract, but abstracted from the world. What is needed in understanding is how the samurai warrior, who is also an apprentice of the Zen master, can kill as beautifully and abstractedly as the master paints the circle. Without feeling moral consequence, the warrior is like the master's egg. By training himself so he is a fused creature with his sword, and when the sword cuts he *is* both the sword and the perfect curve of the cut, he is a body without organs. Even Anouilh's Robespierrean executioners, concerned with how to wash blood off their clothes rather than off their consciences, are bodies without organs. The suicide bomber who calmly, in his view morally, flies a plane and hundreds of people to their deaths, with utter fearlessness and thinking only of Paradise at the moment of impact, is a body without organs. None of this is amenable to Lacan or Deleuze. Its animation may have been crudely approximated by Sartre – crudely, approximately – its seemingly overwhelming absurdity by Camus. Camus at least allowed heroism as a condition of absurdity. Only Malraux was heroic, and only Malraux wrote as if he were *almost* Chinese, half-Japanese, Russian, a host of oriental assassins, whatever.

Whoever. As an Other. Not as a self, consumed by the workings only of the self.

To write as another, to imagine oneself as another: this is not what the self-contained egg can do. The opening pages of *Man's Estate*, however, are a vibrant antidote to eggness. Chen is about to assassinate someone. The victim is sleeping, and Chen is hovering above his bed. Only a mosquito net separates them. As soon as Chen stabs downwards through the net the line between life and death will be transgressed. But Chen hesitates, and the first few pages are a terrifyingly lyrical rendition of the relationship between conscious killer and the unconscious victim. Even when Chen finally stabs down the line is not transgressed. The unconscious body reacts. It reacts unselfconsciously, unreflectively. It jerks – not into death, but into a huge muscular effort to expel the knife. Its power is as if it had never been so alive. Only then does it die, and Chen has been so preoccupied with holding the knife in, wondering how to extract it in case another stab is required, that he does not realise that his victim is dead. What Chen has done in his hesitation has been to begin a process of empathy – not even empathy with another personality, but empathy with another organism, another capacity for personality. Malraux empathises with Chen, Chen empathises with his victim. Malraux empathises with his own fiction, the result of his own capacity; Chen empathises with another's capacity; the chain goes on, all the way to the novel's fiery end. The chain of empathy – and none of this is even *real* – might speak volumes to those who seek to capture, critique and conceptualise, or even deconstruct, reality. To reconstruct ourselves as an ethic for the future is not to reconstruct ourselves as a body without organs, an egg, a thing abstract.

Deleuze is right about one thing, however. That is his suggestion that becoming woman is a transgressive act of great significance. It is not transvestism in its normal sense, but the losing of hierarchies and definitions, of established planes of existence in the act of becoming. Becoming woman, becoming animal, is to make something that had been male or human imperceptible. For Deleuze, imperceptibility was an invitation to abstraction: the in-between of planes is something not open to definition. What I want to say, however, is precisely the opposite. It is not abstract, it is open to definition, it is perceptible, it is to describe a moment of fusion; and this moment of fusion is a moment of hegemony over the fixed places of the world in which some oppress and some others are oppressed, some strike and some others strike back. It is to look at a species whole and to say that empathy is possible to the point where a man might become woman, human become animal, Frenchman become Chinese, terrorist become hero, frenzy become articulation, and madness become a complex if unfixed sense.

To a very large extent, Julia Kristeva expressed Deleuze's essential point more cogently and succinctly than he. Writing on Aragon's later work, she recognises in Aragon 'a cult of the feminine as prototype of the impossible'.[35] For her, an opening out of this sort – towards the impossible – was an intimate declaration of seeking to encompass the world on terms of one's own imagination. It was a revolt against a condensing, stipulative politics. Of course the image of the feminine has been widely used in forms of religious art from India and Tibet. This is unlike the Christian art of Mary, where the female is blessed by virtue of having given birth to the ultimate male. It is an art where the male may migrate and merge into the female, or the female complexly represent the male. Shiva is not only married to Parvati, but can merge into her; or become the hermaphrodite

---

35. Julia Kristeva, *Intimate Revolt: The Powers and Limits of Psychoanalysis*, New York: Columbia University Press, 2002, p. 183.

god Ardhanarisvara, female on her left side with one breast prominent, and male on his right, an erect slightly right-of-centre penis also prominent. The effort at merger may be expressed almost literally, as in Indian paintings that show Krishna wearing the clothes of his female lover, Radha; or impersonated literally in life, as in the case of the sixteenth-century saint Sri Caitanya, who in the second part of his life took on the feminine characteristics and clothing of Radha. He could not merge into Krishna, but the intermediate step of becoming Radha – the beloved of the god – was possible. She had become very much the 'prototype of the impossible', and prototypicality as a woman was somewhat more human than an egg's prototypicality of the abstract. It is the Tibetan sense of androgyny, however, that most consistently represents the possibility and desirability of expanding beyond normally fixed boundaries. The androgynous figurine of a spiritual being is not something worshipped. It is an object of meditation. It facilitates the meditator to escape any fixed notion of a god. Indeed, the meditation's object is to compose or create a *yidam*, a personal god for the meditator, one into which he or she is fused – so that one is not only male and female, but human and divine simultaneously.[36]

The divine creatures of the Tibetan pantheon are also able to be beneficent and burn with cosmic holy anger simultaneously. Originally viewed as reformed demons, the eight *dharmapalas* have ferocious physiques and expressions. They have bestial faces, flowing red hair; they are surrounded by fire rather than haloes; they wear necklaces of skulls; they look as if they have trained in a wrestlers' stable and gorged on the steroids of heaven. And yet they came to be seen not simply as former

---

36. The most elegant and suggestive description I have found of this is by Robert A.F. Thurman, in Thurman and Marylin M. Rhie, *The Sacred Art of Tibet*, London: Thames & Hudson, 1996, p. 37.

demons but as the righteously angry manifestations of exactly those serene, slender, diaphonously clad and androgynous creatures that are now the vogue in both Western spiritual odysseys and art collections. If in New York it is now possible to sell the figurines, possibly looted from Tibet, of ethereal and fragile boddhisattvas – saints who refuse to be become fully fledged gods out of a love for humanity – that is, to sell a pathway to heaven, it is also possible for the same heavenly path to be a river of fire and destruction. The ingredients are not alien to the Western imagination: the same God holds sway in both the Old Testament and the New Testament; but the God of the Old drowned the world, hailed fire and brimstone on Sodom, and approved the tearing apart by ravenous dogs of the beautiful but sinful Jezebel; the God of the New was meant to be the God of Christ, love and forgiveness. It is, however, the distinction that is drawn between Old and New that is absent in Tibetan cosmology. The same god is delicately feminine opening onto the impossible, and demon raining down impossible terror.

The thrower of the bomb is not driven simply by interior abjection. There is a cosmology within the origin of his or her abnegation. The bomb has a programme; the programme is a seamless fusion of what might first appear as opposites. The terrorist has a story. The story has an 'impossible' moral system in its foundation. This is not a story that can be written like an imaginary conversation. It is not a story, like Bernard-Henri Lévy's account of the murdered journalist Daniel Pearl,[37] which, for all its efforts towards empathy, even for the assassins, remains the interrogative work of imagination on the part of a Jewish European philosopher steeped in French thought and consumed by the aspiration towards solidarity – but not identi-

---

37. Bernard-Henri Lévy, *Who Killed Daniel Pearl?*, London: Duckworth, 2003.

fication – with the world of the oppressed. And Lévy's empathy, it must be said, does not match that of his hero, Malraux. It is, rather, a story that bears investigation, just as Antigone bore investigation and interpretation: the frenzied and 'mad' self exists within a society of malediction and aspiration that has been declared impossible. In this impossibility, literalists, fundamentalists and charlatans arise; but atrocious heroes also arise. The *homme engagé* of today may be terrifyingly different to his French predecessor. It is a story that ventures into the terrible and the impossible.

3

The new brutalisms

I n a sense, almost every contemporary savagery is accomplished with the technology of civilisation. In the Rwanda of
1994 the slaughter of Tutsis was mobilised via radio broadcasts.
In the attack against the Twin Towers on 9/11 aircraft were used.
In the war against Saddam Hussein the original rationale was to
uncover his weapons of mass destruction – chemical and biological weapons, perhaps even the first stages of nuclear weapons.
There is no longer a 'primitive' terrorism. Indeed, there is fear
precisely because terrorism is no longer primitive: it is financed
by flows of international capital; it is organised by electronic
communications; it will attack airliners, warships, skyscrapers
– and is able to destroy or seriously damage them. It might even,
one day soon, bring entire cities to their knees. Very little of
this is plotted in a cave in the Afghan hills. It is worked out in
laboratories, modelled on computer screens, and underpinned
by complex philosophies and world-views. None of this can be
ignored. The shift from describing terrorism as 'primitive' to
describing the values of terrorists as both 'primitive' and evil

– hate-filled and therefore hateful – does not solve the great problem of international relations. It is simply expressed as a problem of understanding, but the understanding involved is not simple. Even so, a grand simple image can help. The Czech philosopher Jan Patočka described the scene of two armies clashing. They attack each other and, in the ensuing battle, seem almost to merge into each other. The savagery becomes common. But common also to both sides – before they became one *mêlée* – were motivations, hopes, fears, a belief perhaps in the justice of their cause; what Patočka called a 'solidarity of the shaken'.[1] The British poet Christopher Logue, in his retelling of the Troy story, described the merger of opposed armies and values well.

And when the armies met, they paused,
And then they swayed, and then they moved
Much like a forest making its way through a forest.[2]

Disentangling values in the midst of carnage is not easy. Digging and pecking over the remains afterwards is not pretty. The key time is before.

But it is hard. One of the things that traumatised the European sense of its painfully achieved civilisation and its stumbling towards a political union – based on an integrated economy and integrated values – was the European periphery slaughtering itself in what had been Yugoslavia. The Croatian historian Ivo Goldstein presented an account of competing nationalisms well before the era of Tito. After his death, however, a series of political manoeuvres on the parts of Croatia and Serbia were consistently misunderstood by each other, and were perhaps even wilfully understood in the worst possible light.[3] The wilfulness

1. A particularly sympathetic English-language appreciation of Patočka is Andrew Shanks, *Civil Society Civil Religion*, Oxford: Blackwell, ch. 3, esp. p. 123.
2. Christopher Logue, *The Husbands*, London: Faber & Faber, 1994, p. 51.
3. Ivo Goldstein, *Croatia: A History*, London: Hurst, 1999.

of misunderstanding the other, while justifying the self – even though the self is committing slaughters, or precisely because it is committing slaughters – was caught in a series of newspapers columns, many written during the siege of Sarajevo, by the Bosnian Serb journalist Gojko Beric, who lamented the self-justifying and self-satisfying actions of Serbians against Bosnia.[4] Much of Europe and particularly many French writers were aghast at the crisis in the Balkans. Bernard-Henri Lévy made his much-publicised visits to Sarajevo; and Alain Finkielkraut insisted that the crisis was a crime against Europe, precisely because the Balkans were part of Europe.[5] The American author Susan Sontag famously directed Samuel Beckett's *Waiting for Godot* by candlelight in a Sarajevo under attack – almost as an expression of European despair and absurdity. The question, asked by all, seemed to be 'why can what is meant to be one received set of values, propounded by all, not make sense, not be applied successfully, to this conflict?'

By the time the war was over, it was Serbia that was excoriated by Europe and the West in general. A decade before the war, however, the Serbian author Milorad Pavić wrote an extraordinarily witty and elegant novel which purported to examine one story through three different lenses: Christian, Islamic and Hebrew. It is a story of a people known as the Khazars, curiously proto-Slavic in their origins. And it is a story of a contest to convert the Khazars to one of three religions. If not a debate on three different types of thought, it is at least a disquisition on three different types of perception. It is Pavić's whimsical endnote that contains the moral. 'A book is like a scale – it tilts first to the right until it tilts to the left, forever. Its weight thus

---

4. Gojko Beric, *Letters to the Celestial Serbs*, Sarajevo, 2001.
5. Alain Finkielkraut, *The Crime of Being Born*, Zagreb: Ceres, 1997. (The French edition had appeared in 1992, as hostilities blossomed.)

shifts from the right hand to the left, and something similar has happened in the head – from the realm of hope, thoughts have moved to the realm of memory, and everything is over.'[6] Pavić means a moment of consolidation, a moment when the pearl is fused together and is whole. It can never be the grit or grain of sand again. It doesn't matter then whether you can or want to appreciate different perceptions. You generally can't, since your view of another's perception is bound within your memory of how you came to perceive the world. If you want to escape this bindedness, you must step outside your own memory. In this sense, Pavić differs from Kurosawa and his film *Rashomon*. In that film, all the different points of view were equally presented. Ravisher and ravishee had the same opportunity to persuade an audience with no previous memory or knowledge of them, or what it was like to be them. Pavić himself became a Serb nationalist during the Balkan conflict, and those nationalists hardened their memories against others. The solidity of such memory can be used to oppress others – not only, as Edward Said argued, to resist others. One of Said's interlocutors wrote that, in Saidian terms, 'theories developed in local contexts tend to lose their elasticity and become diluted in power and meaning when transported elsewhere.' They can become mere 'strategic methods, with system and procedure taking the place of genuine thought.'[7] In this sense, theory doesn't travel well. A nationalistic Serb can make no sense to a dislocated Bosnian; likewise an Israeli bulldozer driver to a now homeless Palestinian. There is an impeccable *logic* to the argument for historical and cleansed territory – but that is not enough to make it actually thoughtful; and it certainly does not make it

---

6. Milorad Pavić, *Dictionary of the Khazars*, London: Penguin, 1988, p. 335.
7. Gauri Viswanathan's Introduction to Edward W. Said, *Power, Politics, and Culture*, London: Bloomsbury, 2004, p. xii.

considerate. What Said, by contrast, would have liked to see is an appreciation of infinite logics as a foundation for true thoughtfulness. 'And what is critical consciousness at bottom if not an unstoppable predilection for alternatives?'[8] To see the alternative perceptions – through all the complex ramifications of their development, both in historical and aspirational terms – this is what is lacking in the term 'understanding' when it is applied to international relations. What, after all, is there to understand about an Osama bin Laden, except that he dragged the Twin Towers down and, like no one before him, went to war with the United States? But, even said like that, there is an awful lot to understand. There was nothing primitive either about the ambition or about the technology of execution. Why, then, is only the animating thought primitive – and evil? Do we wilfully refuse to understand or even see bin Laden because he has assaulted our memory of ourselves?

It is not as if Osama was the first to enter a process of demonisation. The Ayatollah Khomenei preceded him. Khomenei did not arrange for aircraft to be piloted into the Twin Towers, but he was regarded as dangerous, and it was within the early days of the Iranian Revolution that the diplomats of the US embassy were held hostage. The Iranian case precisely gives the lie to the notion that what the West has called 'fundamentalist' Islam is a product of poverty and backwardness. The Iran of the early twenty-first century is an Iran thought by many to be developing a nuclear bomb. The Iran entering the last quarter of the twentieth century, and at the time of its revolution in 1979, was a nation of material prosperity. Per capita income was US$2,000, and 1976 oil revenue was US$20.5 billion, with an annual industrial growth of 15 per cent. Half the population was urbanised

---

8. Edward W. Said, *The World, the Text, and the Critic*, London: Faber & Faber, 1984, p. 247.

and this population at least – and it was the one that mobilised for the revolution against the Shah – was prosperous.[9] And in the days immediately following the revolution before the final triumph of the clerical faction, in what was called the 'Tehran Spring', more than 250 publications flourished, women's groups and even Jewish groups sprang into existence or emerged from the shadows, writers banned under the Shah exploded into print as books cascaded off the presses, huge numbers of foreign texts were translated and published, cassette tapes of all sorts of music were mass-produced, and the university district became a bazaar of cultural goods and endless debate. Plays and cinema enjoyed record audiences as unbanned works were staged or screened. It felt like a dawn.[10] To an extent, it was this that prompted the now infamous comments of the French philosopher Michel Foucault, enthusing about the Iranian Revolution – when he thought the tension generated by the dawn of the Tehran Spring on the one hand, and Khomenei on the other, would lead to something new and different in the world of revolutions and the world at large.[11] Something that, by forceful implication, would be historically refreshing – which it has not been, with the hands of the Ayatollahs coming down heavily and the Spring driven deep underground. The point, however, is that it was the complex expression of culture and philosophy that was driven underground, just as it had been driven underground by the Shah before. In the urbanised and middle-class environment of modern Iran, there is a huge subterranean well of complex

9. Fred Halliday, *Islam and the Myth of Confrontation*, London: I.B. Tauris, 1996, p. 51.

10. Annabelle Sreberny-Mohammadi and Ali Mohammadi, *Small Media, Big Revolution: Communication, Culture, and the Iranian Revolution*, Minneapolis: University of Minnesota Press, 1994, pp. 165-7.

11. Michel Foucault, *Politics, Philosophy, Culture: Interviews and Other Writings 1977–1984*, ed. Lawrence D. Kritzman, New York: Routledge, 1988, ch. 12. This is an interview with Foucault conducted in 1979.

thought – and this can be suppressed or controlled only by complex means, allied of course with more brutal ones. But brutality cannot act and succeed alone. And this same grasp of modern complexity leads to the race to go nuclear – to the consternation of a West that fears an Iranian bomb – justified by the Iranian regime as a necessity to propagate further the development and growth and needs of a middle-class Iran with middle class needs and expectations. One of the great laments of US and British-occupied Iraq is that there is no longer the electricity and piped water provided by Saddam Hussein. Next door in Iran there is an accustomed use and expectation of much more than that. *Lolita*, after all, is still read underground;[12] Kant and Hegel and the entire pantheon of the Western Enlightenment are still taught in the universities (not to mention complex Western International Relations theory); and the traffic jams and pollution of Tehran make its atmosphere a rival to that of Beijing, Mexico City, pre-Olympics Athens, anywhere that has industrialised too quickly and added filters too slowly for normal breath to catch up with the pace of change and development. From all of this, there is only a fundamentalism that labels the regime's thought as necessarily primitive and its policies necessarily dangerous and evil. They might certainly be perceived as dangerous to another's interests, but that does not make them evil, nor dangerous to all interests. It is the balancing of interests that, of course, makes today's world so interesting.

I wish to return to Tehran later, but there is for now a side note for wry speculation. In all the war of words between Washington and Tehran, it was the release in 2007 of the film *300* that sparked greatest wrath not only within the Iranian leadership but, to a large extent, throughout the country. Highly faithful

---

12. Azar Nafisi, *Reading Lolita in Tehran*, London: I.B. Tauris, 2003.

to the original Frank Miller 'graphic novel' and its dialogue and visual rendition of the battle for Thermopylæ, it succeeded in distorting even the earliest Greek accounts of the Spartan victory – which were one-sided enough. But, in the film, Spartan King Leonidas abuses and kills ambassadors with impunity, exercises treachery and deception when offered mercy by Xerxes, and is basically a nice guy who is prepared to be a 'hard bastard' when exercising his patriotism. A man's man with Yankee abdominal muscles straight out of Muscle Beach near Los Angeles – not to mention Tommy Hilfiger hotpants straight out of Rodeo Drive. It is a cartoon through and through, but there was enough arrogance in the film and sufficient dehumanisation of the Persian forces for offence to be taken in Iran. A cartoon superpower was insulting and demeaning a civilisation thousands of years old, turning Xerxes in the process into a freak of nature with effeminate gestures and facial piercings that made him look like a high-class punk hooker. There is, I shall say later, not a little sensitivity in Tehran – and Beijing for that matter – which is to do with long prior cultivation of culture and late emergence into modernity, an emergence that found brash young kids dominating the block and demanding to call the shots.

However, I want to draw another contrast between the Western confrontation with a fully fledged nation-state such as Iran, and the Western foreboding of what an organisation ostensibly headed by a sickly man in a Pakistani or Afghan cave might be able to accomplish against a superpower and European major powers. As if the great powers were houses of cards susceptible to storm and battery from a cave with its vestibule lined with carpets and three thousand books of 'fundamentalist' thought. If it takes that much reading to become a fundamentalist, and an evil one at that, why does no one in the West try to read those books to find out what is going on in the animation of thought that plots the downfall of entire super- and major powers? The asymmetry of it all is not just to do with warfare – nuclear powers against guerrilla car bombs – but also to do with a reversal of the brash confidence and insolence Leonidas displayed at Thermopylæ. It is as if three hundred Wahhabi ascetics had decided not, like the modest Leonidas, to make a stand in a narrow pass but to invade the wide urbanised epicentres of every Western project and government. And the final asymmetry is how to balance the interests of these great governments and those that can be physically located only in small mosques and tiny caves.

Before Osama bin Laden and his destiny in a cave, there was Colonel Muammar Qaddafi of Libya. It is already difficult to remember how much of an international menace he was once thought to be. He retains his eccentricity and, if not in a cave, affects a sense of himself at home in a tent. But I recall in 1986, the US having bombed Libya, a summit of what was then still the G7 (the Group of 7 most developed capitalist states) was convened in Tokyo, and I found myself arrested by a very great many highly zealous airport police on suspicion of being an agent sent by the Libyans to assassinate US President Ronald Reagan. I did look on that visit highly disreputable, having just disembarked from the island of Okinawa – the birthplace of Japanese martial arts – unshaven, with long spiky hair, in a olive-green trenchcoat, with bruises all over arms that emerged from roughly rolled-up sleeves, limping from a leg injury, and with a samurai sword slung over my shoulder. Many hours of interrogation followed before, finally, an interpreter was brought – who quickly divined that I was entirely unsuitable for the role of assassin. He apologised profusely: 'You see, Chan-san, they thought you would hide the sword under your coat and wait in the crowds and then, when Reagan-san came by, you would leap out and *cut off his head*!' It was clear that the by now shamed policemen had watched far too many bad movies, but suspicion dies hard, and I was given a personal 'escort' across Tokyo to the other airport and ushered onto my plane. But it would not have been out of keeping with the Libyan leader's eccentricity to send someone who was kitted out as the bad-guy archetype. He was unpredictable and it was this, as much as anything else, that made him seem dangerous. As it was, his eccentricity devolved into a pure unorthodoxy. He believed in his own nation but not its vocation as a state. He was prepared to forge a union with Egypt and, to this day, has called for a union of all states in one Africa. And, in keeping with his affectation and affection for living in a tent, he crafted the image of having sprung out of the desert – pure and uncontaminated – to save the nation. He never once, in his published writings, justified himself by reference to Islam or an Islamic calling – but always by the pure motivation of his forebears, whom he regarded as the upright men of the dry open spaces. 'He is a purifier from the desert, destined to overthrow hierarchies of corruption.'[13]

It is important to remember this image of the desert and its purity. This is because Osama bin Laden has been so closely associated with a form of Islam called Wahhabism – named after its founder, Muhammad ibn-Abd-al-Wahhab (1703-1792), who reintroduced sharia law to the Arabian Peninsula. His followers came to regard all other sects as heretical, and Wahhabism became famed for its austerity and literalism. It was against what it called polytheism – the idea of a god or gods who could be contemplated in the abstract. It became dominant in Saudi Arabia, Kuwait and Qatar – with pockets in Somalia, Algeria, Palestine and Mauritania. It was a sect in favour of reform, and it is thought that Hassan al-Banna, the father of the Muslim

---

13. John Davis, *Libyan Politics: Tribe and Revolution*, London: I.B. Tauris, 1987, p. 254.

Brotherhood in Egypt – a group long and infamously at logger-heads with the secular Egyptian authorities – was influenced by Wahhabism. But, in the case of al-Banna, as with so much else, there are distinctions to be made between what has been derived from Wahhabism. Is it austerity and its associated purity? Is it literalness and its urge to 'fundamentalism'? Is it an agenda of reform against corruption? Or is it a combination of all three, but with different weightings possible for all three key ingredients? Osama bin Laden, although born into privileged Saudi society, came to despise the ease of life and corruption of the ruling house, and went off – like Che Guevara before him – to be the internationalist warrior of his time, only espousing Islam rather than socialism. But was his leaving of Saudi Arabia to do with a sloughing off of ease, or a condemnation of all that emanated from the House of Saud? Certainly he lived a life of ease himself, but his chief luxury was his stable of pure-bred horses. The warrior on horseback from the desert is also, perhaps, a part of Osama's self-image.

As it is, although Osama rails against the House of Saud, money from Saudi Arabia helped finance his community projects during his early years with the Taliban government in Afghani-stan; and it is thought that prominent Saudi figures, themselves rich and corrupt, help keep him elusive in the cat-and-mouse game that he now must play with vengeful Western forces. For, in Saudi Arabia, Wahhabism is still the official state doctrine and, in its official form, must struggle against radical militants.[14] So there are variants and nuances in Wahhabism and it, in itself, should not be taken literally by Western scholars. Having said that, reading the works of Muhammad ibn-Abd-al-Wahhab can only give the impression that the sect's founder intended very

---

14. David Dean Commins, *The Wahhabi Mission and Saudi Arabia*, London: I.B. Tauris, 2006.

much to visit strictures upon the world.[15] One of the first English-men to comment on Wahhabism was Lawrence of Arabia, who wrote on its impact in the region of Kasim.

> The Wahabis (sic), followers of a fanatical Moslem heresy, had imposed their strict rules on easy and civilized Kasim. In Kasim there was but little coffee-hospitality, much prayer and fasting, no tobacco, no artistic dalliance with women, no silk clothes, no gold and silver head-ropes or ornaments. Every-thing was forcibly pious or forcibly puritanical.[16]

The contemporary Western view of Wahhabism has deviated very little from Lawrence's observation. However, Lawrence immediately went on to talk about the ebb and flow 'like the tides or the changing seasons' of the intervals of 'ascetic creeds in Central Arabia'. But each one was destined to encounter the softer values of urban and merchant life and be modulated if not made to succumb to the comforts of urbanisation. Then, it would start again, for 'doubtless they must recur so long as the causes – sun, moon, wind, acting in the emptiness of open spaces, weigh without check on the unhurried and unencumbered minds of the desert-dwellers.' No Englishman has written so romanti-cally of the desert since Lawrence. But that is the point entirely. Wahhabism may ebb and flow into softer urbanised versions – hence the House of Saud is also Wahhabi – and, while desert Wahhabism is a 'fundamentalism', it is also a romance. Osama needs that romance as much as anything else. As long as he is holed up in a cave, he will follow al-Wahhab. An ascetic benefits from the enforcement of asceticism. But this one also reads his books. The combination of asceticism and learning gives rise to

---

15. Natana J. Delong-Bas, *Wahhabi Islam: From Revival to Global Jihad*, New York: Oxford University Press.

16. T.E. Lawrence, *Seven Pillars of Wisdom*, London: Penguin Classics, 2000, p. 152.

the contemporary equivalent of a Knight Templar. History will have its little ironies, and the despoiling and merciless crusaders of the rosy cross are replaced by the despoiling and merciless crusaders of the crescent moon.

But perhaps it is not simply an irony, but one of many parallels and commonalities. Early Islam almost went out of its way to Islamise the figure of Jesus. There are many texts in which Jesus figures as a great and illuminating prophet, second only to Muhammad himself. Some of the stories are direct parallels to those of the gospels, but others are more Quran- and Islam-specific. Even so the character of Jesus as established in Matthew, fasting forty days and nights in the desert and resisting all manner of temptations laid before him by the Devil – including rule over all the kingdoms of the earth – is the character that is most prominent in the Islamic Jesus.

> It is related that Jesus looked at Satan and said, 'Here is the pillar of the world. It is to the world that he went out, and it is the world that he demanded. I do not share anything of it with him, not even a stone to place beneath my head. Nor will I laugh much in it until I have left it.'[17]

Elsewhere, there is Jesus' direct injunction towards asceticism: 'O Disciples, be ascetics in this world and you will pass through it without anxiety.' But the passage where Jesus converses with Satan, remarking that he will not even accept a stone pillow beneath his head, is very directly reminiscent of the gospel lament of Jesus: that even the sparrows of heaven have their nests, but the Son of Man has nowhere to lay his head. Whether Jesus repudiates the pillow or simply finds himself without, his condition is that of a person who does not use pillows – even stone pillows. He lives

---

17. Tarif Khalidi, ed. and trans., *The Muslim Jesus: Sayings and Stories in Islamic Literature*, Cambridge MA: Harvard University Press, 2001, p. 117.

the life he urged upon the rich young want-to-be believer: 'Go and sell everything you have and give the money to the poor.' And when the young man could not, Jesus said, 'it is easier for a camel to go through the eye of a needle than for a rich man to enter the Kingdom of God' (Matthew 19:21-24).

The example of Jesus was not in itself new. In a sense he was in a long tradition of Semitic ascetics, even though he was in contest with some of their sects in his time – the Essenes for instance, with whom, in some traditions or revisionisms, Jesus was associated. But the Essenes, about 4,000 of whom lived in Jesus' era, pioneered some of the rules of later Christian monasteries – except that men and women lived together, but in a state of chastity (apart from one sub-sect) and certainly in communal poverty and extreme rituals of cleanliness and piety, all in isolated desert groups. And the image of Jesus resisting temptation and enduring privation in the desert parallels the tradition of Muhammad receiving the first words of the Quran from Gabriel on a desert mountain; it veers back to Jerome translating the Bible into Latin in his wilderness cave attended by a wild lion converted to companionship because of Jerome's piety; and, all the while, the desert saints are counterpointed with the splendours and vanities of great cities – Jerusalem, Mecca, Rome – so that the historical traditions of the religions of 'the Book' are interweavings of austerity and sumptuousness, of communal faith and an early capitalist mercantile ethos, the two being transacted by hostilities and condescensions. In this sense, Osama is not new, and nor is the thinking behind his attack on the Twin Towers of the World Trade Center.

The point is that austerity, asceticism, privation, the lying on stone pillows or directly on the ground, are part of a symbolic practice; they are in themselves a symbolic 'form': that is, they are what enables a subjectivity to emerge, the 'I who suffers',

and this subjectivity depends upon a 'form' of existence that is
rendered almost mythological in itself, in order that the partaker
might become closer to the larger, enveloping and 'substantial'
myth that is the 'objective reality' of God, so that the subjective
experience of renunciation and purification leads towards the
Greater Purity.[18] And, just as a dialectical relationship exists
between the lesser subjective and the greater objective reality,
so also a dialectical tension exists between purity (combined
subjective and objective), on the one hand, and desecration and
apostasy, corruption and capitalist exploitation, on the other.
For Osama, as agent of one order, it is natural enough to wage
war upon the other order.

But war means sacrifice, and all the privations are themselves
rehearsals for the final great sacrifice. What might a person
sacrifice? In the desert mountains Abraham sought to sacrifice
his son, Isaac. Jesus sacrificed himself. In the final biblical book
of Revelation he is revealed as an existence identified by many
codes – the 'Alpha and Omega', and the 'sacrificial lamb'. Even
as a great ruler in heaven, his name is still as a self-sacrificer;
and, not only that, he went to the *sacrificium* as meekly and
as calmly as a lamb. The point is that every sacrifice brings a
return, a renewal.[19] Jesus was himself resurrected, renewed as
himself and in order to bring renewal to all the earth – to rule
over it in a way that Satan could never have offered. But, before
his sacrifice, he suffered agonies of apprehension and, indeed,
fear and weakness in the Garden of Gethsemane. God had to
send angels to lift his spirits. Even then, having gone through
with the sacrifice, at the very last, entering his death agonies

---

18. This formulation is drawn from Ernst Cassirer, *The Philosophy of Symbolic Forms*,
Volume 2: *Mythical Thought*, New Haven: Yale University Press, 1955.

19. Mircea Eliade, *The Myth of the Eternal Return: Cosmos and History*, London:
Arkarna, 1989.

on the cross, he called out to ask why God had abandoned him to such a hideous death. To go to the *sacrificium*, no matter for what renewal, is no easy thing. Many things must go into the preparation, and the hardening of the spirit through privations is only one. No one goes forward only as a fanatic.

But one does go forward on the basis of the mythological foundation of righteousness that one has developed through privations and purification that *surmount* the written word; that is, the Wahhabism of Osama is different *experientially* from that of the House of Saud – albeit that Osama's is suffused with idealism and disgust. Yet both he and the House of Saud read the same texts by al-Wahhab. What Osama has done is to have made the progression from *logos* to *mythos*, but his *mythos* could not exist without the *logos*. The *logos* animates the *mythos*, just as it might – in a palace in Jeddah – animate nothing at all. To understand someone like Osama, it is necessary to read the texts he reads, but it is also necessary to take a leap. His followers, in any case, were not reading any books at the moment they piloted their planes into the Twin Towers. We shall have to make a psychological excursion – but should do so first by elaborating the parallels in Western thought and foundational histories and mythologies.

The first point to be made is simple enough in its outline: that the move from *logos* to *mythos* is not something that traces a rational path. It might have its logic, but that does not mean it has a traceable rationality. It has a certain metaphoric leap, not unlike that associated with poetry. It recalls to mind what the philosopher Hans-Georg Gadamer once said: 'Without poets there is no philosophy.'[20] What he meant was that literature, particularly poetry, is a partner to philosophy. Literary language uses irrational devices and in so doing has the attribute of

20. Hans-Georg Gadamer, 'Without Poets There is No Philosophy', *Radical Philosophy* 69, 1995, p. 27.

'coaxing prereflective knowledge out of its depths'.[21] In short, irrational language stimulates rational thought. It acts as the provocation for rational thought and language to come into its ordered existence. Certain theologies might serve in the place of poetry here; but what I want to say is not that prereflective knowledge precedes reflective knowledge, not that the irrational precedes the rational as its stimulus – but that there is also such a thing as post-reflective knowledge, where the rational thought gives rise to the irrational action. How this takes place is the subject of what follows.

My second point is that this post-reflective knowledge is deontological. This is from the Greek *deon*, or 'duty'. It means the capacity to sacrifice oneself or one's interests, even those one loves, for the sake of a greater duty. This is not something that happens automatically or intuitively. It requires an act of imagination and will. It is not a reflex conditioned by lifetimes of practice, as in the case of the great Buddhist boddhisattvas (saints who renounce Nirvana for endless reincarnations in which they help humanity advance towards the Nirvana they will now never see). The boddhisattva has sacrificed him- or herself by chosen vocation, and is good at sacrifice both because of unending practice and, finally, because of accomplished character. It's just what he or she does. The *sacrificium* is his or her calling, justification, and is accomplished without thought at all.

> When the Boddhisattva was an elephant, roaming in the wilderness, he could not bear the suffering of a hundred travelers who had lost their way. He fed them with his own flesh and blood. He consoled them and gave them his own life.[22]

21. Hans-Georg Gadamer, 'Text Matters', in Richard Kearney, ed., *States of Mind*, Manchester: Manchester University Press, 1995, p. 270.
22. Marylin M. Rhie and Robert A.F. Thurman, *The Sacred Art of Tibet*, London: Thames & Hudson, 1991, p. 94.

Of all the boddhisattva stories, I like that one best. It gives a new twist to the idea of the saint offering succour. It is an ultimate deontology, but it is not the sort at stake here.

The sort at stake may be both chillingly and sentimentally told. Chilling in the case of the early Roman republican leader Brutus, who sentenced his own sons to death for plotting against the republic. The French revolutionary artist David painted a haunting picture of a disconsolate but bitterly determined Brutus, brooding in his chair to one side of the room as, in the background on the other, the corpses of his sons are brought in. This man is determined not even to mourn – even though it is a phenomenal act of will and duty. Here, duty is greater than love, the republic greater than family, the city and nation greater than blood. It may be sentimentally told, as in the case of the fourteenth-century English poem, *Sir Gawain and the Green Knight* (not an epic as such, but written to be recited or sung to audiences in instalments – the pre-technological 'soap' of its day). In this poem Gawain answers a challenge made by a giant green stranger who has thundered into Camelot at Christmas. The challenge is to decapitate the stranger and, later, suffer decapitation in turn. Gawain beheads the stranger, but then, to the court's horror, the green knight picks up his head, remounts his horse, and announces that he expects Gawain to seek him out at a most imprecise location and, in exactly a year's time, suffer his turn at being beheaded. Then he thunders out. Now there is no 'normal' compulsion on Gawain, no legal summons, no oath on the Bible – nothing but his own word. But, true to his word, Gawain seeks the green knight and does so with great suffering (it is clear from the poem that he has had to wander into Wales). In the week before his due date he is given shelter in a stunning castle, where the beauteous hostess does her best to seduce him while her husband is out hunting. Gawain courteously, wittily and stubbornly refuses her. However, he cannot resist her offer of a green sash that she says will make him invulnerable to any blade. Finally, wearing the green sash, he goes out and finds the green knight. Even then, after so many adventures to come to his death, Gawain flinches at the last, seeking to avoid a fake blow. So, on two occasions – the acceptance of the sash, and the attempt to roll away from the blow – all of Gawain's deontology is called into very human question. For, otherwise, Gawain is perfect. Some of the Arthurian legends have him, rather than Percival, attaining the Grail. He is certainly the most courteous and chivalrous of the Knights of the Round Table. And he certainly sets out stubbornly, and within his duty as a knight of his word, to seek his own decapitation. The author of the poem clearly loves him, but is also keen to make a gentle example of him – for when Gawain finally arrives back in court, having been spared by the green giant, all the knights resolve to wear a green sash out of solidarity with Gawain's two moments of fear. But, until those two moments, Gawain was the walking and curiously noble embodiment of a deontology that expressed itself gently but was as ferociously stubborn as anything Brutus might have felt.

However, both Brutus and Gawain had to steel themselves to it – and Gawain did not quite do his sense of duty full justice, though Brutus certainly did. There is one final Western example I wish to recount, involving not the giving up of one's own life, or the lives of one's family, but one's own honour. This is the story of Priam, King of Troy, last ruler of the great city besieged by the Greek armies, a king who has watched his sons fall in the city's defence one by one; and now his favourite son, Hector, has fallen at the hands of Achilles. That duel between Hector and Achilles was less mundane than depicted by Eric Bana and Brad Pitt in the awful film. Hector had earlier killed Patroclus, the best friend (and, some latter-day commentators insist, the lover) of Achilles. Patroclus had been wearing Achilles' armour at the time and Hector had looted it. So, when he confronts a vengeful Achilles at the gates of Troy he is wearing that armour and, in fact, looks like Achilles. At heart, Homer was saying that all men are one, and certainly that all men are heroic in tragic circumstances. The most moving scene in the *Iliad* is in fact of Hector about to go out to face Achilles. His wife brings their son to see him and the child is startled by the father's great horse-plumed helmet. Hector, laughing, removes it to embrace his son one last time. Once outside the gates, however, he sees that the Achilles who rushes towards him is not only the invulnerable demigod he knew (he had prepared himself to face and try to overcome such uneven odds), but a demigod clothed in new divinely made armour. So it is a man in human Achillean armour facing a demigod in heavenly Achillean armour. Hector breaks and runs and the battle between the two is in fact a race around the walls of Troy until Achilles overtakes Hector. It is against the mythic proportions of that contest, and against the atrocities Achilles tries to commit upon Hector's body, that the excruciatingly human act of Priam should be seen.

It is dawn. For days, Achilles has been desecrating the body of Hector before the walls of Troy. Not a soldier, not a surviving son of Priam, dares to sally out to rescue the corpse. It is all clearly lost. The champion of champions has fallen and the city is doomed. At dawn the gates open a little, and an old man riding a cart emerges from Troy. The gods suddenly divine what he is doing and are startled, then moved, by an act of agency that none of them had contemplated might be in the human lexicon. They come down and help Priam enter the Greek encampment unseen. He comes to the tent of Achilles. The Greek hero has very long hair. It has not been cut since birth. He is having breakfast with his friends. Out of armour, he partakes in a curiously domestic scene. Yet he is the one who has killed Priam's son and committed sacrilege upon the body – for Achilles, by refusing to bury Hector, has defied the natural laws of respect and the rituals that facilitate the migration of souls to the afterworld. So the person sitting there is also monstrous. Achilles has not seen Priam. But then he feels lips upon his hand, and he looks down to the side of his chair. Priam, who is a very old man, and a king, is kneeling there: 'Forgive me, Lord Achilles, for I have kissed the hand of the man who killed my son.' And Achilles instantly knows that he has gone too far with his atrocities, but that the old man has gone even further with his self-abnegation. Achilles raises Priam up and gives him back the body of his son.

My third point is that the drive towards this sort of deontology, whether it commits familial murder like Brutus's, whether it proceeds gently like Gawain's, or whether it wears the most human and humane proportions like Priam's, is made possible by *ate*, by the frenzied madness Lacan deciphered in Antigone – except that the frenzy is not that of a madman who raves and storms, but of one under full control, and that control is to obliterate the irrational qualities of what one is about to commit. The frenzy is like a state of grace; that is, it has a calm centre that radiates outwards, and it bathes its host in a certainty that can seem positively serene. The problem with a one-dimensional reading of Lacan on Antigone, taking madness and frenzy as agitated qualities, is that Antigone is never less than self-assured. She is able to debate with the regent Creon, whose law she has broken. She goes to her death calmly. Even Anouilh's Antigone, after all her performances as a *demandeur mal*, is restored at her execution to a teenage state of dithering about almost everything except her death. She is as calm as a teenager can be and amazingly offhand about her impending demise.

My fourth point is that this calm frenzy can be extremely lucid. Sartre's introduction to Fanon painted a picture of a 'native', weary beyond comprehension, his muscles tensed and twitchy. It was almost a racism. To the 'native' the only thing denied him in his vengeance was the condition of philosophy. It was not so much himself impelling the bomb forward as himself impelled by his weary, driven-to-despair, nothing-left-to-lose, acted-upon condition – until, finally, his only remaining act of self-agency is to destroy. He has a muscular back, a 'permanent tensing of powerful muscles which are afraid to relax'.[23] This is a caricature – and it is particularly a caricature of Fanon's own writing. In Fanon's most famous work, *The Wretched of the Earth*, there is only one chapter on anger and violence, even if a long one. Much of the rest of the book is a psychiatrist's case studies of those traumatised or otherwise affected by violence. In this sense the acting outwards of trauma, through violence, was the recourse of those traumatised. But there have been very few global revolutions plotted only on the basis of trauma. And even the footsoldiers cannot be made easily into the traumatised dupes of cooler leaders. The phenomenom of videoed 'last wills and testaments' by Islamic suicide bombers, about to go out to explode themselves into gory smithereens, and explode all those around them, are calm expositions of determination, with very clear – if not fully reasonable – explanations for why they have chosen to die and kill in this manner. Moreover, it takes time, effort and organisation to become a suicide bomber: one must find a militant cell; one must convince that cell of one's voluntary bona fides; one must undertake a form of training – if only in appearing inconspicuous and positioning oneself for maximum effect. If a fully solo act, one must organise and assemble the

---

23. Jean-Paul Sartre, 'Preface' to Frantz Fanon, *The Wretched of the Earth*, London: Penguin, 1967, p. 15.

explosives oneself. With all of this, the last moment of lucidity in pressing the button merely follows upon much lucid preparation and mental rehearsal. Suicide bombing is a weapon in a new war. In its militant Islamic guise it is a major international problem, but it is not a new device. Japanese kamikaze pilots flew what were in fact glider-shaped bombs into the US naval fleet. A female Tamil Tiger operative blew herself and Indian prime minister Rajiv Gandhi to kingdom come. The kamikaze pilots were imbued, even if sometimes forcibly, by a philosophy of *bushido*, or warrior self-sacrifice. It should not be the case that the condition of philosophy, no matter how reductionist, should be denied the bombers of today. Clausewitz, the Prussian general who deciphered how Napoleon smashed his way through the best armies of Europe, wrote that 'war is policy by other means'. That has become a dictum ever since, and one which contemporary generals labour upon their political masters. There has been more than one delegation of brass to the summits of power in Whitehall and Washington, asking what clear political and military objectives one is being called upon to fight for; asking 'where and what is the policy?' In a sense, the strategists behind suicide bombing, whether they know it or not, are applying another of Clausewitz's precepts, the concentration of forces upon the enemy's weakest points, and doing so with a mobility and speed that confounds the enemy. But they probably *have* read Clausewitz. Every military cadet in every military academy all over the world still reads his great book, *On War*. But what we are witnessing today – and it is confounding us – is not only terrorist war as policy by other means (we just haven't understood the 'policy'), but also the philosophy of other means of war.

As for Fanon, in his other works, he sought not a destruction of the masters but the equality of master and slave. *Black Skin, White Masks* was probably the first draft of his medical thesis, before it was substituted by a document more obviously scientific. The book of the thesis-that-wasn't is an amalgam of existential philosophy and despair, cultural crossovers, early Lacanian psychoanalysis, some medical science, and pure if angry youthful idealism. It is a most imperfect work – but it is the best of Fanon. It is also one of those books with an endless array of reference points – Adler, Hegel, Tchaikovsky, Van Gogh, the empathy possible between discriminated blacks and discriminated Jews – and is, far from a manifesto of black purity and black anger, a manifesto of black equality within a global cultural mix. It is not Fanon who can be easily applied to today's rash of global anger and violence, but even in Fanon's day – with the cool lucidity of bombers and condemned prisoners in the Algerian independence struggle – there was much more than mindless anger and violence at work. Anger and violence, certainly. Mindlessness played a smaller part.

My fifth point is that, nevertheless, the experience, memory or imagination of enforced abnegation does play a key role. Years of real or imagined oppression – or a solidarity, even an identification, with those who have been oppressed elsewhere – lead to a rebellion. The question missing from most analyses, however, is that the oppression that is resisted is not only a political oppression of a people – for example, the Palestinians (which almost every Islamic state and militant organisation has conspicuously failed to help beyond very limited points) – but a perceived oppression or denigration of a sense of self and a sense of core belief; and it is perceived as applied personally, but also as systemically applied to the collective manifestation of this core belief. To that extent, it is belief that seems as if it is called upon to fight back, because it is belief and philosophy that have been subject to abnegation. It is not, however, just the philosophy that fights back, but, as mentioned above, the philosophy of the means chosen. Does abnegation justify a *sacrificium* in which huge numbers of innocent people are swept into death? Does the *sacrificium* necessarily sacrifice others? In so far as the memory or re-created memory of abnegation is strong and made stronger, it triumphs over the memories and values of self held by others. Terror thus becomes a requital and ruthlessness – requital for sins committed perhaps against self but certainly against self's historical and contemporary cohorts, and ruthlessness in an exploding outwards. In this requital and ruthlessness there is a disproportion. I am here applying a variation of Paul Ricoeur's 'disproportion of subjectivity', the 'vehement ontology' of a 'wounded *cogito*'.[24] But, as with all memory, it is a wound that is as imagined as it is real. It is adopted as a badge and rationale as much as it has been branded by another onto one's skin. It is the adoption of abnegation, often by those who have never personally been steeped in abnegation. Osama grew up in privilege and luxury in an independent state, where the national religion was his religion, and the global capital of his religion was in his country, and where the footsteps of the Prophet were all around him. But it was precisely the perception that all these surroundings were also being imprinted by the footsteps of those who saw the House of Saud as clients, who thought they could and would buy the loyalty of a holy land, that acted as the steeping in abnegation. The site of memory was being contaminated. The global city was sweeping away the desert. In a way, Osama felt like Jesus, wanting to whip the merchants out of the temple; but the merchants have held firm in his temple, so Osama wants to whip them in their own parts of the global city.

---

24. These terms from Ricoeur's life's work are best summed up by himself, in 'Intellectual Autobiography', in Lewis Edwin Hahn, ed., *The Philosophy of Paul Ricoeur*, Chicago: Open Court, 1995.

What does Osama want? What does the varied collective we might label 'Osama' want? Let me here speculate rather than demonise. Like Qaddafi before him, he seeks the *umma*: the stateless unity of the Islamic nations, a unity forged on faith and not on secular governments. He wants the worldwide homeland of the faith. Unlike Qaddafi, he anchors this desire precisely on faith, whereas Qaddafi wanted an Arab unity and an African unity. Qaddafi wanted the unities of what he perceived to be the two most benighted peoples on earth. Osama wants the unity of the Prophet to stand up to the atheistic and polytheistic infidels of corrupt global capital. This *umma* of his will be a vast international land of true faith. It will be austere within its environment. And it will become an international superpower and, as a superpower, challenge the West. That is the prime goal. For now, the West is attacked only because it prevents the cohesion of the *umma*, installs and insists upon its client governments (Iraq being only the latest of many examples), and stamps itself militarily on the lands of the holy places. Osama wants the West to withdraw militarily from the Middle East in particular and all Islamic countries in general. If the problem of Palestine can be addressed as a by-product, that would be welcomed – but Palestine, although part of the badge of abnegation, is not key to Osama's agenda. Then Osama wants to compete economically with the West and show the triumph not of an anti-capitalism but of a clean and equitable Islamic capitalism.[25] And he will have the economic weapons to do so, since the West will still be hostage to the oil reserves of what will become the *umma*. It is the great global revolution of the twenty-first century that Osama seeks. It is prosecuted through

25. For the philosophic ingredients of such a thing, see Charles Tripp, *Islam and the Moral Economy: The Challenge of Capitalism*, Cambridge: Cambridge University Press, 2006.

requital and ruthlessness, but is also about a sweeping idealism. It is a pure desert idealism that, all the same, imagines its way forward into a very complex world. Osama experiences Wahhabism differently from his Saudi countrymen – and he imagines it differently from anything al-Wahhab might have managed in his desert of the eighteenth century. After all, in the deserts of the twenty-first century, Osama plots his revolution with the best technological weapons available. He uses television, the Internet, mobile phones, camera crews and even image-makers. The transition of Osama, from ascetic fighter in his irregular broadcasts to presidential figure seated behind a desk with not a gun in sight – offering respite to the West on certain conditions – is not accidental. In some ways, his *umma* will have within it the seeds of the negation of its own austerity.

If even some of this speculation is correct, then what can the West do? Thus far it has called every wrong shot possible. What it fights against grows as a result. In its pomp as the 'last man' of consummated history, it is now unable fully to contemplate the 'first men' of a renewed history and what they have in mind. The West, in its anxiety to demonstrate it still has *thymos*, will and strength, the courage and power of its convictions and self-recognition, thinks the struggle is about *thymos* alone. But the struggle is indeed about desire and reason, and not about the puffing out of the chest of *thymos* alone.

The city grows everywhere. Everywhere the desert shrinks. The shrinking of the desert is the key to Western strategy. But this is not a planting of trees alone. It is not just about accelerating development in the Islamic world. In Turkey, it took a certain stage of more equitable development for a new, more expansive and inclusive middle class to vote into government an Islamic party. It is precisely about accelerating development to grow on purpose an Islamic middle class. And this is not a strategy devoted only to the Middle East and other parts of the Islamic world. In Europe, the way forward is to help build the agenda of what Tariq Ramadan has called a 'European Islam'.[26] This is certainly an Islam better able to understand and work within Europe. It is not necessarily an Islam *integrated* within Europe. This has to be understood. It is not an appropriation of Islam by Europe. It is as much an appropriation by Islam *of* Europe. In short, it is not the sort of multiculturalism that seemed to emanate from British reformers such as Parekh,[27] and not the sort of majoritarianism espoused by influential journalists such as Goodhart,[28] where every core 'European' value is sustained and strengthened. It is the sort of interaction where Islam becomes more European in some ways, and Europe becomes more Islamic. What I mean is a proper cross-fertilisation. I do not a mean a Europe that embraces Islam with all its 'nasty' bits chopped off. I mean a Europe that embraces Islam and engages in dialogue with the nasty bits, and perhaps is even changed by them. After all, the Islamic laws against usury might be of very great benefit and relief to millions of mortgage-bearing homeowners – even though it would transform the banking system. Europe as its present whole might find that difficult, but the European residue of socialism should establish the imagination to recognise that this is exactly what it also has sought – on the foundations of the finest European thought and idealism. In short, radical examples apart, the exercise might be far more resonant on all sides if entered in literal good faith.

---

26. Tariq Ramadan, *Western Muslims and the Future of Islam*, New York: Oxford University Press, 2003.

27. Bhikhu Parekh, *Rethinking Multiculturalism: Cultural Diversity and Political Theory*, Cambridge MA: Harvard University Press, 2000 – a brave rethinking of the Western foundations of liberalism, but one which recognises the power of liberalism and its limits in tolerance, yet doesn't really propose an exceeding of this tolerance.

28. David Goodhart, 'National Anxieties', *Prospect*, June 2006.

What this would do, above all, is build a model for emulation in precisely those middle classes arising in the developing Islamic world. The voters of Turkey should recognise that Europe is as much their city as ours; the citizens of the Islamic world should recognise it is their world as much as ours. When everything is everybody's, there is nothing left to bomb, no one left to fight. The memory of the world's next generation will be a common memory. Otherwise, without this fusion, there will be no way to disable the dragon's teeth now being sown as the children of Osama.

4

Mercy and the modern world

One of the great African novels is by Ayi Kwei Armah, and it is called *The Beautyful Ones Are Not Yet Born*. It is about a plangent stubborn refusal to enter corruption, even though everyone around the central character survives and prospers through it. The refusal of corruption means a life of poverty and its journey through literal shit. There is not much beauty, and even the central character is far from a Beautiful One. But at the very end of the novel he sees a single flower, and in that flower, in the emergence from shit to see that flower, there is every possibility and every incarnation of the Beautiful. It is an image with an odour. Anyone who has trekked the slums of Accra in Ghana, where the novel is set – and anyone who has traversed the slums of Indian cities – will remember how necessary it was to become accustomed to the smell of shit, to make it ordinary and everyday. But, at the end of it all, anyone traversing, trekking through, will come again to a life of air-conditioning, clean chrome and comfort, will come to the Bollywood movie existence that other people's lives will gape at in hopeless aspiration.

For those who have nothing, what flower might be seen as they glimpse the world from the mouth of their sewer?

The Indian film industry has come a very long way. Like early Chinese cinema, its first production standards were execrable – those of Satyajit Ray being a conspicuous exception. I remember, in the early 1950s, being dragged by a harridan grandmother to awful Chinese films. One stood out in particular. Clearly shot with one camera, clearly unedited, clearly with all the scenes shot sequentially and, with just enough film stock to last ninety minutes with exactly twenty scenes of about five minutes each, the actors had to get everything right in the first (and only) take every single time. It was a historical musical. Halfway through the film, the lead actor's trousers began to fall down beneath his medieval robe. In full view of the camera, but as quickly as possible – the show had to go on – he adjusted his trousers upwards and, since it was his turn to sing next, pulled his robe back down and burst into song on a great moral question to do with true love versus a lovingly arranged marriage. I had barely begun school, but insisted on never going to these films again. A quarter-century later, stranded by a typhoon in Mauritius, the only thing to do in the storm-lashed little hotel where I, one other guest and an endless contingent of refugee mosquitoes were staying, was to watch Indian films on Mauritian television. But I was more patient now, and found it quite amusingly artful that the depiction of Shiva, a god with many arms, was accomplished by framing the actor front-on, with two other actors behind him, trying very hard to ensure their own bodies were hidden by his, waving their arms as if they emanated also from Shiva's body. Shiva was thus able to have his six arms, although, thankfully, did not try to dance in front of the camera. There is a limit to ambition, which only today's technology has extended. That same year I was again stranded, this time in what was still called Bombay, and acquired a huge stack of volumes which covered, sometimes in comic-book format, many of the stories of the great Indian legend-cycle the Mahabharata. I have never ceased to be a fan of these amazing stories and their beautiful heroes and even more beautiful gods.[1] And, driving the streets by day and walking them by night, I realised that if you, your life, your surroundings, and your prospects are ugly, your gods will be very beautiful. The English romantic poet's injunction that truth is beauty and beauty is truth was never more true than in India where, amidst squalor, the truthfulness, beneficence and beauty of the gods were co-equal. Such a god was a Beautyful one.

And the depiction of the Beautyful ones was, whether in comic-book illustration, on film, or in the sculptures of ancient times, of such extreme beauty that they – even as visual representations – seemed to radiate perfume. The image as scent was of great importance, so that as many senses as possible could be engaged – in reality or imagination – in the adoration of the gods. They wore few clothes – India generally being hot – so corporeal smell and extrusion would be an all-too-human reality, had not the gods emitted perfume instead; and, as far as I know, there are no instances of their needing to shit. Permanently constipated, they nevertheless conspired to be fully slender, to have volumised hair piled up from their shoulders, and to wear in place of clothes necklaces, bracelets, rings, earrings, jewelled belts and sashes, diadems, crowns, mascara and eyeshadow. Male earrings were different from female earrings, but both were weighted, and from both the ear lobes hung distended as a clear

1. For commentaries on the aesthetics involved, see Vidya Deheja, *Indian Art*, London: Phaidon, 1997, chs 6 and 10; and Roy C. Craven, *Indian Art*, London: Thames & Hudson, 1997, which discusses the aesthetic qualities of Indian art historical epoch by epoch.

metaphor that other parts – barely hidden under diaphanous silk wraps – also hung; for the gods, although not needing to shit, had a propensity for fucking that led to the cosmic orgasms that shook and reordered time and space in the tiny human salient of their universe.

This much is to paint a colourful picture – but one not far removed from the pictures of the gods that have descended through Indian human history to the cinema of today where – amidst much higher production standards and much song and dance – the gods look as ever they did. And their timelessness is important, because they represent both antiquity and the projection of antiquity into the future – where memory will be re-remembered, reinscribed in future consciousness like a wave that washes constantly to shore. Like the great forebear god Brahma, each night in his sleep or meditation, emanating the universe into existence for the following day, and reabsorbing it again at close of day – everything that is material is emanated from a dream of cosmic power; the insubstantial having more creative power than the physically substantial; and physical substantiality flows into existence only to ebb away again, and is then re-created both just as it was but different – from a different dream. Each reinscription of the dream, each rememory of an earlier dream, carries antiquity into futures where antiquity is viewed differently. It is the same god dreaming, but each new reality interprets the dream for itself. Until finally it is the human reality that triumphs over the dreaming god and appropriates the dream while offering deference to the dreamer.

In a contemporary world of Islamic revivalism, contesting both individual nationalisms and dreams of a transnational *umma*, the renaissance of *hindutva* or Hindu nationalism is often ignored or regarded as 'safely' contained within India. But there are many revivalisms and nationalisms at play in today's world. The Tibetan independence movement is a pacific but militant Buddhism, and the Dalai Lama himself heads a Yellow Hats faction of what was a monasticised state, a faction that struggled against and overcame the Red Hats in the seventeenth century, with not a little conflict. But that episode of strife does not obviate a curious Tibetan vision of *shambhala* – not the nirvana of accomplished bliss, but a pure land, already in physical existence, probably within the ice wastes of Greenland, shielded by forcefields from the knowledge of a corrupt world, already sending out its agents to convert the world to pacificism. And, when that is accomplished in 300 years' time, the global age of *shambhala* will begin, introducing a worldwide legal and moral framework. Even the most non-violent of nationalisms will have an internationalism in its core vision and animation, and *hindutva* has as well – but these days as an antidote, an alternative vision to what has been accomplished by the arrant rationality of the West.

So that precisely the image of Brahma dreaming the universe in and out, or the parallel image of Shiva as *nataraja*, Lord of the Dance, dancing the universe in and out (it comes alive when he dances, relapses out of existence as he tires), dancing in the sculptural representations in a perfect circle, become for the advocate of a Hindu or Vedic science an antique but fully correct representation of the origins of the universe – from Big Bang to the farthest extents of Big Bang's explosion, to the contraction again over trillions of years of all that Big Bang flung out. For the Vedic scientist, the *metaphor* of science is as strong as the science itself; and – here is the point – the Vedic metaphor was both more beautiful and, above all, more original than anything that emanated until recently from Western science. The Vedic metaphor, the Vedic explanation of life and the universe, was first. Throughout India there have been for years faculties of Vedic science, of Ayurvedic medicine – so that Malraux's depiction of Benares Hindu University as a perfect site of fusion, with its holy trees, robed monks and English gothic buildings, is something that is more than meets the eye. It is an assertion of mind. And it is an assertion of primacy – over Western rationality, over secularism, in its most narrow-minded localised fundamentalism regarding the beliefs and rights of India's Muslim citizens. This last assertion, very often inflamed by politicians seeking scapegoats to explain away the poverty of their Hindu voters, inflaming riots and pogroms against Muslim slum dwellers, is the banal and violent end of a wide, rich and problematic spectrum. For the linkage between the poor and popular aspiration to embrace an image of the Beautyful ones, and an elite manifestation of the same thing in claiming this Beauty for science – claiming that the origin of science is in this Beauty, is located in metaphor – is astounding. It is one of the great political accomplishments of the world's post-independence history. And the claim is that this sort of foundation for India's nationalism is also the foundation upon which India will stand as it rises, matches and finally surpasses the West. There is no lack of antiquity in India, and no lack of international ambition.

Nor is India alone in its methodology – even if few others match it in Beauty. The fundamentalist end of the Zionist spectrum is precisely that, in King Solomon's day, about 950 BC, the extent of Israel's borders were set. These were at their widest mark, not surpassed before or since, and they now constitute the imagined borders of *Eretz Israel*, the old and true Israel, to which modern Israel is entitled. The only problem is that these borders were set almost three millennia ago, were held briefly, were achieved as much by alliances and treaties as by heavenly gift, and might in fact never have existed because – outside the scriptural accounts – there is no verifiable evidence of such an extensive kingdom, and indeed there is no verifiable evidence that Solomon himself ever existed. What there is, in both Hebrew legend and Islamic renditions, is accounts of Solomon's amazing fecundity for fusion. He married widely, thus establishing the alliances and diplomacy that allowed him wide and friendly borders; and, when he didn't marry, but courted with great lyricism, it turns out that the beautiful dusky Shulamite woman in his 'Song of Songs' was a Canaanite, in today's terms a Palestinian; international trade and commerce were active, so that the beams for his great temple were floated down from Lebanon (the famous cedars of Lebanon); Sheba came from Saudi Arabia, Yemen or Eritrea (all three countries claim her, though the Eritreans call her 'Magda') to test his famed wisdom; and the temple was itself built – an architectural and engineering feat of its time – with the help of demons whom Solomon tamed and trained, using the occult elements of his extensive and eclectic knowledge. Legend has it that in no other way could such an architectural marvel be understood – it was a building beyond man's ingenuity. And, when Solomon tired of wise discourse among even learned people, he wrote treatises on botany and 'spake also of beasts, and of birds, and of creeping things, and of fishes' (1 Kings 4:33). Perhaps he also spoke *to* them, as he spoke to demons and spirits. Solomon is a legend of knowledge, and a legendary architect not only of a temple but of a nation and its borders. But, to this day, those legendary borders constitute a very real and fiery political issue.

Legend begets struggle: Israeli against Palestinian; Hindu against Muslim; even Buddhist against Buddhist (the ideological wars of the competing Buddhist states in ancient Sri Lanka were as bloody as any). There have been 'clashes of civilisations' long before Samuel Huntington and the loose school descended from him imagined such could only be between Islam and the West. And these are clashes of aspiration, established on beauteous cultures that have been painstakingly laboured into place, and linked to and furbished with much thought. It is the linkage to thought that is everything; for thought is what gives justification to everything, whether those things were originally just or not. But, probably in legend and metaphor, they were. And, in the science derived from metaphor and legend, they are.

Except that, in the case of Indian legend, there is less surety than first meets the eye. A superficial fundamentalism is possible here too. To avoid this, let us look at some key elements of the foundation legends. One of the great heroes of the Mahabharata was Arjuna, the Pandava prince and great archer. It is he who features in the intersection between heroic epic (the Mahabharata) and scripture (the Bhagavadgita); it is in the latter that the god Krishna adopts the guise of Arjuna's charioteer on the eve of the great battle of Kurukshetra, where the decisive struggle to settle the great Indian civil war will take place. Arjuna goes forth in his chariot to survey the enemy ranks, and is dismayed when he sees an array of cousins and friends leading the lines against him. He loses heart and, very humanly, laments that he cannot fight and kill his own. It is at this point that Krishna delivers his great sermon to Arjuna about a greater cosmic justice that must be pursued through this battle. Some have seen this as the ruthlessness of a supervening good. Others have seen it as an expression of the smallness of humanity and its concerns in the great cosmic wheel. Yet, to this day, the Hare Krishna devotees in the streets will make available to you books and pamphlets depicting the scene of this sermon. In them you see Arjuna and Krishna between the opposing ranks of the great armies that stretch into the distance. The chariot is equipped with an umbrella, so the two can sermonise and listen in comfort.

Arjuna has stacked away his bow and quiver of arrows, but still wears his golden armour and helmet. His long curly hair trails out from under the helmet, and he wears a neat moustache. He is seated with one hand on his knee, and Krishna is standing over him. He is blue – the traditional colour to depict a god who was in fact black – and he talks of the need for slaughter with a beatific smile on his face. He waves an admonishing finger in Arjuna's face, and the prince, once assured by Krishna that his reincarnation prospects will not fully diminish if he loses stomach, is visibly galvanising himself. You can almost picture his fingers beginning to twitch towards the bow. I want to come back to what this scene more complexly represents.

First, another Arjuna story. He is by far the most human character in the Mahabharata, if only by virtue of being the most promiscuous. It is perhaps for the reason of his imperfect human-ity that he is the perfect foil for Krishna's cosmic presence. The other story has Arjuna on a ten-year exile from his court. He is following a white horse that wanders in front of his army. The horse wanders randomly. Whenever it comes to a new city, that city must either surrender to the Pandava empire, or stand and fight. Given the strength of Arjuna's army, fighting en masse was an unattractive proposition for most cities; but they had the option of sending out a champion to face Arjuna in lone combat. That champion must have quivered as he went out, knowing he was facing the world's greatest archer. For Arjuna could look at a pond and see, in its reflection, a bird flying in the sky; and, by looking only at the reflection, aim his bow and arrow upwards and bring down the bird – the arrow through the eye every time. One day the white horse came to the great walled city of Manipur. The gates were locked. Waiting in front of the gates, standing in his golden chariot, was the city's champion. But he was Arjuna's own son, sired on his earlier romantic interlude in Manipur with the Princess Chitrangada. Arjuna had lingered awhile with her, and as the boy grew taught him everything he knew about the bow. For the first time, at the gates of Manipur, Arjuna would be evenly matched. A furious battle takes place. Arrows fly like flocks of swallows diving through the air. But it is the son who slays the father, and as the city gates open Chitrangada rushes out to survey and lament her early husband. However, observing the action had been a princess of the snake kingdom. She also had been an earlier lover of Arjuna. She brings from the snake-world the means of resurrection. Arjuna gets two lives in one incarnation and the scene fades with a reunion involving Arjuna, his son and two brides. There is, to put it mildly, a degree of ambivalence in the emotional wanderings of Arjuna.

It is precisely this ambivalence that humanises both Arjuna and the foundation legends of *hindutva*. The American religious scholar Ruth Cecily Katz makes this point in her (rather more than) full-length study of Arjuna. However, her treatment as to why Arjuna fought at Kurukshetra is cursory. It was, she says, for the sake of *dharma*, for the good of human law and justice that guides human affairs. For all good *dharma* an element or depiction of sacrifice is required, but order – through just human institutions – comes at a price. The enemies of Arjuna and the Pandavas had upset the moral and legal order and it was in *dharma*'s interests that they be defeated. Here, it was not the cosmos that was greater than family member against family member. It was law and justice, the surety of human order, that was greater.[2] What this does is at least establish the very human context in which Arjuna went to war. However, the Bhagavadgita is not only a sermon from Krishna, but a discussion between Arjuna and Krishna. The ebb and flow of this discussion estab-

---

2. Ruth Cecily Katz, *Arjuna in the Mahabharata: Where Krishna is, There is Victory*, Columbia: University of South Carolina Press, 1989, pp. 117-18, 242-5.

lishes the full parameters of human doubt and unease, as well as humanity's transcendent aspirations. If the two characters could be taken as one person's interior dialogue, then what we have is a perennial human dialectic – as positions are advanced and checked, get-out clauses are offered and dismissed, proper conduct is the goal but a tally of the costs is itemised. Arjuna finally goes forth – he even needs to cheat on the battlefield – but only after going through what in fact every military man goes through on the eve of battle.

For Peter Brook, the great theatre director who went to India to research for months his own production of the Mahabharata and who finally staged it as an all-night performance in Paris – ending at dawn, when the back of the stage would fall away to flood the theatre and audience with the first rays of sunrise – dharma was something far more personally intense than Katz suggested.

> Something immense, powerful and radiant – the idea of an incessant conflict within every person and every group, in every expression of the universe; a conflict between a possibility, which is called dharma, and the negation of that possibility... The Mahabharata does not attempt to explain the secret of dharma, but lets it become a living presence.[3]

As the drama of the Mahabharata unfolds, scene by scene, we find in Arjuna a conflicted personality – one who wrestles heroically with this conflict and, in fact, with his personality as a cosmic speck that is nevertheless a part of the cosmos. Arjuna wrestles with himself as a human dwarf in the Vedic order. When, finally in the Mahabharata, Arjuna's brother Yudhishthira alone makes it to heaven (Arjuna is having to spend some time in hell for

---

3. Peter Brook, *The Shifting Point: Theatre, Film, Opera 1946–1987*, New York: Theatre Communications Group, 1987, p. 164.

cheating at the battle of Kurukshetra), he finds even there illusion and ambivalence – so that no human appropriation or
understanding of anything, even the divine, is transcendentally
divine.

What alone is transcendent in the human condition is love.
Here, the work of the great Indian poet Rabindranath Tagore
reveals a very different Arjuna in his brief relationship with
Chitrangada. In many ways, Tagore's play *Chitra* is an equivalent
of Solomon's 'Song of Songs' in its lyricism and beauty. In some
ways it is more beautiful, for it is not a lovelorn and helpless
Shulamite slip of a girl pining for Solomon, but an accomplished
princess, herself an archer, someone who revels in her independence, but who proposes herself to Arjuna as a lover who is both
earthly but immanent – true love is immanent within her if
Arjuna can let himself uncover it.

> I am not beautifully perfect as the flowers with which I
> worshipped. I have many flaws and blemishes. I am a traveller
> in the great world-path, my garments are dirty, and my feet are
> bleeding with thorns. Where should I achieve flower-beauty,
> the unsullied loveliness of a moment's life? The gift that I
> proudly bring you is the heart of a woman... Herein lies an
> imperfection which yet is noble and grand.[4]

It is an immanent love with bleeding feet, a noble and grand
imperfection, which should form the foundation of *hindutva*,
and it is this that would allow the thought that aspires out of
legend – in this case, Gadamer's post-reflectivity at work – to be
less opportunistically fundamental and oppressive. The human
condition is grand and imperfect. It is transcendent in love,
but not in myth. It cannot attain the condition of the gods – so

---

4. Rabindranath Tagore, 'Chitra', in *Collected Poems and Plays*, London: Macmillan,
1980, p. 172.

that a God of Mercy is indeed composed of mercy. Buddha is not simply compassionate; he is the incarnation of compassion, the essence of compassion. An act of compassion is simply a radiation of his core.

The line of descent from Hindu gods to the Buddhist pantheon is one in which both aesthetic and moral qualities were transferred. Indeed, in the Hindu capacity towards inclusiveness, the Vaishanava system regards Buddha as the ninth avatar or earthly manifestation of God. Nevertheless, Buddhism took on new characteristics as its migration spread. In Tibet, it assumed aspects of the native Bon religion, so that the Tibetan spiritual world is a trans-border synthesis of both good and bad, with the bad gradually transmuted into the righteous temper and fury of the good. It is the depiction of Tibetan spiritual personages that has much captured the contemporary art market's fascination and devotion – and there is not a little looting of artefacts from the high mountain temples.[5] And I should say that there is not a little inflection of contemporary taste into the contemplation of the figurines and statues of the Tibetan boddhisattvas. Of the chief of these, in the sense of his incorporation of compassion and mercy, Avalokitesvara, the Victoria & Albert Museum catalogue almost drools: 'The stillness and serenity of this figure speaks of the state of harmony to which the Boddhisattva aspires, while the sensuous contrapposto of [his] sleek, androgynous body ties him to the human world.'[6]

---

5. For commentaries on Tibetan holy aesthetics, see Philip Rawson, *The Art of Tantra*, London: Thames & Hudson, 1995; Robert E. Fisher, *Art of Tibet*, London: Thames & Hudson, 1997. For how Buddhist aesthetics changed in its migrations, see Robert E. Fisher, *Buddhist Art and Architecture*, London: Thames & Hudson, 1996.

6. John Guy, entry 89 in *A Grand Design: The Art of the Victoria and Albert Museum*, New York: Harry N. Abrams, 1997, p. 241. This 93 cm tall object is in copper gilt, gold in colour, with the boddhisattva's typical pose – one leg bent and carrying most of the body weight, thus making the curve of the waist pronounced – with eyes modestly downcast, heavy earrings falling in line with the long hair escaping the crown, and strands of jewellery slung across the largely naked body and its diaphanous short skirt. The hips

Indeed, as the cult of Avalokitesvara spread eastwards, the female qualities of his body grew into female qualities overall. By the time he reached China, he had fully transgendered into Guanyin (or Kuan Yin; Kwannon in Japanese), with not only an overall purpose of mercy but special qualities of merciful rescue towards shipwrecked sailors, chained prisoners and, above all, women in the distress of childbirth. She became a spiritual version of Florence Nightingale and, by this time, was no longer the personification and embodiment of compassion and mercy – that is, no longer a quality with human characteristics, but a person with merciful qualities. It was a significant shift away from the possibility of mercy as an abstract quality, existing *a priori* to any human or worldly attempt to manifest it. It ceased being, in terms of a parallel with the eighteenth-century thought of Kant, a 'categorical imperative' – a moral course drawn from a universal template and impulse towards morality, a human course drawn from the highest, almost spiritual, course of cosmic nature – and became something performed in individual acts and in specific cases for specific people in specific conditions. A thoroughly Chinese peasant pragmatism reduced the god to a mother who comes running when the child is hurt.

It was also a Chinese sense of order and propriety. Confucian overlays on all behaviour made everything performative. Provided it was *seen* to be righteous, it was. And it could be gauged as righteous if its performance accorded with the *Analects* of Confucius – and this performance was within a strict order of hierarchy, obligation and prescription. A wise man, a *junzi*, was one who could make all this appear seamless and also make himself appear at one with his performativity. If he had inner qualms about his performance, if he had moral misgivings, he

are exaggerated sweeps from the slender waist and the pectorals are like prepubescent breasts. In short, this would serve as a certain form of gay iconography.

kept them to himself. Outwardly, he had to manifest a form of Lacan's *jouissance* with its perverse capacity to garner pleasure while hiding a sense of turpitude. He had to conform to Aristotle's *eudaemonia* – the good demon of good public behaviour whereby one was constituted as both 'good' and 'happy'. In Chinese history, only the wild poets would sometimes rebel on moral grounds – the inner urge becoming too much to be contained by public expectation – and they were, in generations afterwards, held up for admiration. But not for emulation.

But, as often as not, the wild poets rebelled precisely because the official rulers were themselves not performing public morality correctly. Nor was this performativity only Confucian. The Chinese approach to Buddhism was to codify it.

> All living things are tainted by Causation,
> Six Directions of Reincarnation bind us fast.
> Seven stages of cognition succeed each other,
> Round Nine Abodes we are forever moving.
> How painful are the Five Aggregates,
> How wearisome the Four Causes...[7]

The codification of belief preceded the ordering of behaviour; and the observation of that ordering became a social value and a state requirement. There is not a huge step forward into the contemporary equivalent. In a sense, as late as the Tienanmen Square protests of 1989 – savagely crushed by the authorities – the complaint of the students and their supporters was that the Communist Party had turned against its own people and its own values. 'I gave up my youth for the Communist Party in its struggle to seize state power. And now a handful of tyrants have

---

7. Hsieh Ling-yun, excerpted in *An Anthology of Chinese Verse: Han Wei Chin and the Northern and Southern Dynasties*, trans. J.D. Frodsham and Ch'eng Hsi, Oxford: Clarendon Press, 1967, p. xxix.

betrayed the Party."[8] The Party had determined what right action was in accordance with right ideology. Misgivings were for the individual soul, but not for individual expression in public.

Having said that, there were extreme extents to which right-eous public performance could be taken, thus binding together public approval and Buddhist compassion. There is a famous story of a great general who was ordered to subdue a persistent rebellion. Seven times the general overcame the bandit king and seven times allowed him his freedom. After the seventh time, the bandit king realised how righteous the general was – allowing him his freedom to comprehend gradually how mercy and kindness could be expressed by the state. Accordingly, he withdrew his rebellion permanently; because he had not been executed or imprisoned, his followers could not attack the state in revenge. The general was praised as an epitome of wisdom as well as propriety – for, by his wisdom and compassion, he had in the end rendered a far more substantial service to propriety than if he had punished the bandit and incurred the continuing resentment of his people. This was Taoism blending in with both Buddhism and Confucianism.[9] But even Taoism, in the end, becomes the 'formless form'. It is far from anarchy or licence. It is a derogation of law to nature's impulse towards order and balance, which re-emerges all the same as a form of law. The sage obeys the law; he simply ignores its *value* in the cosmic order, but re-expresses it as integration with a holistic balance.

Those who are not Taoist sages, who have been conditioned away from mercy and compassion as an abstract universal qual-ity, nevertheless seek for mercy almost as an artefact of what it

---

8. Liu Binyan, *A Higher Kind of Loyalty: A Memoir by China's Foremost Journalist*, London: Methuen, 1990, p. 282.
9. See *The Tao of War: The Martial Tao Te Ching*, trans. Ralph D. Sawyer, Boulder CO: Westview Press, 2003.

once was as represented by Avalokitesvara: seek the ray rather than the sun. And seek its instances in time of distress. Seek it as an interim blessing in lives that do not recognise a supervening and overarching condition of primal Buddhist mercy.

It was the French philosopher Simone de Beauvoir who in a long-forgotten interview employed, almost casually, the term 'interim mercies'. She meant that, in a world of injustice and inequality, in a world of dire need and urgencies, it was not appropriate only to work for the great redemptive revolution. Some succour and relief had to be delivered in the interim. It seemed both a humane and a hopeless prescription – humane in the sense that, certainly, there must be help given to those who stretch out their hands; hopeless in the sense that the systemic and structural cruelties of the world could not be overcome in any immediate future. And yet she defined our basic condition as citizens and human actors who care for other human actors. She defined us effectively as Gawain – failing in the end to be the corporeal embodiment of gallantry and fidelity to his word to the death. By flinching, he revealed himself to be a human actor with a great and generous store of courtesies and gallantries and fidelities – but he was not their embodiment. There is in today's world, de Beauvoir meant, no supervening condition of redress and correction to make right so much that had become wrong. But the world's condition allows the human condition to be exercised. It is, as it were, *permitted* for interim mercies to be exercised and extended – almost to take the strain off a structure that cannot in itself embody mercy. It is almost like the interim chivalry that, even at the height of the Crusades, was possible. During a truce at the great Battle of Acre, the Saracen sultan Saladin (Salah-ad-Din Yusuf ibn Ayyub) invited King Richard the Lionheart to his tent. Richard came in, all bombast, took out his great English broadsword and with one huge stroke chopped a thick firewood log in two. 'This', he beamed, 'is the sword of England!' Saladin in response threw a square of silk into the air, drew out his scimitar and sliced it cleanly in two as it fell. 'This', he said, 'is the sword of Islam.' Then, having paid their kind respects to each other (and gained an appreciation of contrasting sword methodologies), the two rulers parted and the terrible Battle of Acre resumed with great bloodshed on both sides. And yet, despite the Lionheart's victory in that conflict, it was Saladin who entered Christian folklore. The entire Third Crusade in which Richard the Lionheart fought had been occasioned by Saladin's capture in 1187 of Jerusalem – capital of the Kingdom of Jerusalem established in the Second Crusade. But Saladin had treated the Christian population with great mercy and clemency. He killed and plundered no prisoner, ransomed huge numbers for nominal sums and let the rest go free. In the aftermath of this, the eventual explanation in Christian legend was that Saladin, being more Christian than a Christian in his behaviour, had to have been an incipient Christian; he later received a Christian baptism and was made a Christian knight.[10]

This bears a likeness to one of the last great battles of the Maori uprising against white settlerdom in New Zealand. Surrounded by European rangers, the Maori garrison in their fortified *pa* (hilltop town) were taking a hammering. Under shellfire, they had run out of ammunition for their rifles, and both male and female fighters had taken to firing wooden bullets carved from their own palisades. Yet the Maori warriors would still crawl out to no-man's-land to rescue wounded European rangers, even while under shellfire. The European commander was so impressed by this chivalry that he offered honourable surrender. The reply of the Maori chief, standing on the ruins

10. Karen Armstrong, *Holy War: The Crusades and their Impact on Today's World*, London: Macmillan, 1988, p. 185.

of his earthworks, resonated in both Maori and European minds
for a century afterwards – during which the defeated Maori kingdom entered a period of dejection, but maintained solidarity,
and eventually re-emerged in a great cultural renaissance with
political assertion and assuredness in the 1970s: 'Ka whaiwhai
tonu ake! Ake! Ake!' – We shall fight forever, and forever, and
forever. Sometimes it is the gesture of mercy – no matter from
which side – even if all else has failed, that sets the stage for a
push against the merely interim. The New Zealand philosopher
Andrew Sharp has not called this a mercy. He argues that, at
day's end, despite all cultural differences, what can be universally transacted is kindness.[11] But, if it doesn't set the stage,
if it doesn't lead to great reconciliations and historical leaps
forward in human satisfaction and interaction, is an interim
mercy or kindness enough? Is it enough, for instance, to send
food to the victims of famine one year, but not help them settle
their conflicts over land in the years to come? Is it enough to
fulfil the UN overseas aid quota – that is, observe the code of
desired benefaction? Reach the targets? Give up x percentage of
y income? Throw pop concerts where the great screens at Hyde
Park fill with images of starvation, while those who dance wear
either designer clothes or their clones from Asian sweatshops? At
what level of thought and concern can our imperfection become
noble and grand?

Problems of interim mercy

In 1984 I was living in Zambia. It was the time of the great
Ethiopian and Sudanese famine, and international aid was being
mobilised – often on real but highly emotive grounds. The State

---

11. Andrew Sharp, *Justice and the Maori: Maori Claims in New Zealand Political
Argument in the 1980s*, Auckland: Oxford University Press, 1990.

of Israel concentrated its relief activities on rescuing the Falasha Jews of Ethiopia – sometimes colourfully described as the lost 'thirteenth tribe' – and flying them from Ethiopia to Israel, where they would be safely resettled. This caused an outcry, both because of the highly selective nature of the rescue effort, and because the rescue involved a transplantation to a strange and foreign land. What about all those who were starving in the same areas but who were not Falashas? How would the Falashas integrate in Israel, a land which already had a sharp 'class' difference between European and 'oriental' Jews? Stung by this criticism, the Israeli authorities decided to cover their rescue operations with secrecy. The Falashas would now be smuggled by land out of Ethiopia across the border into Sudan. There, military transport planes would fly them unseen to Israel. The guards and government authorities on both sides of the border would have their cooperation and discretion purchased and, just to keep it all deniable, those escorting the Falashas from Ethiopia to Sudan would be non-Israeli operatives – non-combat (hopefully) mercenaries. So, one day in Zambia, I received a visit from a gentleman, clearly an Israeli Mossad (intelligence) operative, who recounted how my reputation as a reliable and robust individual in righteous operations had come to his organisation's attention. Would I be prepared to ride shotgun to escort the Falashas into Sudan? It seemed a stunningly inept approach, and even the flattery seemed under-researched. I very politely declined, but this was harder than it first seemed – for, after all, was it not better that some be saved than none at all? And, in the matter of selectivity, how many people in how many missions of mercy had been left behind on the most arbitrary grounds of selection? At least the criteria to be used were not arbitrary. And it would not be as heart-rending as *triage* – where the surgeon walks between the beds of the maimed and twisted and says, 'this

one... this one... not this one... not this one...', indicating who
will benefit from scarce medicines and his surgical skills, and
who is condemned to complete the process of dying; deciding
life and death necessarily on the grounds of limited resources,
but doing so on a walk that could appear as casual, and would be
as scientific, as a stroll in the park. I did very little to help those
suffering in Ethiopia and Sudan. Would it not have been better
to have done *something*, no matter how ambivalent the process
and criteria? At God's judgement seat, what will it matter if the
people you saved were Falashas or not? Would you not have a
better case than having to look downcast and mumble that you
saved no one at all? I drank much alcohol the night I sent the
Israeli gentleman on his way. But, even though a very young man,
I had already been blooded into the *problematique* of mercy. The
quality of mercy might not be strained; it might drop like the
gentle dew from heaven; but it is a damnably vexatious quality
to put into operation – and all those who want a straight-line
clean conscience had better not dabble in mercy.

As it was, it was precisely this famine in the Horn of Africa,
stretching into Sudan, that both alerted a generation to the
need for help and made reductionist its sense of what help was
needed. Alex de Waal has written about the famine as it affected
Darfur in 1984–85. He found that people generally did not die
of starvation, although they certainly died as a result of disease
occasioned by both weakness and social dislocation, when their
patterns of life and sustenance had been disrupted. The over-
riding concern of the people during this time was not to save
as many individual lives as possible, but to preserve their *way*
of life. To that extent, although the huge scale of food aid had
meaning, it had no long-term purpose.[12] The struggle of ways

---

12. Alexander de Waal, *Famine that Kills: Darfur, Sudan, 1984–1985*, Oxford:
Clarendon, 1989.

of life in Darfur has returned to haunt the world's headlines today.

There has been huge growth in both the aid and development industries. Like any other industries, they have targets, appraisal and audit procedures, and impositions upon their client groups as well as benefits. Often, these organisational and self-justifying procedures (self-justifying in terms of their annual reports and regular appeals to their donors) take precedence over actual on-the-ground need. Or need can be simply, even sometimes maliciously, misread in order to preserve a mode of operation that suits the speed, delivery mechanisms and approved 'project stock' of the agency concerned.[13] And the agencies' own need for short-term, verifiable results ('successes') often obviates the importance of the longer-term, less quantifiable, less-actual-need-for-the agency-to-be-there efforts to restore ways of life. For how does 'helping to restore a way of life' show up in an annual report to donors? Numbers of wells dug, tonnes of food distributed – anything quantifiable – are what donors wish to see and auditors need to see. The agencies are also largely unable to grapple with the politics, often violent, of the regions in which they work. But Amartya Sen wrote, in his famous study *Poverty and Famines*, that there are very few famines in which there is genuinely not enough food in the country to go round. There is, however, a politics of *entitlement* which, depending on whether you are entitled or not, determines your access (or lack of access) to food.[14] Now, all the sources I have cited in these last two paragraphs are two decades old. The deeper analyses have been around a long time. But there is both an industrial need,

---

13. B.E. Harrell-Bond, *Imposing Aid: Emergency Assistance to Refugees*, Oxford: Oxford University Press, 1986.

14. Armatya Sen, *Poverty and Famines: An Essay on Entitlement and Deprivation*, Oxford: Clarendon Press, 1981.

and a simpler mobilisation need, to present tragedy simply. To assemble hundreds of thousands of young people in Hyde Park requires, if not a jingle, a simple message that can fit into a sound bite. In order to attract donations, what has happened is that we have commodified suffering. Here is a 'thing' that is simple to understand; it stinks; so all you have to do is also simple, and that is to give some spare money and sign a petition that blames someone. But the blame is part of a complex game of global critique and reform, often of institutions not only dear to the capitalist heart, but integral to the very developed economies that allow people to have spare cash in the first place. The Bretton Woods institutions of the World Bank and the IMF were first established to regulate the capital flows of the post-war Western world; even with austerity packages visited upon countries as developed as the UK and New Zealand in the 1960s, they succeeded in keeping together an international capitalist system – now, with the fall of Communism, global – that informs every aspect of our lives. Reforming these institutions to help far more fairly the developing countries might require more change than even Joseph Stiglitz has recommended.[15] And it might mean, finally, a change in our own way of life, which, like every Darfurian perhaps – though more perversely – we might fight to sustain.

Probably the most admirable and honest of the aid agencies is Médecins Sans Frontières, founded by the maverick doctor and socialist activist Bernard Kouchner – now, in typical maverick fashion, appointed to Nicolas Sarkozy's government as foreign minister; and the on–off friend of Bernard-Henri Lévy. Kouchner is described by Joan Juliet Buck having a Chinese dinner with

---

15. For a post-Stiglitzian agenda of more radical shape, see Jonathan Pincus and Jeffrey A. Winters, eds, *Reinventing the World Bank*, Ithaca: Cornell University Press, 2002.

Lévy: 'They are both idealistic and jaded in the way that only men who have tested themselves are allowed to be.'[16] There is not a little of the still-starry-eyed fashion writer and gamine gadabout girl of *Tout Paris* in Buck, and she is clearly in love with the two men. But Kouchner, more than Lévy, has the right to be jaded – even if, telegenically, he chose to be filmed carrying a real rice sack on his back into Somalia, whereas Lévy was dodging only fake bullets for the camera in Sarajevo. The former head of the UN's civil administration in Kosovo, and the familiar of trouble spots from Afghanistan to – sometimes it seems – the ends of the world, Kouchner is the template from which the doctors with the contempt for borders are sprung. They are the ones who do not break and run when the shells start falling; the ones who do not need, like other agencies, to inflate the death toll in the tragic case of twenty-first century Darfur – they say what it is and get on with it, and see no need to scandalise their donors into munificence by raising the numbers and the apparent stakes.

Before Kouchner founded Médecins Sans Frontières, I was put firmly in my place in the early 1980s by a young Swiss medical worker. He could have been a forebear of the Médecins. Stranded by heavy rains in a remote corner of Zambia, we entertained each other with stories. His story was to do with the fall of N'Djamena in Chad. In the periodic civil wars of the time, the capital was about to fall again and the warlord presidents forced to rotate. This time, Libyan warplanes had come to the assistance of the faction attacking the city. My friend was with the Red Cross delegation and they prepared to evacuate themselves in a small twin-prop Cessna. By the time they reached the airport, it was coming under shellfire. Just as they were about to board, my

16. Joan Juliet Buck, 'France's Prophet Provocateur', *Vanity Fair*, January 2003, p. 93.

friend saw, struggling to hurry towards them on the runway, an old man whose son he had saved in an earlier day of the siege. The grateful father was carrying a special meal he had cooked to say 'thank you'. The Swiss doctors looked at one another. They looked at the shells landing closer. Then, without a word, they sat down on the runway and ate the meal with the old father. Only after all honour and custom had been satisfied did they fly out. I was not sure I could have done that. I would perhaps have made a great show of accepting the meal, say we would take it with us and eat it later with all due ceremony, but for now, well, we'd better go.

If anyone had put it to the Falasha Jews that they had a choice, exodus to Israel or a sustained intervention to help them survive the famine and then redevelop their way of life in Ethiopia, they might perhaps have asked for the second option. And the option I would have had, in my days of globe-trotting idealism, would have been to go there, stay with them, work with them, and learn a thing or two from them, then affect jadedness in my stories back home in the metropole. But to discharge idealism's true mercy, which is not to cargo-cult aid from the fund-raised skies, is twofold: to change the structures of the world's capital flows; and to be humble enough to live within the structures of those we seek to help. The Tartarus in between might be a place of interim mercies – and Simone de Beauvoir was right, they are better than none – but it is not the interim which, by itself, can save or change the world.

Philosophies for mercy

Human history has been a search for utopias or the imagination of them – from the 'pure lands' of Tibetan Buddhism to Thomas More's famous book. In the twenty-first century, there is the imagination of an ecotopia. The search for the possibility of utopia and its sceptical, realist backlash has infused literature, prophecy and every millennial sect on earth.[17] In utopia, every living thing and every impulse is reconciled to its fate as part of a fruitful cooperative paradise – and everyone cooperates because everyone believes the communal vision; believes, in the William Morris vision, its artisan work ethic; believes, in the Nazi vision, the advent of purity and the dawn of the *Übermensch*. The problem with utopias is that there is little imagination of dissent within them. They are perfections that have driven out all imperfections of social organisation, and dissent has been logically and rightly abolished. There are laws within a utopia, and they are never broken. There is thus an ideology of utopia, but not a questioning philosophy. Let us begin by saying that an international paradigm of mercy is not utopian; is imperfect and noble; screws up and argues; has difficulty even agreeing what mercy is. Not unlike the great theologian Hans Kung's 1987 Parliament of the World's Religions – a truly heroic convention that sought to agree a global ethic and global responsibilities.[18] After considerable debate, if not heated argument, both ethic and responsibilities were largely agreed. Then the Islamic delegation proposed that the declarations be prefaced – not unreasonably, given that they were a parliament of religions – with the words, 'in the name of God'. At this point, the Buddhist delegation objected, given the fact that Buddhism is essentially atheistic – there may be spiritual personalities and spiritual forces, but no overarching God. So the wonderful declarations were held up for weeks as debate raged back and forth among holy men as to whether it could be said that a God

---

17. Krishan Kumar, *Utopia and Anti-Utopia in Modern Times*, Oxford: Blackwell, 1987.

18. Hans Kung and Helmut Schmidt, eds, *A Global Ethic and Global Responsibilities: Two Declarations*, London: SCM, 1998.

existed, and whether something could be done in His/Her/Its name. I am sure that the bespectacled Kung must have vacillated between bemusement and suicide, thinking that the inquisition he had faced at the hands of the Vatican had been a mild experience by comparison (he had questioned papal infallibility and been threatened with excommunication). In the end, God was omitted from the preface but, should He exist, He would have appreciated the efforts on His behalf. A philosophy of mercy might be a little like that: unable to command agreement. But, if we are largely condemned to committing only interim mercies, there had better be a philosophy about why we do it, and what we should be doing if only we could.

The problem is that the philosophy should not be totalitarian; that is, not so prescriptive that all one's life is spent seeking to attain a condition in which one might be *rightly* merciful. The Buddhist eightfold path is in fact an invitation to an unending road of self-cultivation and self-perfection – certainly self-critique – for the second of the eight 'right' paths, right thought or right intention would invalidate thousands of acts of generosity made with 'tainted' motives. The others – right speech, right action, right livelihood, right effort, right mindfulness and right concentration – can mean, under the instruction of strict *roshi* (senior temple teachers), no cursing, blaming or lying; no vengeance, stealing or drunkenness; no stockbroking, investment banking or tobacco farming; no arrant ambition on the one hand and no laziness on the other; no pinpoint concentration that is not part of a holistic vision; and no pinpoint concentration that is self-centred, and no goofing-off. The very first of the eightfold paths, right understanding, basically prescribes faith as the precursor to all the effort to follow. The faithful Buddhist will accept the need for constant effort in all eight aspects of a human life. All this is much harder than the Ten Commandments:

if I do not steal, I am covered; I've fulfilled the commandment; it doesn't matter that I was tempted to steal and hatch
all manner of undischarged fantasies to steal a million pounds
for my retirement fund. Even if I did not steal because of a loss
of nerve, I am still in fulfilment of the commandment. I might
have trouble with another of the commandments, not coveting
my neighbour's wife, but, if I do not actively covet, do not flirt,
do not arrange 'accidental' encounters when my neighbour is
absent, then I might think that an untold number of fantasies
in which I possess my neighbour's wife are within the bounds of
the commandment. In short, prohibitions are easier to observe
than paths of self-perfection. The impulse to self-perfection
was also the root of Gawain's sense of self – over which he was
bitterly disappointed when he found he was only human after all.
But all his paraphernalia had been established around the icons
of human perfection. The emblem on his shield, the pentangle,
represented a different moral quality for each of its five points,
as did each of his five fingers – and so did each of his five senses.
Five was a magic number, so Gawain represented a magical combination of moral attributes – and it was an emblem (somewhat
controversially) attributed to Solomon, who, having built his
temple with the help of demons, needed a magic symbol to ward
them off afterwards; so that, in these legends, the pentangle star
preceded the Star of David.[19] None of this disguises the key point
that both Solomon and Gawain – the first for all his wisdom and
the second for all his courtesy and chivalry – fell from grace.
The first might have fallen from pride (and the exhaustion of
maintaining a harem of 1,000 – although the Bible suggests

19. Brian Stone, 'The Pentangle and Its Significance', in his translation of *Sir Gawain
and the Green Knight*, London: Penguin, 1974, pp. 148-9. Stone does make the clear point
that the issue of which star preceded the other is an area of controversy and there is no
real evidence the Pentangle was a Jewish star at any time. It was a Pythagorean device
and an Arab symbol, although the star does feature modestly in the Kabbalah.

the multicultural assemblage corrupted the singularity of his faith rather than merely his flesh); but the second fell because his justifying template was too perfect for human exercise. He fell out of template, was stamped 'imperfect', and himself swore to wear forever the mark of failure and frailty.

And yet it is Gawain who probably best fits the characterisation of a person of mercy – even though it was as a person of honour that he sought to see himself. He tries. He really works at it. His hostess is magically beautiful, and on three successive mornings he patiently withstands her efforts to seduce him; he is determined to die in order to honour a gory but play-time Christmas wager; he seeks out his executioner across the wilds and perils of Wales in winter; and he only utters a profanity at the very end – when he knows he has screwed up. Until he realises he is imperfect, he behaves perfectly with a passion. It is Gawain who fits well Martha Nussbaum's description of who and what should be celebrated: 'Abandoning the zeal for absolute perfection as inappropriate to the life of a finite being, abandoning the thirst for punishment and self-punishment that so frequently accompanies that zeal, the education I recommend looks with mercy at the ambivalent excellence and passion of a human life.'[20] This was the reassurance Arjuna sought from Krishna between the armies at Kurukshetra. What happens to – with what cosmic regard is he held – the man who screws up? 'Does he, both objects unachieved, come crashing down and perish like a riven cloud, his firm foundation gone, bemused on Brahman's path?' Arjuna's reply is that the man of effort is never lost. He will be born again, given a second chance, perhaps have to start from a lower base, 'and once again he girds his loins, struggling for Yoga's highest prize' (Bhagavadgita VI:38–43).

---

20. Martha C. Nussbaum, *The Therapy of Desire: Theory and Practice in Hellenistic Ethics*, Princeton: Princeton University Press, 1994, p. 510.

And when Arjuna presses Krishna, asking about the qualities
of a person who has transcended his mortal limitations and is
in a position to accomplish perfect good, Krishna nevertheless
replies that the transcendent person is still marked by 'radi-
ance – activity – yes, delusion too – when they arise, he hates
them not; and when in turn they cease, he pines not after them'
(XIV:22). Because, finally, the condition of cosmic good is not
a realm for humanity. But it is a realm from which humanity
derives inspiration and motivation. This balance between the
reality of accomplishment and the aspiration towards a perfect
good, a perfect condition for our imperfect efforts at mercy, is
perhaps what Altaf Gauhar meant with his own translations from
the Quran. Gauhar was a refugee in London with a controversial
past – a one-time-imprisoned opponent in Pakistan of Prime
Minister Ali Bhutto; in 1977, he tried tentatively and briefly to
inaugurate my study of Islam. He finally gifted his new book
to me, one which it was rumoured he completed in prison, and
there was a passage which struck me. In most translations of
the Quran, Sura 2:143 reads: 'We have made you into a just
community, so that you may bear witness before others and so
that the Messenger may bear witness before you.'[21] Others use
the term 'central community', or 'a just people', or 'an exalted
people'. However, Gauhar translated the verse as follows: 'This
is how We ordained you to be a people most balanced so that you
may be a model to others and the Prophet a model to you.'[22] Now,
in fact, the Arabic term at stake is *ummatan wasata*, and it was
an act of ingenuity on Gauhar's part to render it 'a people most
balanced' – but his commentary on his translation was to the

21. M.A.S. Abdel Haleem's new translation of *The Qur'an*, Oxford: Oxford University
Press, 2004, p. 16.

22. Altaf Gauhar, *Translations from the Quran*, London: Islamic Information
Services, 1977, p. 80.

effect that only a balanced people could be a moral people and thus a just people. I liked his translation a great deal. As a young man I believed fervently that this, and his other translations, were the inspired achievements of a man suffering in prison and rescuing himself through meditations on the holy book. Even now, Gauhar's passage gives a way forward to an association with the quality of mercy; for each sura of the Quran begins with the words 'In the name of God, the Lord of Mercy, the Giver of Mercy' (Abdel Haleem's translation), or 'In the Name of God, the Merciful, the Compassionate' (Gauhar's translation), the implication being that Allah's mercy is infinite; it is a divine quality ('His Grace is unbounded, His Mercy infinite'). The attraction of Gauhar's rendition is that it takes a balanced people to use justice and morality to enact God's mercy on earth. And, in my limited reading, 'balance' includes the capacity to screw up, as well as the capacity to move onwards and try again. It is by this constant effort that humanity seeks to sacralise its existence – rather than live in awe of the accomplished sacred.

Can there be nationalisms and an internationalism of mercy, both interim and with an overarching philosophy of effort that renders its imperfections noble and grand? This is part of the contemplation that follows. There is a great novel, *Petals of Blood*, by the Kenyan writer Ngugi Wa Thiong'o. In it, a motley band of outcasts – who include a disillusioned freedom fighter and a prostitute – set out, like Yeats's beast slouching towards Bethlehem, to find justice in the nation's shitty and corrupt capital. It is a heroic but hopeless march. But they recount tales along the way of the primeval impulse to do what they are doing. The spirits and ancestors bless them. But the beast that slouches towards Bethlehem is ugly, ponderous and awkward. But it is tougher than a flower. It is also new.

5

The Tao of international relations

I t was the Chinese film director Ang Lee who once spoke of the need for an 'industrial Tao'. There can be too much retreat towards, and contemplation of, mountains, streams, clouds and the wholeness and friction-free quality of nature. We cannot all become hermits and, in any case, finding an uncluttered mountain-top is these days somewhat harder than in Lao Tzu's. What about those of us who must work and live amidst the industrial skyscapes of the world's oxygen-starved cities? Those of us who see grime and smog instead of clouds and blue skies; who perch in tower blocks rather than on mountains; who must meet deadlines and face intrusions rather than wander aimlessly; who must present ourselves to the interrogating and jealous world rather than become one with the spirits of our surroundings? Why cannot we, who wander by toxic rivers, have the balance of the sage who drinks from his crystal clear stream? Ang Lee was refusing withdrawal and isolation as a condition for enlightenment. There should be no problem for the wise person to operate as a just and enlightened person in the clamour and angst of product, production, promotion, proscription and defeat. There should even be the possibility of a sage in today's Beijing, with its choking exhaust and pharmaceutical atmosphere – where, if you have sensitive skin and have, by exposure in the world's cities, become a connoisseur of pollution, you come back from a summer walk bathed in what others will think is sweat and feel on your bared forearms how much of what chemical wash with what nitrous burn has sloshed onto your body and into your invisibly corroding lungs of iron.

As it is, the uses of the Tao have varied greatly. Whether as an appreciation of Taoism proper, or of the Tao as the 'way' espoused by Buddhism, or as the more likely syncretic Tao beloved by Chinese pragmatists – in which various spiritual persuasions are integrated to form a likeable whole with which one can live, and in which one can believe without dislocation – the Tao has been used, or misused, differently from epoch to epoch.

In the somewhat infamous case of the Shaolin Temple, notwithstanding its habitation by Buddhist monks, there is in fact scant evidence that there was ever a Tao of martial prowess – whether within Shaolin or within the practices of the more purely Taoist monks and hermits of Wu Tan. The contemporary folk legends that there indeed were such martial monks, particularly as the 1960s kung fu movie craze began, prompted much scepticism from religious historians, who doubted if there ever had been such a thing as Shaolin. It was the New Zealand poet Rewi Alley[1] – one of the acclaimed foreigners, like Norman Bethune from Canada, who went to live and work in China out of solidarity with the revolution – who first claimed that the

---

1. His most famous poem, 'Boiler in Sandan', was republished in *New Argot*, July/August 1974. This was a New Zealand arts newspaper, participating in efforts to commemorate Alley's seventy-fifth birthday; but, even in New Zealand now, he is little remembered – nor even in a China that once made heroes of him and Bethune for their efforts to help the Chinese.

footprints he found worn into the stone courtyard of a ruined temple could have been caused by the repeated patterns of the ritual exercises of Shaolin (although they could as easily have been caused by ritual dances). However, the myth of Shaolin really draws from two key moments of uprising over the last 200 years. The later event was in the early years of the twentieth century, as the Boxer Uprising gathered its recruits for the onslaught against the foreign enclaves in Beijing and elsewhere. Unable to match the modern firepower of the European and Japanese occupiers, the Chinese resort was to condensed and intense training of volunteers in 'traditional' martial arts; and the most important element of this training was the steeping of fighters in esoteric teachings and rituals that would protect them from bullets. Now, in fact, much of this 'tradition' was improvised, some of it was invented, and all of it was certainly condensed. It didn't take much time for a raw recruit to be piled into the front lines. But the esoteric teachings, rituals and protective potions and medicines were derived from the herbal arts of the Taoist sages in their searches for immortality. Far from seeking to wander in the mountains peacefully and forever, the Boxers wanted to storm and kill the Europeans immediately. Effectively, the Boxer Uprising defined Chinese popular martial arts for ever more. It was the widespread recruitment of fighters that led the survivors to teach their 'traditional' arts afterwards, taking at face value their induction into the supposedly authentic. The Shaolin legend was, to this extent, an invention for the Boxer Uprising. Even so, what had been passed onto them as 'traditional' owed to an earlier uprising, the great Tai Ping revolution of the nineteenth century, when, with an invented tradition of biblical authenticity and an overlay of colourful Taoist teachings and emblems (not to mention genuinely revolutionary breakthroughs such as the equality of female fighters), 2 million fighters rose up to challenge the emperor of the Manchu Ching Dynasty. China was plunged into turmoil as the Tai Ping came close to toppling the empire. But their martial teachings, heavily influenced by their strange synthesis of Christology and Taoism, had a marked impact on the development of Chinese martial arts, just as today the so-called Shaolin monks and the refurbished temples for martial arts tourism are cynical concoctions of theatre for the gullible and enthusiastic. It is the Chinese tourism gimmick of the era, and what the 'monks' are really doing is a form of Beijing Opera gymnastics, combined with Qigong (a form of Chinese yoga) breathing and body-control techniques. Today, the combination is marketed as 'Shaolin', and the Buddhism of 'original' Shaolin has been lost, although a patina of Buddhic performance is preserved with the employment of appropriately dressed 'Abbots' at each temple. It is the latest in a series of retailorings, retellings, reinventions and outright inventions. But all to the purpose that the Tao may be violent; it may rebel; it may be commodified; it is not, any more in the last 200 years of the industrial age, a core spirit through whom one communes with an unpolluted and unspoilt environment. As it was, there probably was a Shaolin martial element – but not as practised by monks. More likely, the monks were pacific, but they were defended in their violent times by 'unshaven disciples', fellow travellers who had not taken religious vows, basically sympathetic mercenaries. But that does not sit well with the syntheses that embrace the Shaolin of contemporary imagination and expectation.

That process of synthesis is what makes the Falun Gong dangerous to today's Chinese government, just as the Tai Ping were to the government of the day. Not violent, indeed until recently pacific to a fault, the Falun Gong is one of those interesting instances of created belief, of a created Tao, which abjures the harsh meditative efforts of old, allows practitioners to be natural in their breathing (although not necessarily in a natural environment, the Falun Gong's recruits being mostly urban), and alarms the authorities because the one thing missing in its synthesis of Taoism, Buddhism and other beliefs is any acknowledgement of Communism and the state created by the Party. It is not that, originally, it was against the state; its teachings just saw no need for the state.

Outside of Chinese propaganda, and the equally unhelpful Falun Gong propaganda in reply, what *is* the Falun Gong? In a way, its generic prototype was the Maharishi Mahesh Yogi's 1960s Transcendental Meditation – the TM beloved of the Beatles and other celebrities (and which continues to have its contemporary devotees and practitioners; for example, Joaquim Chissano, the second president of Mozambique) – what John Lennon later rather sardonically called 'instant karma'. The difference between becoming a worldwide cult or a suppressed cult lies entirely, in the Falun Gong case, with having its base in China. The frontispiece to all Falun Gong books by its founder, Li Hongzhi, is the movement's symbol. This is a circle within a circle. The central circle contains the Buddhist cross – or swastika – with each arm pointing in the direction of the next, representing continuity, repetition and the leap of faith. The outer circle becomes something like a solar system, containing planets that orbit the sun and its swastika. Each of the four planets is the Taoist yin/yang symbol of mutuality and flowing interaction. In lighter colour are four stars, and they are the Buddhist swastika reshaped to looked like the flow of the Taoist yin/yan device. This is typical Chinese fusion religion. They're going to have the best of both worlds. And they're going to have it easily. Just as TM promised cosmic results from just two sessions of fifteen minutes a day – a sort of meditation-lite – so

Falun Gong makes a point of abjuring the harsh regimens of the ancient sages. No endless, austere mountain-top sitting in a double-jointed posture, looking relaxed and serene – except that getting to that point and achieving the breath control necessary to activate the *tantien*, the central energy-point just below the navel, actually requires the sort of muscle-control that builds abs of steel. Just try sitting with perfectly upright posture in a double lotus. Provided your knees and hips will let you do it in the first place, the real stress is carried by the lower abdominal muscles. The posture is derived from yoga, and there are some yogis with six-packs that make an Olympic athlete look like a sissy. Li Hongzhi says that you do not have to do this. Speaking of the movement's core Qigong exercises, he says 'a practitioner of our cultivation system need not adjust his respiration or pay any attention to his breathing. Such methods are used only for elementary cultivation ways. We don't need them ... it is not the result of artificial refinement.'[2] So, at a stroke, the Falun Gong exercises are easier, superior to those of old, and replete with natural goodness – without the need also for mountains and forests. They can be done in Beijing on its most chemicalised atmospheric days. But the key is not so much with the exercises as with the conduct of both exercises and life within the *fa*, the Buddhist law. Now, strictly speaking, there can be no Buddhist law. There can only be continual efforts towards the rightness of self in all aspects of thought and behaviour. There is certainly a highly codified Buddhist cosmos but, within it, no law in the normal sense. There are no commandments or prohibitions. *Fa* shouldn't really be translated as 'law' at all; it is much more a variation of the Tao, or the Way. But, translated as 'law', it allows the organisation, and Li Hongzhi, great control over the

---

2. Li Hongzhi, *China Falun Gong*, Hong Kong: Falun Fo Fa, 1998, p. 154.

Falun disciples. And, just as Li Hongzhi's 'cultivation system' is greater and better than any other, so also the *fa* is a greater and better law than any other, including any legislated by the state. There is no need for the state and, on an everyday basis, no need for its laws. Indeed, the cultivation of *qi*, through Qigong, is the cultivation of a cosmic energy. It is the energy that, in the comic books and films of Ang Lee, allows heroes and heroines to fly. It is the energy that flows within the body's meridians, susceptible to acupuncture. It is the energy that melds with the energy of the spheres and the cosmos. It is an energy within the body, above the state and beyond the planet.

Li Hongzhi never instructed his followers to disobey the state and its laws. He has not made a personality cult of himself. The pictures of him demonstrating Qigong in his books depict only a person who seems in fact quite good at the exercises. But it is the suggestion of two things – the lack of primacy for the state and the Party, indeed the lack of acknowledgement of either; and the repudiation of remoteness, for it doesn't need the mountains, it is a movement in the cities – that alarms the authorities. They are alarmed not for what the Falun Gong did before its proscription, but for what it might do – and, indeed, is now doing as it fights back. And, as it fights back, it is showing a harder edge than anyone might suspect of a Buddhist and Taoist movement.

And, in fact, there has been Buddhist fightback for some time in a number of the world's arenas. Pacifically but famously, Buddhist monks protested the US presence in Vietnam by dousing themselves in petrol and burning to death before the world's cameras. A platoon from a Buddhist sect turned up one day in Afghanistan to fight with the mujahideen against the Soviet occupation. They weren't of much help, armed only with *nunchaku*, the swinging rice flails made (in)famous by Bruce Lee in his films. And, no matter how hard he denies it, it is the case that the Dalai Lama has within his coterie hotheads who plot resistance to the Chinese occupation, despairing of the old man's unsuccessful diplomacy and periodic negotiations (through intermediaries) with the Chinese. But the hotheads are as Buddhist as he – and the shapeless, parameter-free joy of *tantra*, that blissful state of perpetual pre-orgasm that is the sign of communion with the energies of the pure-lands, the cornerstone of Tibetan Buddhism, may one day be lost in an armed uprising perhaps as shapeless and doomed as the terrifyingly motley and hapless Tibetan army that resisted, with flaccid ineffectualness, the modern Chinese advance into Tibet in the first place. The archive photographs of that army, standing under arms, have made every two-bit banana-republic tin-soldier army since look like the epitome of precision and professionalism.

In a sense, the hotheads are asking the same question Nietzsche asked of Buddhism. It is often overlooked these days that Nietzsche was deeply interested in Buddhism, having been greatly impressed by Schopenhauer's rendition of what it meant. It was, at that time, a primitive knowledge of Buddhism, but both Schopenhauer and Nietzsche were serious in what study was then possible of the faith.[3] But Nietzsche asked the same key question about Buddhism as he asked about Christianity – although he thought Buddhism superior to Christianity. The question was: where was the point of *responsibility*? It was well and good to recognise there was eternal suffering in the world, indeed endless cycles of it, but who was responsible for it? Who would accept responsibility for it? Who would *will* a moral responsibility for it?[4] Nietzsche proposed the moral impossibility

3. David Loy, 'Beyond Good and Evil? A Buddhist Critique of Nietzsche', *Asian Philosophy*, vol. 6, no. 1, 1996, pp. 37–58.
4. Friedrich Nietzsche, *The Anti-Christ*, trans. R.J. Hollingdale, Harmondsworth: Penguin, 1968.

of quietude. The minute you insert responsibility into either the Buddhist or the Taoist universe, the 'Way' and the Tao are lost or compromised. The hard has been introduced into the serene. It must be reindustrialised to survive in a world that breathes acrid chimney and exhaust fumes, and that recognises the need for responsibility. In Ang Lee's greatest film on a Chinese subject, *Crouching Tiger, Hidden Dragon*, the young and wilful heroine, Jen Yu, by Ang Lee's own admission the embodiment of freedom over a life of rituals and codified behaviour,[5] has inadvertently lured the righteous hero, Li Mu Bai, into a fatal trap. The last scene of the film has her, even with the prospect of union with her outlaw lover within her grasp, choosing to throw herself off a mountain bridge to her death as an admission of responsibility. In the end, even freedom must recognise responsibility. In the end, a life in the mountains is impossible.

Just as the hard may be seen in the serene, so beauty might be necessitous within evil

The Japanese Shinto belief in *kami* is multifaceted. In some ways it is a religion of localisation. Whereas the grandeur of Taoism is to see the cosmic, spiritual and energy-laden connections among all things and their universal wellspring, to achieve a holistic vision, Shinto is more pedantically animist. Each rock can have a spirit or *kami* within, each tree, each blade of grass. This is notwithstanding occasional teachings, such as those by thirteenth-century Ise Shinto, that have seen the entire universe as one great *kami*, or by teachers such as the seventeenth-century figure Razan Hayashi, who identified the Way or *do* (the Japanese equivalent of Tao) of the *kami* with the

---

5. Ang Lee, in the published screenplay of *Crouching Tiger, Hidden Dragon*, London: Faber & Faber, 2000, p. 138.

Way of the Emperor – that is, the Emperor embodied the spirit
of all that was in Japan and as its embodiment was also its most
naturalistic expression. Certainly in *ko* Shinto (ancient Shinto)
there were celestial *kami* or *mikoto* that predate Buddha and
stand in a hierarchy between an original creator and all else.
However, on an everyday basis, *kami* were found within specific
objects, particularly in nature; and, above all, they were not only
spiritual beings or spiritual qualities, they not only inhabited or
infused natural and beautiful things, they were amoral. They
were a quality unto themselves and observed no principles except
that of their being the latent environment in which all humanity, usually unknowingly, inhabited. However, in folklore they
also shared certain desirous characteristics found in European
ghosts: they could desire to become fleshly. They could desire a
love-object. They could become a beautiful, amoral woman to
acquire the man of a *kami*'s dreams – acquire, enjoy and destroy.
The great Japanese novelist and playwright Yukio Mishima, in
his *Noh Plays*, depicts the *kami* as the spirit of the moon come
down to earth with very earthly intent;[6] and a theme of this sort
haunts many of Mishima's works. The debate is not whether the
kami are amoral because of a lack of morality, but whether they
are *above* the moral universe, which is therefore restricted only
to the affairs of human beings. Despite many efforts to establish
a synthesis between Confucian ideals and Shinto, therefore, such
a project has always been problematic. The necessary linkage
between the right conduct of heaven and that on earth is broken
if, in key parts at least of the spirit realm, there is no intrinsic
quality of rightness.

Christian theology has always had a problem of this sort with
Satan – notwithstanding his evolution as an entity within human

6. Yukio Mishima, 'The Damask Drum', in *Five Modern Noh Plays*, New York:
Alfred A. Knopf, 1957.

religious thought over the millennia.[7] Certainly early Christianity, before it was consolidated in a number of authoritative (and
authoritarian) councils and, finally, imperial Roman edicts,
enjoyed an amazing pluralism as beliefs contested with one
another to attain the rank of orthodoxy. The Gnostic persuasions
of the church certainly had a sense of Satan as equivalent to God
– a balancing principle; a contestation that gave creation more
than one dimension; almost a Yin to God's Yang.[8] Over the years,
artists and legends have ascribed to Satan – as oppositional
principle – amazing beauty, even if only the beauty romanticism associates with heroic rebellion. Gustav Doré's etchings
of Satan's fall and rousing of his fallen colleagues depict an
angel of charismatic musculature and almost fragile features.
Doré merely continued almost a tradition of such depiction,
inspired by Milton's characterisation in *Paradise Lost*. Satan's
beauty is rendered by artists such as William Blake, the French
symbolist Jean Delville, and the Pre-Raphaelite painter Edward
Burne-Jones, whose 'Satan Being Cast Out of Heaven' shows a
pageant of immaculately armoured men with female faces slowly
walking down the steps from heaven. There is no rout here. It
is almost as if they are leaving as a result of negotiation. They
are sad, but they are beautiful. On their black armour there is
not a speck of angelic blood. They have lost something but are
not defeated. These are problematic depictions when contrasted
with the medieval representations of Satan and his demons as
lizard-like, as the flying Godzillas of their day. But even these
medieval portrayals were to the effect that this is what happens
when beauty falls. God has (rightly) turned the beauty of the
fallen angels into the horror of the demons. The clearest first
step is the transmogrification of feathered bird-like wings to

7. Elaine Pagels, *The Origin of Satan*, London: Allen Lane, 1996.
8. Elaine Pagels, *The Gnostic Gospels*, New York: Random House, 1979.

the leather webs that God gave first to bats – the creatures of darkness who cannot even see the light by virtue of not being able to see at all.

However, it would also seem that medieval Christianity conflated two types of spirit creature. In Hebrew mythology – which generally tells stories that parallel but also greatly embellish and qualify the biblical accounts – the fallen angels retained their beauty and, indeed, remained in (fractious) dialogue with God and were even used from time to time to discharge missions by God. They became, as it were, a small opposition party within heaven – although heaven remained firmly what we would today call a 'dominant-party state'. The debate between God and Satan that opens the Book of Job is a case in point, and I shall return to that in a later chapter. But Hebrew mythology treats the demons as a separate spiritual species. Angelo Rappoport argues that they acquired 'citizen rights in Jewish myth and legend' from Persian origins.[9] Rappoport's description has them almost as an equivalent to *kami*: omnipresent, multifaceted, but sentient entities rather than immanent in nature (although they often roost in trees); and not amoral as much as consumed by an *im*morality – that is, they are formed in such a way that it is necessary in their identity as demons to obstruct that which is moral and right. They are the gutter opposition to heaven's declaration of what is right, and even the fallen angels don't want to have too much to do with them. They are ugly, but they do have wings; they procreate, so they must discover beauty and attractiveness among themselves. And they can be pressed by extraordinary means to be of constructive service, just as Solomon was able to force them to help build his magical temple. There is an irony here of course, in that the temple of God was built by

---

9. Angelo S. Rappoport, *Ancient Israel*, Volume 1, London: Senate, 1995, p. 71.

the demons. But, in this theology/mythology, the demons were almost beneath contempt, for debate in heaven was reserved for those, faithful or fallen, who were radiant and unquestionably beautiful. That the fallen became over time also 'evil' is a parallel to the Christian Church also becoming not only monotheistic (the Gnostic 'Demiurge' rival to God fell into apostasy), but dictatorial. There could be no opposition on earth, so there had better not be any in heaven – and those who tried it were to be condemned after first having been labelled.

In a sense it was inevitable that Satan would be rehabilitated as a balancing and oppositional principle – not to mention a beautiful one – by the generation of Milton and those who followed him. The struggle against the divine right of kings became also a questioning of the right of the divine. And, as the struggle for democratic rights evolved, whether it took wrong turnings or not, it was not surprising that conservative satirists would depict Robespierre in France and Fox in Britain as demonic. But the hard-won struggle to evolve parliamentary democracy was a struggle to evolve a sense of balance in institutional domains and in public expression. To a significant extent, freedom became nothing absolute, but a centralising principle located in the capacity for dissent – the absence of which demarcated a 'democracy' losing its way. The theological parallel to this has seen a return of Gnosticism – not so much in the format of the Church and worship, but in popular science-fiction literature. The other-worldly is now either technologised, in one branch of science-fiction, or fantasised, in the other. I would like to look at two fantasy examples, one English and one Chinese. And, after all, in the bookshops of today, popular angelic literature sits in the stacks next to sword-and-sorcery fantasy and the same illustrators are happily migrating from one to the other. The genre in depiction is now homogenous, and not only in the image on paper, but in the image as generated by the writing. So Michael Moorcock's description of the Lords of Justice descending from heaven to confront on earth the Forces of Chaos is an almost exact echo of Burne-Jones's painting of 'Satan Being Cast Out of Heaven' – except of course it is Moorcock having his typically pleasant and 'here you see it coming a million miles away' irony – for the Lords of Justice are not the Legions of Satan; they stand for the opposite principles. Or do they?

Michael Moorcock is the foremost science/fantasy author. At first glance, his genre seems entirely sword-and-sorcery fantasy. However unlike, say, the contemporary 'Harry Potter' series, the sorcery does not stand alone as a given, explained only by the unique laws of sorcery. In Moorcock's case it fits into a speculative physics of multitudinous dimensions in equally multitudinous times and spaces – what he calls the 'multiverse'. The key hero in his novels is an albino prince of an almost extinct race, whose name is (often) Elric. Moorcock, true to his ideas of the multiverse, however, reinvents Elric as a host of other protagonists in other times and spaces. Elric, who begins life in a prehistoric age, is the same as Dorian von Hawkmoon in another early age; they are the same as Von Bek, who fights in the endless wars of an emerging modern Europe; and as Jerry Cornelius in a more fully modern time. But it is Elric who is the archetype and it is in the cycle of novels devoted to him that Moorcock first fleshes out his sense of a balance in his multiverse. The scene where the Lords of Justice descend from a sort of heaven is found in the last of the original Elric sextet[10] (although Moorcock later reprised this hero).

---

10. Michael Moorcock, *Stormbringer*, collected with the other five in an omnibus volume, *Elric*, London: Gollancz, 2001. This was first published as a separate novel in 1965.

Elric has almost served his incarnation on earth, but the primeval planet cannot enter its new and more human phase until a balance is struck between Law and Chaos – so that the emerging human species can live tolerably. The great forces of the two elemental opposites assemble on a battlefield almost drawn from the biblical legend of Armageddon. Certainly, for the evening of Elric's era, it is apocalyptic; indeed, although Moorcock's writing gradually became more elegiac and almost literary, at this stage it was so apocalyptic that St John would have been humbled to be in his company. The Lords of Law wear armour made from white mirrors and glide through space. Their emblem is a single straight arrow – for law allows no deviation. The Forces of Chaos, by contrast, ride weird beasts and are multicoloured. They include in their ranks the scarlet Dukes of Hell, and all assembled on their side are dedicated to colour, variation, confusion and dissent. In a very clear way, the Forces of Chaos are as attractive as the Lords of Law, and the great battle merely clears the earth of any hegemony from either.

The balance that results is not symmetrical, however. It is a jagged affair, so, to that extent, Chaos takes an edge into the future. Law becomes the opposition party, holding the multiverse in a sense of direction and evolution, but the balance is a condition of ebb and flow, of struggle, and often it is tenacious struggle. The Taoist symbol of seamless integration of opposites can never have the smooth operation its curved lines suggest. It is only in a much later novel, when Moorcock reprises the Elric character, that he finally reveals the symbol of Chaos to be two jagged and ragged lines of forked lightening, one yellow and one black, crossing each other.[11] It is an electric swastika – but nothing even Li Hongzhi, in his manipulation of the symbol, would have wished.

---

11. Michael Moorcock, *The Revenge of the Rose*, London: Grafton, 1991.

The second example derives from a Hong Kong comic book series titled *Tien Ha* – Heaven and Earth (The Cosmos).[12] This has been a bestseller for years on a fortnightly basis throughout Asia and the world's Chinatowns, and has spawned at least two films. The series actually has two quite separate or separable parts. Up to issue 259, the serial adventures concern the fathers of the sons who assume centre stage from 260 onwards. My disquisition is about the fathers. One is called Wind and the other Cloud. They have magical qualities drawn from the Taoist elemental universe. Wind in particular, though blinded in one eye, is very beautiful; his long hair swirls in the wind as he, true to his name, flies through the air as a circling vortex. But there is a third fighter in the story. They were all friends and training partners once and, despite possessing different fighting skills, are evenly matched from having shared the same teachings. Their destiny is to acquire the magic swords of the cosmos: there are just and unjust ways to do this.

The third fighter, flame-haired and also very beautiful, goes down the path of injustice. He takes the dragon potions and gradually acquires the flaming energy – not just the hair – of a dragon. It is not by that he becomes evil. In Chinese mythology dragons are benign creatures, usually depicted as messengers from heaven. It is because he seeks the dragon's power in order to use it unfairly and unjustly. But, as the dragon's personality also takes him over, his immoral characteristics are subsumed by an amoral character. Shortly after issue 200 he has lost re-flectiveness. He becomes evil not because evil has triumphed in his internal balance; he no longer has an internal balance. He is evil because good has no place in him. Yet he retains his beauty until, in the final issues, rage at encountering defeat allows

12. Published by a group called Magnum Consultants Limited. Their comics are represented on www.comicworlds.com.

ugliness to well within him until it erupts to overcome all that he is on the surface – and he dies as a hideous flaming monster, his hair burnt to cinders by his own raging fires. However, in the issues after 259, as the sons of Wind and Cloud grow into their parents' places, the son of the dragon fighter also appears. There is an eternal return here. But the sons of Wind and Cloud cannot balance the dragon son as their fathers had. The sons are much more complex and are themselves susceptible to evil. They struggle with each other and within themselves, and even form alliances with the dragon son. The issues of the fathers are more comic book than the issues of the sons – but the earlier issues were more successful as moral fable precisely because they set out to be moral fable.

The key centrepiece, from issue 242 to 247, is the Temple of Heaven, which still stands as a tourist attraction in Beijing. In the comic books it is constantly enveloped in swirling winds and sandstorms as the heroes battle it out – much as it is mostly enveloped in haze and smog today. But the artists might have been forgiven if mistaken as the prospective architects of the temple. In fine Chinese traditional etching style, they depict the temple tile for tile, beam by beam, exactly as it is when one visits it in Beijing today. It is not the only borrowing. In issue 243 there is an adaptation of Doré's etching of Satan being cast out of heaven; only it is not Michael casting down Satan, but the dragon fighter (Satan) casting down one of his old teachers. The theme, all the same, is about titanic struggle between good and evil at the very centre of heaven and earth, to command the very purpose enshrined in the name Temple of Heaven; and it is fought by characters drawn as anatomically beautiful as any artist could render them. There is a struggle, if not a debate, in heaven about good and evil; about its fractious balance; about which opposition or ruling party might attain ascendancy; and both sides display exceedingly beautiful qualities. There is a political struggle with the usual seductive instruments.

The beautiful history of Iran

Given the fractious and dangerous tensions between the USA and Iran in 2007, it was perhaps not surprising that the Iranian political establishment found the comic-book-turned-film *300* offensive. Even the original legend (for there is no historically sound evidence for the event) of a handful of Spartans, with their Theban allies, holding firm against the unconvincing number of 2 million armed Persians is demeaning. It suggested that one Westerner was worth, in fighting prowess at least, 6,666 Persians. Even then, the Persians needed treachery on their side to overcome the least cultured of the Greek city-states. But the comic and the film reduce even the basic legend to a travesty of itself. Xerxes becomes a kind of transvestite giant; the Greek who betrays the Spartans becomes the hunchback with the hump that a hundred gargoyles could not match; Spartan women suddenly have rights that sit in contradistinction to those enjoyed even by Persian men; and, when the Spartan warriors sally forth, their fighting moves seem suspiciously drawn from the Samurai spins and swordplay that are seen in electronic games and are, in any case, entirely unsuited to the primitive stabbing swords of the Spartans – and Persians fall like chaff before scythes. Only long-distance archers and swordsmen on horseback attacking footsoldiers have any success at all against the Spartans, who, thanks to computer enhancement, never stop flexing their abs – even in their final death, where they are laid out and filmed from above as if they had become a tapestry, or a variation of Michaelangelo's Sistine Chapel mural, all God's judgement represented as a sprawl of Western sacrifice, but in Caravaggio rather than Michaelangelo colours. It is a beautifully and artfully uncouth film, but I don't doubt the offence it caused.

The compelling aspect of the Persian and Greek wars, however, was precisely the superior arts of the Persians. Greece, and particularly Athens, never entered its fabled golden age until the rebuilding of Athens after it had been sacked by Persian fire. It was only then that the temples of the Acropolis and all of Athens' legendary architecture became possible – and became the appropriately grand and geometrically rational site to host the sense of Western democracy beginning in all its (nevertheless) fractious marketplace shouting and oratory. But the empire of Xerxes, which Greece had been invited to join, was the first true global empire in terms of the races and nations that were called to Xerxes' arms. The Mesopotamian empires had been Semitic, the Egyptian ones localised alongside the Nile. The Persian empire was never democratic, but it was tolerant and pluralistic. And its founder, Cyrus the Great, around the mid-500s BC, established not the first code of laws (that was the stele of Hammurabi, about 4000 BC, which was Sumerian, or in today's terms Iraqi) but the first bill of human rights, to do not with political freedoms but tolerance and the rights of religions and different beliefs. In 539 BC he took Babylon, and afterwards freed the Jews, who returned to Israel to rebuild the temple overthrown by the Babylonians. The work of Solomon (and the demons) was refabricated by the facilitation of a Persian.

But it was the close descendant of Cyrus, Xerxes, who ascended the throne in 486 BC, who has more than one identity. In the biblical book of Esther, he is called Ahasuerus, and is the husband of Esther, a Jewish exile who, after much court intrigue, succeeds in persuading her husband to promulgate a specific bill of rights for the Jews. So, whatever debt or lack of debt owed to the Persians by the Greeks, that other strand of Western ancestry owes much to them. The rebuilding of the temple at Jerusalem also allowed the emergence of a new priestly class in Israel, and it was Ezra and his cohorts who set about basically compiling from scattered documents and manuscripts, and editing folklore, to write much of what has now been accepted as the Old Testament – certainly key legal and behavioural elements of the Pentateuch, or the seminal first five books which contain, in addition to the stories of creation and exodus, the laws of Israel which, even today, form the core of orthodox Jewish behaviour. To the Persians, even to Xerxes, much is owed by the West and even by the Israelis, who fear the development of a bomb to rival their own.

The Persia that Alexander of Macedon later came to face and conquer was thought by many Greeks to be the degenerate descendant of Xerxes's empire. In any case, it was time for revenge, an invasion for an invasion, and one against something overripe and past its sell-by date. Except that it was anything but. Once having conquered Persia, right up to and beyond its borders with India, it is the case that Alexander himself was conquered by the culture of what he had invaded; and, to the consternation of many of his followers, he became a fusion of Persian and Greek, establishing a particular Hellenic period which was far from the triumph of the West, but a triumph of a multiculturalism that eventually made his Ptolomaic successors seem more un-Greek than Greek. When, much later, Persian painters depicted him, he was building walls of iron and brass on the frontiers of his conquests in India to keep out a threat common by now to both Christian and Islamic apocalyptic fears: the peoples of Gog and Magog. Alexander was never fully nativised, although many paintings show him with the beard and costume of Persian nobility, but he became an intimate feature of Persian and Middle Eastern discourse as the almost domiciled representative of the great 'Other', the 'out there', and the way it thought. He became the intimate oppositional principle, without which Islamic thought had no possibility to prove its superiority. What was called 'the thought of Alexander', including the preservation by Islamic thinkers of key aspects of Aristotelian and Platonic thought, when it had died in the West, was as essential to the development of Islamic philosophy as Islam itself.

This sense of contested fusion is found also in Indian art. The northern Indian Gandhara sculptures of the second century AD are often cited as evidence of Greek influence, and, with their Hellenic naturalism and fully human features, they were. Buddha became a robed Greek athlete seated in his meditation pose. However, there were other forces also at work. The artistic movement at Gandhara was more influenced by the Roman take on Greek art than Greek art in its original: that is, it had more to do with new trade routes between East and West than with the residual influence of Alexander, although there was indeed some of that. More importantly, however, the new artistic influences were precisely what was needed in the religious movements of the day, as monastic Buddhism gave way to Mahayana Buddhism, a 'great wheel' Buddhism that was not like the small wheel of the enclosed priestly spaces. This form of Buddhism was expansive and humanistic, and devoted much emphasis to the newly emergent figure of the boddhisattva, the saint who refuses nirvana for the sake of an endlessly reincarnated messianic mission to help humanity on earth. The huge pluralism of boddhisattvas meant that humanity was suffused with them. Anyone could aspire to their mission and, with proper care and devotion – later incorporating rituals and vows – become one of them, even if just a very junior member of the species. The idea was to make earth a better place, not get to heaven. The humanistic Buddhism welcomed the humanistic sculpture. But the humanistic sculpture did not stay Greek or Graeco-Roman for long. It stopped posing as an athlete with the dignity of a senator presiding over a congregation. That admixture had the capacity for an immediate stiltedness. It was Afghanistan that, by the late Gandharan period of the fifth to seventh centuries A D, saw the fully realised fusion of Greek humanistic and naturalistic features (though now orientalised rather than Caucasian) with the idealised sweeping and androgynous curves of Indian art and later Tibetan art. There is a surviving head of the Buddha in the Victoria and Albert Museum in London where the Buddha looks contemplatively and almost seductively downwards to one side, his eyes half closed. If the original paintwork had survived he would seem to be fluttering his eyelashes – a coyly flirting Buddha. The surviving neckline can only have belonged to a torso held in a curve and probably weighted on one leg more than the other – the classic pose of the later Tibetan sculptures of boddhisattvas. And, in the Fondukistan region of Afghanistan, there is a monastery where this combination of naturalism and sensuality is combined once again with a form of mannerism in gesture and adornment. What is still Greek in this went on to have an influence on Chinese art, although this was Sinophiled very quickly. Basically, both Alexander and all that came in his wake – the Western influences that reached India and beyond – were appreciated, copied, absorbed and transmuted. In the Hellenic empire of Asia Minor and in Persia and the Middle East, what was from Alexander became part of debate and, as something intrinsic to the discourse of the period, became naturalised as a key influence within, and also in contradistinction to, what was argued to be original local cultures and their teachings.

From Persia, however, came something that may have influenced the West far more than either Persia or the West realises.

Certainly there are some traces of Zoroastrianism in Afghan
Buddhism and in the famous Tibetan rendition of Buddhism
– but the teachings of the great Persian Church have quite possibly underpinned everything the West holds dear in the Christian
side of its Judaic-Christian heritage; and we have already seen
how Persia facilitated the readvent of the Judaic tradition.

There are very few Zoroastrians left today, and those who
survive dispute the purity of their members – so that Persian
Zoroastrians dispute the full authenticity of the Parsi Indian
Zoroastrians who were part of an early diaspora from Persia.
Marrying only within pure bloodline means that, inevitably,
like any small and closed community, the group will die or be
forced to expand its sense of inclusiveness. Many of its rituals
survive, however, such as the Persian new year ritual of jumping
over fire – uttering the chant, 'My whiteness for your redness
and your redness for my whiteness' – which is still a nationwide
custom, even in today's Ayatollah-dominated Shia Islamic Iran.
Zoroastrianism is generally tolerated in Iran, if only because
it was a belief system prior to Islam – that is, it did not try to
challenge or supplant Islam; whereas the more recent Baha'i
faith, founded by Baha'u'llah between 1853 and 1873, is persecuted. Baha'i is a universalistic faith, in that it hopes for a
universal government and foresees not only a time of justice but
an intermediate point of interim justice – an interim mercy for
humanity. In some ways it is clearly partly derived from Shia
Islam, with its belief in an era to come of justice and the advent
of just men. In other ways it is a conflation of the nineteenth-
century remnants of Enlightenment expectation and a yoke
of laws and procedures that make the Book of Leviticus seem
pedestrian and modest.[13] But the original mission of conversion

13. See one of the faith's key books, effectively a scripture: Baha'u'llah, *The Kitab-
i-aqdas*, London: Baha'i Publishing Trust, 1993.

undertaken by Baha'u'llah was to Zoroastrian communities in both Iran and Bombay; and his work might best (if contentiously) be described as an exposition of key parts of the 'mother book' (the Quran) with a Zoroastrian commitment to ceremony and rituals of cleansing and remaining clean of misconduct, many of which were prefigured in works entitled the *Bab* (the Gate) by Mirza Ali Muhammad, a precursor of Baha'u'llah, almost as John the Baptist was to Christ. But the *Bab* seems very derivative from Persian tradition and Zoroastrian conduct, even though one of Mirza Ali Muhammad's key expositions was to do with the Quranic story of Joseph and his brothers in Egypt (Sura 12 of the Quran). However, all these writings are deemed heretical by the Shia Islam regime in Iran, because they give an exposition of the Quran that is no longer orthodoxly Islamic; they claim to surpass the Quran as a means of instruction for a new age; they are not a safe and colourful antiquity that re-manifests itself in folk customs. The Baha'i are a harmless people but inhabit the same ecological niche as the Falun Gong in China. They seek to elide the state religion, rather than oppose it; but, in so doing, they seek to bypass the instrument of totalitarian governance. Notwithstanding this, the point here is that Zoroastrianism may be waging a vain fight to remain 'pure', but its descendant forms and influences are problematically widespread.

But the figure of Zoroaster first came to its European audience in the form of Nietzsche's Zarathustra. Nietzsche knew as little about Zoroaster as he did about Buddha, and his Zarathustra is in fact a curious blend of Jesus (he leaves on his search at age 30, just as Jesus began his ministry at that age), transcendent Sufi Islam (of the sort that did reach Europe via its contacts with the Ottoman Empire), a Buddhist recluse (he lives sometimes in a cave), and someone finally committed to the 'eternal return' – the endless cycle of resurrection or resurgence, which, as

Mircea Eliade noted, is a universal religious motif,[14] but which is also a feature of Zoroastrianism. What is strange about Nietzsche's book *Thus Spoke Zarathustra* is not the compilation and integration of eclectic personages into Zarathustra, but the overwhelming melancholy of the penultimate section where Zarathustra is drunk. He has just triumphed over the 'higher men' and given an ugly man his life's meaning, but he now sings of the joy of opposites: 'All joy wants the eternity of all things, wants honey, wants dregs, wants intoxicated midnight, wants graves, wants the consolation of graveside tears, wants gilded sunsets.'[15] But that is because Nietzsche wrote the book in a matter of just a few weeks, emerging from a period of great despair and mixing his relapses with moments of great exhilaration.[16] In the end, this best-known of his works, immortalised further by Strauss's musical composition of the same name (and even more when this music became the overture to Kubrick's *2001: A Space Odyssey*), was about the nobility of Zarathustra when he believes in nothing anymore except the drive of humanity towards hope. Despite despair, the work of humanity is to achieve the eternal return of hope and all its works. The work towards hope is the point of responsibility. This is not the central message of Zoroastrian thought, but it becomes so when associated with a balance in the universe. But Nietzsche illustrates certainly the historical effect of Zoroastrianism: it keeps returning to our consciousness in ever more mutated forms – whether Nietzschean, Baha'ian or Christian.

Just as it is itself something of a mutation, the problem of Zoroastrian thought is that, like Buddhism, it was recorded

---

14. Mircea Eliade, *The Myth of the Eternal Return: Cosmos and History*, London: Arkana, 1989.

15. Friedrich Nietzsche, *Thus Spoke Zarathustra*, London: Penguin, 1969, p. 332.

16. Curtis Cate, *Friedrich Nietzsche*, London: Hutchinson, 2002, pp. 392–426.

only many years after the death of its founder. Zoroaster himself lived about 1400 to 1200 BC but the Zoroastrian equivalent of the Bible and Quran, the Avesta, was written only in the fifth or sixth century AD, using a specially composed alphabet. Both the alphabet and many parts of the original Avesta are now lost. What we have are translations, not of the full book, from 1323 AD. The English translation is a century old and is out of print. The entire scholarly history of Zoroastrianism, from the time of Nietzsche onwards, is problematic. Like Nietzsche, people have sought to impose their own normative assumptions on these teachings. However, it would seem clear that this was a monotheistic religion with one supreme God, Ahura Mazda (of whom, I am told, the Japanese car makers were indeed aware and sought to exploit). It was also dualistic, in that time within the universe was a constant battle between good and evil, with the efforts of Ahura Mazda's Holy Spirit and his 'Holy Immortals' (something like archangels) devoted to maintaining the balance towards good. Depending on one's reading, this battle occured one level below that inhabited by Ahura Mazda himself. Good, in ritual terms at least, is represented by fire, and this is why Zoro-astrian ritual privileges fire as its key symbol and metaphor. The religion is highly ceremonial and ritualistic, and very concerned about cleanliness – another metaphor for goodness.

Zoroastrianism probably had a marked influence on the development of Christianity, both the early Gnostic variant with its privileged place for dualism as coexisting and largely equal principles of good and evil; and the more literal aspects of key foundational characterisation. Both strands fed into the debates and arguments of the embryonic Christian Church, as it struggled for an orthodoxy; and they were probably introduced via the descendant Zoroastrian sect devoted to Mithras, which had become popular with Roman soldiers who had served in

Persia, and the sect having spread widely in the proletarian suburbs of Rome and other Italian cities. As it happened, the consolidating Church embraced the characterisation and declared heretical the dualism. That characterisation is notable in the parallels between Zoroastrianism and Christianity. In the struggle between good and evil a saviour will appear, called the *Saoshyant* (Messiah); he will be born of a virgin mother; as a result of his second coming (Zoroaster's was the first coming, cut short by his assassination) there will be great strife between good and evil with the apocalyptic triumph of good; at that point cataclysms will take place, mountains will melt, the dead will be resurrected and be reunited with their souls and all will be brought to a last judgement. The good will be saved and become immortal, whereas the bad will be plunged into hell. The kingdom of Ahura Mazda will descend to earth and rule in righteousness forever. The parallels with the Gospel accounts, particularly Matthew and the Book of Revelation, are strong enough to seem like borrowings, and if not direct borrowings then clear influences. Scholars are reluctant to emphasise this, as the evidence is circumstantial. Even so, there was an early empathy between the Zoroastrian Church and Christianity.

I referred in an earlier chapter to *The Epic of the Kings* (the *Shahnameh*) by the eleventh-century Persian writer, Ferdowsi. The translator likens the huge epic to the *Iliad*, but it is probably more like the Mahabharata, with Rostam as an Arjuna figure. By the time of this epic, Persia had become part of Islam, but the great poem is a writing-back to a Zoroastrian age of chivalry. It gives, among other things, a rendition of Persian victory over the Roman Caesar Valerian – very different to the Roman account – and it is a depiction of magnanimity and multicultural wisdom. In a cosmopolitan setting, where Chinese, Greek and Hindu influences and thought are part of the discourse, the Zo-

roastrian philosopher lectures Caesar on Christianity. He gives
a stirring picture of Jesus and how he went with equanimity to
his death; then immediately conflates Jesus, as the son of God,
with God Himself, who, 'as the Lord of the world is one and that
to serve any other is without reason'. Here there is an explicit
linking of one monotheism to another. And it is clear that the
philosopher approves of the teaching of Jesus, as he rebukes
Caesar's imperialism:

> The Spirit of the Messiah bears witness to this. Do you not see
> what Jesus son of Mary said when he was revealing the secrets
> which had been hidden? He said, If someone takes your shirt,
> do not contend too fiercely with him, and if he smites you on
> the cheek so that your vision darkens because of the blow, do
> not put yourself into a rage nor let your face turn pale. Close
> your eyes to him and speak no harsh word. In your eating be
> content with the least morsel of food, and if you lack worldly
> possessions do not seek about after them. Overlook the evil
> things and pass meekly through this dark vale. But for you
> now lust has become dominant over wisdom and your hearts
> have gone astray from justice and honour. Your palaces soar
> up to Saturn and camels are needed to carry the keys to your
> treasure-houses. With the treasures you have arrayed many
> armies in resplendent proud armour. Everywhere you fight as
> aggressors, destroy the peace with your swords, and turn the
> fields into pools of blood. The Messiah did not guide you along
> this path.[17]

In early Islam, and to an extent to this day, Jesus features
as a major prophet; but he was also a conscious feature in Zoroastrian thought as a variant of the characterisation within

---

17. Ferdowsi, *Shahnameh: The Epic of the Kings*, trans. Reuben Lévy, Tehran: Yassavoli, 2001, pp. 180–81. I hasten to add that this is the Iranian republication of the
Routledge & Kegan Paul translation of 1967, published in Boston a dozen years before the
Iranian Revolution – and that Reuben Lévy is Jewish. There is no bias in the translation
against the United States, despite a clear parallel in today's politics.

Zoroastrianism itself – not to mention his teachings being a close variant of those in the Avesta. Zoroastrianism embraced a hugely pluralistic and cosmopolitan environment. From Cyrus and Xerxes onwards, Persian outreach had been multicultural, and this never really ceased. The 'thought of Alexander', for instance, was always present as one part of discourse, even if it could be demonstrated to pale before the revelation of divine light from God. But in early Islam there was enough self-confidence to engage sympathetically with Western thought, of which Alexander was merely a personification. The great discursive poem of the thirteenth century, *The Speech of the Birds* (sometimes rendered as *The Parliament of the Birds*), by Faridu'd-Din 'Attar, represents extensively the Persian Sufi Islamic tradition – something directly paralleling the work of the thirteenth-century Anatolian poet Yunus Emre,[18] and of course the thirteenth-century Persian poet Jalal al-Din Rumi, around whom an industry has spawned and commodified a 'Rumi-lite' – he is the best-selling poet in the United States and his work may be found in bookshops alongside collections of aphoristic wisdom and new age mysticism. He doesn't deserve this, and it is well to remember that he came to Sufism from a Sunni and legalistic background. He was a student of Hanafi jurisprudence, one of four Sunni legal paradigms, and his sense of logic and order were greatly influenced by it. So he is no transcendent stand-alone mystic. Just as his dancing followers – he in effect founded the whirling dervishes – needed first the dance before attaining transcendence and union with God, so the law is like a candle that lights the way. It is not the way – but, without it, the way cannot be seen. The Rumi-lite of today was satirised, ahead of time, by Rumi himself. His poem 'The Parrot and the

---

18. The finest translation of whose work was prepared by Talat Sait Halman: *Yunus Emre: Selected Poems*, Ankara: Ministry of Culture, 1990.

Oil' concerns a talking parrot who spills precious oil and, when chided by its owner, enters a silent sulk, until one day he spots a hairless monk and bursts back into speech, comically accusing the monk of having been made hairless as a punishment perhaps for spilling oil himself. Rumi writes about the fallacy of supposing someone holy to be like oneself.

> Don't suppose the pure your mirror image,
> Though it's true ewe and you may sound the same;
> The whole world's gone astray for just this reason;
> So few can recognise the saints of God.
> Folks compare their own selves to the prophets,
> and take God's saints for mortals just like them.[19]

There is, in fact, very little parroting 'gee whiz, he speaks so directly to me and my problems' in Rumi or the Sufi poets in general. And 'Attar is a further case in point, where the speech of the birds is a metaphor for a communion with God that logical human speech can never approximate. In one of the lengthy disquisitions in his poem, Alexander has died and is praised by Aristotle as having lived 'in the way of faith'. Indeed Aristotle calls him 'King of the Faith' – and there is an Islamic tradition that supposes Alexander a man protected by God and even a minor tradition that accounts him one of the prophets in the line before Muhammad. Nevertheless, his thought and Aristotle's, 'the philosophy of the Greeks', cannot evade death and cannot transcend it. But birds always fly their roost before they die. They sing in a language that is to do with God's love and light, but – and here is the key interesting point – it is not a light that can be rendered in literal terms.

---

19. I am told that in the original language this is hilarious. Cited in full in Franklin D. Lewis, *Rumi: Past and Present, East and West*, Oxford: Oneworld, 2000, pp. 375-6. This is an extensive and fully sensible study of Rumi.

The 'p' of 'polytheism' in this, with the truth of
        intuitive knowledge,
Would I prefer to the 'ph' of 'philosophy'.[20]

The love and light of God is like God himself – abstract, not
able to be rendered in a single definition, not susceptible to any
fundamental statement that 'I have understood and proclaim
God.' It is, by this Sufi Islamic approach, antipathetic to the
Wahhabism behind the Osama bin Ladens of today's world. It is
the 'polytheism' denounced by the founder of the Wahhabi movement in his desert, bird-free retreat. It is the birdsong celebrated
by the great French composer Messiaen – beyond the formal
strictures of music. It is also the great fissure within Islam today,
in key senses greater than that between Shia and Sunni, because
it cannot be appropriated within fundamentalist assertions of
how the world should be. In so far as non-Kurdish Turkey retains
a descendant version of Sufism, albeit made more pragmatic
not only by modern times but by an internationalised sense of
Islamic decorum, it becomes the key Islamic country with which
to engage; but it is the fundamentalist fires of European politics
and fears that will prevent this from becoming a moment of
actual union. In the absence of union, other fires burn and the
Iranian fire is again sensing its ascendancy.

For, far from Fukuyama's dancing philosophic attendance on
George Bush's sense of triumph after both the fall of the Berlin
Wall and victory in Gulf War I, far from the liberal triumph that
proclaimed the 'end of history' – that is, the accomplishment
of history, the future with no need for history because history
had delivered the best result it ever could – far from the bom-
bastic conceit that liberal democracy was all there could ever

20. Faridu'd-Din 'Attar, *The Speech of the Birds (Mantiqu't-Tair)*, trans. Peter Avery,
Cambridge: Islamic Texts Society, 1998, pp. 402-3.

be in terms of destiny, there was the sense of another history beginning. The revolution in Iran, before it succumbed fully to the clerical faction, was highly utopian. By that I include a Shia utopia which simultaneously looked backwards as well as forwards into the future. It looked backwards to the foundation of Shia, when the Twelfth Imam (the Shia are sometimes called the Twelvers), a direct descendant of Muhammad, entered 'occultation'; that is, he disappeared from society with the promise that he would one day reappear – the Shia equivalent of the Christian Second Coming, the *parousia*, even of the Zoroastrian Second Coming. And, when he did come again, history would start anew, and it would not be Fukuyama's era of the 'last men' of history, but the first men – who would be the new just men – of a new history. Ahmadinejad believes he rides on the horse of history – the hidden Imam's second coming is imminent – while, in theological terms at least, the Horses of the Apocalypse bear down on the West. But, as we shall see later, there is much more to represent within Shia Islam than what Ahmadinejad might tauntingly say.

The Tao of birdsong

There are typecastings, un-typecastings and re-typecastings in any imagination. A 'healthy' type might be one with a balanced mixture of all three. Demonisation should not be swamped by its antidote. Scepticism is always welcome in a world where few things can be as they seem. The work of international relations might be to see the fused layers of every actor and its background, and not just a layer which is forcibly represented as the worst aspect possible. It would of course be reflective if each actor could see its own fused and often contradictory layers – and they are fused together; they can be analysed in their component parts, but they can't be unglued completely. However, in a world of ascendancy and descendancy in the international, every actor essentialises its historical glamour and greatness as an underpinning for victory. The trick for the observer – and the wise statesman – is not to believe anything, but to believe *everything*; to know and believe each and every single layer of the whole even when, often, the layers are far from neatly stacked but are jumbled materials that form a living collage of interchanging shapes and colours – Jackson Pollack in 3D. It would certainly make the study of international relations, and even more so its practice, quite fascinating in more than its present morbidity of power relationships.

When Kent Nagano conducts the great orchestras of the world what immediately strikes the viewer is how his long hair bounces in time to the music. What strikes the listener is that this is clearly a disciple of Messiaen. Nagano works almost exclusively with modern repertoire, including highly experimental work. As a young man, with the London Symphony Orchestra (and he has red-facedly omitted this from his discography), he even recorded a double CD of Frank Zappa's music (actually it wasn't that bad). His technique is a simple crystalline layering of a music's clearly differentiated component parts. This is partly why he so likes working with the soprano Dawn Upshaw. Her voice is not sentimental and rounded, but crystalline in its clarity. Many critics can't stand what he does, but there is a genuine case to be made for approaching almost atonal and serial work in this way. If there is no lyricism in the melody – melody in its traditional sense having been banned by the harsh industrialism of modernity – there has to be lyricism in how the working tools of the composer play their individual parts in constituting a whole. And it doesn't even have to be because of industrialised modernity. Messiaen's entire *œuvre* was how to transcend the industrialised

Tao, to escape into the music of the spheres; and, if the music of the planets was not always successfully rendered, the music of the birds in the skies that intervene between heaven and earth was caught by him wonderfully. *Oiseaux exotiques* remains one of the high points of his work. The irony, of course, was that he could catch it only with orchestras playing the pure notes of modern instruments, and it has come down to us on digitised recordings where every natural impediment to purity has been electronicised. To escape the industrialised Tao, one must first embrace it. And, by embracing it, every bird-sound Messiaen sought to represent can be distinguished one from the other, even if they imagine themselves in a dawn chorus.

Can there be such layers in international relations? Layers, say, of compassion and mercy, ambivalence and imagination, abjection and horror, forgiveness and history, industrialism and birdsong, power and faith? Well, there had better be. The world is not getting any easier to navigate. Might as well navigate it in all its layered complexity. It is the sort of 'long revolution' the Welsh thinker Raymond Williams once sought to impose upon cultural and intellectual work within a capitalist society – to subvert and change it from within its very structures, not of exchange, but of communication.[21] Well, I think it just got harder, because we must seek to understand communication and its foundations within societies we have never approached on their own terms before. And, in the clamour of industrialised and industrialising world politics, we must seek still to do it serenely. Seek to appreciate the flower, with myriad colours in its petals, surviving still at the mouth of the sewer that carries our fetid human and chemicalised wastes towards the gasping ocean.

---

21. Raymond Williams, *The Long Revolution*, London: Chatto & Windus, 1961.

6

What should God do about evil?

Of all the French symbolist painters of the last two hundred years, it is Jean Delville who is most like the English Pre-Raphaelites in his choice of mythical and classical themes, and in the androgyny of his subjects. His *Academy of Plato*, where the nude male students sit in contemplative awe of Plato (who in turn sits under a purple wisteria), is at first glance a study in homoeroticism. The students sit arm in arm and strike languorous poses. They are perfect athletic specimens and, clearly, are developing minds as idealised as their bodies – which are curiously sexless despite being male. In fact, they are probably not meant to be homoerotic at all, not in today's terms anyway – which ascribe contemporary queer interpretations to all historical subjects. They are, instead, the objects of an 'urning', a term taken from the planet Uranus – with the emphasis on the first two letters rather than the last four – which was adopted by men of the Victorian era and its continental equivalent to depict a passionate but asexual longing for a male companion. Alfred Lord Tennyson's pining for Arthur Hallam is a case in point. The lack of consummation was the point of idealism. It was a longing that was perpetually tantric in the mental sense – enjoyed and never fulfilled, because the longing was more enjoyable than the fulfilment. Beauty was separate from gratification. The loved one was not a lover, and always pure and never owned. In this sense he could be forever idealised.

I raise this because of Delville's other famous painting, *Satan's Treasures*, in which Satan dances with pleasure above his captured sleeping souls. These perpetual captives are not corrupted by death but are a beautiful nude colony, neither aware that they are damned by God nor in fact giving a damn. Delville's Satan is the most beautiful of them all, however – more beautiful than his captives and more so than Gustav Doré's or any other post-Milton depiction of Satan. He dances because he has a dancer's body. His bat and flying-lizard wings seem part of a detachable cloak, and his billowing hair is flame red. He resembles almost exactly the dragon warrior in *Tien Ha*, the Hong Kong comic book series of cosmic struggle under heaven, and it would not be surprising if the artists had been inspired by Delville. This painting has illustrated the cover of science-fiction novels and a recording of Messiaen by Simon Rattle. It is, in some ways, the most universalised image of Satan in the early twenty-first century. It can be downloaded from at least twenty websites dedicated to Delville and makes the perfect desktop wallpaper. Satan is here idealised. It is he, not God, who is unattainable. This creature is, we might imagine, the same Satan who appears one day in the courts of God, who at that moment is basking in the devotion of His servant, Job.

The Book of Job is one of the most problematic in the Old Testament, if not the entire Bible. It seems composed of three parts: the temptation and obstinate faith of Job, despite the scepticism of his friends; the oratorical defence of God by Elihu;

and God's own self-enunciation as creator of the leviathan, in the language that inspired Milton, and also in a language that is almost Quranic in the splendour of its rhetoric and didacticism. In fact, they were probably three separate works, glued together by the revisionist nation-builders of Ezra's generation, seeking to rebuild not only the temple but the body of faith which it represented. Certainly most scholars seem agreed that Elihu's part is the last addition – almost as if Job's interrogators and sceptical friends had done too good a job in questioning God as a source of mercy; for, by then, with God's full permission, Job has been reduced to a wasted, diseased, suppurating and bereft shadow of his former self. His family, by this same permission, has been annihilated and his extensive wealth and beautiful possessions have been swept away. He has left only the ashes in which he rolls and a shard of pottery with which to scratch and relieve the oozing sores that have swarmed all over and penetrated his now-skeletal body.

Chapter One of the Book of Job opens with an inventory of Job's wealth: he had 7,000 sheep, 3,000 camels, 500 teams of oxen and 500 female donkeys (we do not know how many male donkeys, but this many livestock could only have grazed the land of Uz, where Job lived, to desert). He had seven sons and three daughters, many servants, and was famous for his parties, which he threw seven times a year, 'and sometimes they lasted several days... [when] they would eat and drink with great merriment' (Job 1:4–5). His loss of all this was occasioned by a great cosmic wager. It began one heavenly day when the angels presented themselves to God, and Satan came as well to do the same. Now there are some interesting features here: first, the angels would have come in their finery, and Satan likewise, not having been made ugly because of his rebellion; second, he was able to talk to God as an equal, offering no ritual *politesse*, and even scoffing at God's statements; third, he seems to have been given dominion of the earth but is not banished from heaven. He appears as a prince in controlled tetchy conversation with a slightly greater king, and both are prepared to lay bets against the other. There is no sense of hierarchy, of prior triumph or defeat, of stigma, or of deference and pleading for readmission to heaven. The two are, for the only blatant moment in the official Old Testament, the central Gnostic pairing, where equal but oppositional principles are in a discursive relationship with each other. This is the first problematic aspect of the Book of Job – the absence in the first section of the unchallenged and almighty creator. The second problematic aspect is in what little regard human life is held by God. He gives Satan full rights to kill everyone who is loved by Job, and, by the end of the book, Job having held firm in a rather sulky and imperfect way, his possessions are restored and doubled (so now he has 14,000 sheep, etc.), and he is able to sire more children – as if love and fatherhood involved simple replaceable numbers. And the third problematic aspect is that this numbers game is predicated on a wager – as if humanity was simply a plaything of the gods and possessed no intrinsic merit. The wager is that Job loves God only because he loves the blessings of God – that is, his riches. Satan bets that, once they are taken away, Job will curse God. Worshipful or cursing, Job's happiness or unhappiness stems from God. Indeed, all the debate that follows, from both Job's sceptical friends and Elihu as protagonist of God, depicts humanity in the full Quranic sense as a contingent species. Its subjective agency and self-conceived sense of individual worth count for nothing. The only difference is that, in the Quran, God is the absolute first principle upon which humanity is contingent. In the Book of Job, God is not absolute in the opening exchanges – although he protests Himself to be so in his leviathan speech at the end. But he opens that speech by the suggestion that only He can command the morning to appear and the night to recede. In short, he has been able – through Job's obstinate faith in fact – to win the bet against Satan and to defeat the Angel of the Morning Star. Until then, God is not an absolute first principle but one half of a symbiotic pairing, with each half seeking to tilt the advantage one way rather than the other. God is part of a conjoint principle of contested balance. In so far as Satan represents evil, evil is also part of God's work, and it is evil that Satan, with God's permission, has wreaked upon Job. What, then, is God to do about evil, when He Himself helps to originate it?

This is a question that extends beyond theology, for it involves the same principle by which humanity organised itself on a 44-year cold war precipice, from 1945 to 1989. No one moved back from the sheer drop but stood, armed and balanced, at the very edge – each side daring and betting against the other's nerve. What was called the balance of power involved massive nuclear armament; and the principle of armament was not deployment and use, but the threat of it. It was the careful preparation of a threat to do great evil, ostensibly (on both key sides) for the sake of a foundation good – whether for the good of democracy and 'American values' or the socialist values of the proletariat. But, just as economics has become a discipline in love with its key instrument of econometrics – the elegance of the equation is everything and its applicability somewhat less so – so the balance of power became a love affair not with power and its possible final triumph, but with the balance. Herman Khan's elaborate series of scenarios, arranged over seven sets with a total of forty-four steps, was a game-theory elaboration of how war, and even low-level nuclear war, could be taken forward step by step, without loss of balance until the final forty-fourth step of no turning back – when the world ends in 'insensate war'.[1] The elegance of the calculations was matched only by the fury of the denouement – but the trick was to avoid the denouement and wager humanity's fate against the ability to control threat and violence within a balance.

By the time of Henry Kissinger, the balance, and the rivalries that sought to tilt the balance one way or the other (but never too far, for it had to be recognisably maintained), had entered the high arts of diplomacy and the lower forms of political trading. It had become refined into what Kissinger called a 'geo-political equilibrium', and this equilibrium was the context in which the world survived and even made progress towards not peace, but stability.[2] This equilibrium became refined, after Kissinger's day, into a kind of 'steady state' – with two rival theories both describing systems of stability and equilibrium. One is called neorealism, in which a hegemonic power or coalition of like-minded powers holds the world in a suspended capsule of shared values and principles.[3] The other is called neoliberalism, in which international institutions (often driven or heavily influenced by the great powers) bind the world together in shared protocols and formal cooperations.[4] Either way, there is no escape for those of deviant values or who wish to establish alternative frameworks of cooperation. This is why the advent of Islamic forces has been greeted with dismay. Radical Islam proposes new and different values, and consortia of Islamic states – or consortia of outlaw groups – introduce new forms of international organisation,

1. Herman Kahn, *On Escalation: Metaphors and Scenarios*, London: Pall Mall, 1965.

2. Based on views Kissinger developed as a Ph.D. student, from which he never swerved. The published doctorate is Henry Kissinger, *A World Restored: Europe after Napoleon*, New York: Grosset & Dunlap, 1964.

3. Stephen Krasner, ed., *International Regimes*, Ithaca: Cornell University Press, 1983.

4. Ernst Haas, *When Knowledge is Power: Three Models of Change in International Organizations*, Berkeley: University of California Press, 1990.

none of which is regulated by Western hegemonic influence. In the days of George W. Bush the recourse of the neoconservatives in Washington was to return to sheer power politics, of the crude sort that existed at the very beginning of the cold war.[5] Before the Soviet Union developed atomic and nuclear capacity, the USA sought to lord it over the Soviet Union with its unmatched arsenal. Without the atomic bomb itself, the Soviet Union could not match the power of the USA. The problem with applying this type of power-play to today's world is that the 'fundamentalist Islamic enemy' has neither need nor desire to match the US strength, but will seek to contest international relations by tactical victories in diffuse and asymmetric war. The Iranian impulse to develop nuclear capacity is a side-show and, even if it came to possess a nuclear weapon, the balance of that sort of power would be overwhelmingly on the side of the USA and the West. However, if the US hawks ever sought a new balance of power, there is no ready means by which the world could achieve or find comprehensible a balance of faiths or, in Samuel Huntington's brazen formulation, a balance of 'civilisations' otherwise inclined to clash. Thus the emphasis on Iran, since it gives strategists something to which they can apply old strategies. Beyond the Iran issue – and, as we have seen, there is more to Iran's contribution to the West than meets the eye – there is a huge variety of Islams, just as there is a huge variety of Christianities; and it might be instructive to review the latter, particularly if many US voters and politicians think and talk in terms of the included and excluded angels, the saved and damned, the righteous and evil, the perfect fundamental binaries of God's heaven and earth.

5. Robert Kagan, *Of Paradise and Power: America and Europe in the New World Order*, London: Atlantic, 2003.

There were always distinctions made within God's heaven
anyway. Jewish, Gnostic and residual Christian traditions, for instance, postulate several classes of angel – archangels, seraphim,
cherubim, and so on. One of the recently uncovered Gnostic
gospels, that of Judas – offering a somewhat distinct stance on
the relationship between Jesus and Judas, and the nature of the
'betrayal' – posits particularly low forms of angels assigned
solely to the earth, who do not and cannot understand the nature
of the higher heaven.[6] Not so much a hierarchy as a pluralist
sociology, Christian churches and groups form far more than
the typical Catholic, Protestant and Orthodox communities. It
might be more helpful to view them as:

1. *Truly luminous* – where the worshipper is transcended by
   his or her direct communion with Christ (in which there are
   direct parallels with Sufi Islamic practice).
2. *Fundamentalist* – where the received Biblical canon is read
   literally, to the point where it is proposed as superior to science and political and social pragmatism, and international
   neighbourliness (in which there are at least suggestible parallels with Wahhabism).
3. *Christological* – where the spirit and practice of Christ, and
   his example, are seen as even greater than his recorded teachings; where his love and compassion form the guiding principles for a tolerant and embracing Church (in which there are
   parallels with the image and compassion of Buddha).
4. *Merely ethical, with spiritual enhancement* – both the lowest
   common denominator of ecumenicalism and Christianity's

6. There has been a rash of commentaries and translations of this gospel. The best,
though written far more simply and speculatively than Pagels's earlier work, is Elaine
Pagels and Karen L. King, *Reading Judas: The Gospel of Judas and the Shaping of
Christianity*, New York: Viking, 2007. Pagels wrote the commentary and King provided
the translation.

key engagement, not only among a variety of faiths, but with secularism (which is what many Western politicians, away from the tub-thumping, would wish a well-behaved Islam to become, with the ethics consonant with those of the West and the spiritual enhancement enacted in mosques as if they were museums and the Imams curators – and multiculturalism become a parade of festivals in which all can have a good if exotic time).

An international balance of faiths would be as difficult as a balance of faiths within Christianity – where the Irish cleric and politician Ian Paisley will still stand up in Brussels and condemn Catholic papism; where the Catholic Church will itself suspend its Zambian Archbishop Milingo for 'witchcraft' (even though, throughout his enforced residence in Rome, far from his Zambian congregation, he was a popular preacher at meetings of Italian charismatic Catholics who sought his blessing and healing); where the line-up for ecumenical summits has as much difficulty with protocol and precedence as any political and diplomatic gathering (does the Greek Orthodox patriarch stand to the left or right of the Russian Orthodox patriarch, and where do you put the Coptic prelate who, after all, represents the earliest Christian Church of them all, even though he comes to the metropolis from a church dug out of the ground in Ethiopia?). But the determined effort to ignore the place of faith in international relations has had dire consequences. Faith has risen up in, or been planted upon, the wastelands that followed the US and British occupation of Iraq. Egypt, Algeria and Turkey – all secular states – must devote much attention to the interface between faith and state, and must sometimes do so violently. The Henry Kissinger sort of stratagem, of balancing Egypt out of the power struggles in the Middle East – removing Egypt from the balance of power with Israel – cannot be advanced in the twenty-first century. That sort of secular geopolitics faces the limitations of power that must accommodate faith – or of faith that uses power.

A crooked line of history

The Oxford philosopher Isaiah Berlin once wrote about 'the crooked timber of humanity'.[7] By this he meant the variegated and plural history of human thought and different human subjectivities. We don't get it 'right'. We might all separately think we get it right, but half the world might think we got it wrong. By a melange, even a *mêlée*, of different arguments towards different forms of rightness is humanity formed as a crookedly righteous species. The same sort of judgement, but differently presented, by Paul Ricoeur provides a French counterpart to Berlin. Ricoeur's entire life was a sensitive investigation of how *all* arguments are right – except when they claim that someone else's is wrong.[8] These two thinkers were perhaps the twentieth century's greatest protagonists of tolerance and the imperfection that, nevertheless, tries to get it 'right'. But what they also implied was that all versions of human history are sorts of crooked lines – both history/ies past and history/ies to come.

But many crooked lines tend naturally to intersect – a bend in the line crosses the bend in another line. They are not geometric and endless parallel lines. At the point of intersection, what hopes lie there for fusion? This is where the Chiapas rebellion in Mexico, involving the Zapatista guerrillas, is fascinating and

7. Isaiah Berlin, *The Crooked Timber of Humanity: Chapters in the History of Ideas*, London: John Murray, 1990.
8. Paul Ricoeur, *Oneself as Another*, Chicago: University of Chicago Press, 1992.

instructive.[9] Although the figure of Subcomandante Marcos has been somewhat overwritten and romanticised, his major use to the Zapatistas is precisely to be their public (if enigmatic) figurehead – a figurehead without an identity who wears a balaclava as a constant mask (quite postmodern, quite comic-book superhero). He smokes a pipe (quite academic, giving a deliberate tantalising clue as to what he was); he suffers from asthma, so the pipe is not helpful to him apart from imparting some air of learning and mystery (but his hacking and wheezing undermine the superhero effect as another deliberate postmodern irony). He strokes a hand-held mascot, a stone turtle (or perhaps a tortoise, a reference to the ancient Greek riddle and mathematical demonstration that the slow tortoise would always beat the swift rabbit). His guerrillas in fact very seldom fight: they are an army that postures rebellion, and such war as takes place is in fact a war of manoeuvring, positioning and denial of territory, and a war of public relations (something like a militarised form of Gandhism). He likes to lie in his hammock (affecting an Ernest Hemingway pose) and read aloud Shakespeare (particularly *Hamlet*, offering therefore suggestions of angst, Lacanian guilt and guilty pleasure, *jouissance*, and certainly melancholy); meanwhile government artillery shells fall nearby and others prepare to evacuate (but the shells seem to fall accurately short of the encampment, so the government forces are in on this game, as if this war were a gigantic *double entendre*, as if it were a comedy of manners by Mozart or Molière). Marcos adorns innumerable posters, the Che Guevara of his day (only he hasn't Che's handsome features; he hasn't *any* visible features; he is an anti-hero like Ellison's Invisible Man); and he facilitates an

---

9. I think by far the best work on this is Nicholas P. Higgins, *Understanding the Chiapas Rebellion: Modernist Visions and the Invisible Indian*, Austin: University of Texas Press, 2004.

Indian rebellion and expressionism against and within a Mexican political environment with its Hispanic sense of Spanish high culture and its motifs of an Aztec glory now 'disappeared' (so both Marcos and the Chiapas rebellion are a crucible of fused and interlocking, mutually undermining and ironic, and symbiotic fusions). Marcos is crafted to be mysteriously something for everybody, while being in fact nothing at all, the Man with No Name (no real name, but it allows a Clint Eastwood reference point), the No Man (showing off a knowledge of Homer) who is in fact Everyman. Marcos and his rebellion are crooked, knowingly and cunningly. But his war of public relations was won by all these intersecting reference points. Everyone could find an intersection which chimed with him- or herself (many of the female Zapatista fighters wear balaclavas as well).

The history of Satan is crooked as well. The revisionist Gospel of Judas shares with many of the Gnostic gospels the sense of Satan as a balancing principle to the weight of God – only this balance and this God are a level below a higher and 'truer' God, reminiscent of Zoroastrian thought, reminiscent also of the idea of an Adibuddha (a primeval Buddha from whom all other Buddhas emanated or evolved), the origin of which may also have been from Zoroastrian thought. But, if Satan was ripped out of the balance and beastialised as the Christian Church achieved its orthodoxy, and became satisfied with the conviction or conceit that the earth was the centre of creation – not just a lower and subsidiary creation (with subsidiary creator) – so his cohorts of fallen angels achieved a demonic apotheosis as lizard-like creatures, as flying Godzillas who tormented people in hell, looking exactly like the baddie monsters in today's *Power Rangers* on children's television. We have at least outgrown the fear of humanoid lizards/monstrously deformed angels/Satan with horns. But we still ascribe malevolent *looks* to whatever we think is evil.

And that much has a historical continuity – because the visual terror of demons as lizards faded quite quickly after the middle medieval period and was replaced quite emphatically with the visualisation of the demon realm as being oriental. This was in part caused by church leaders proposing holy crusades against the Middle Eastern kingdoms – but leaders such as Saladin soon put paid to the notion that Islam and devilry were synonymous. It was in greater part caused by the Mongol hordes, who swept not only across Europe as far as Austria and Poland but also through Persia, meeting defeat only at the hands of the armies of Egypt. The Mongols became 'the devil's horsemen', and no European army could stand against them. Europe was spared only because the Mongols themselves decided to withdraw, leaving a legend regarding their prowess and their savage looks.

But Satan had more than his horsemen. He had two key lieutenants, Gog and Magog. At the end of history, after savage early defeats, Gog and Magog would muster Satan's forces one last time for one last stand, the immensity of them like numberless grains of sand. Satan 'will go out to deceive the nations of the world and gather them together with Gog and Magog, for battle – a mighty host, numberless as sand along the shore ' (Revelation 20:8). 'Leur nombre est comme le sable de la mer.' The French version of the Bible has a slightly more subtle account. There, Satan goes out not to deceive, but to seduce, the nations of the world. Regardless, Gog and Magog over the years came to represent the last cosmic stand of evil. They became the inspiration for Michael Moorcock's Dukes of Chaos preparing for the decisive battle with the Lords of Law. And they changed in appearance. If you go today to the boulevard Saint-Germain in Paris, to Les Deux Magots – the café where Sartre, de Beauvoir, their camp followers, and all the baggage of wannabe philosophers went to write and debate – you will see the carvings of two old

Chinese gentlemen. They are the two *magots* – the two Magogs – orientalised, seductively benign in appearance, but mustering the last stand in a slightly more subtle way than St John or Moorcock might have imagined. Sartre and the wannabes must have thought it a great joke to impersonate the disciples of Satan, writing their philosophy against the superstitions of the world, looking out across the square at the neighbourhood church, with the somewhat more beautiful church of Saint Sulpice just a block away to the south, and the sight of Notre Dame just a two-minute stroll to the north, at the end of rue Bonaparte. And here they were, at the epicentre of revolt against church, state, sense, sensibility, whatever caused nausea, whatever claimed not to be absurd – and all superintended by the oriental Gog and Magog. They were young then, Sartre and the others, and it must have seemed delicious.

But there is an intersection here too. For Gog and Magog were not only Christian emblems of devilry and savagery – the enemies of godly civilisation. They were in the Islamic world too. In the Quran, Sura 21:96–97, there is a prophecy that 'when the people of Gog and Magog are let loose and swarm swiftly from every highland, when the True Promise draws near, the disbelievers' eyes will stare in terror'. Here, too, the sweeping advance of Gog and Magog is a sign that the final resolution of war between good and evil is near, that the True Promise is imminent. In the interim, however, Gog and Magog press hard. Well before the time of the True Promise they lay siege to the believers and attack them unremittingly. One of the most enigmatic suras concerns a figure called Dhu'l-Qarnayn. He appears out of nowhere, but it is claimed his power to accomplish all he wished originated from God. One day, he travelled his lands, dispensing justice as he went, judging cases brought before him, and moving in the direction of the rising of the sun. 'Then, when he reached a place between two mountain barriers, he found beside them a people who could barely understand him. They said, 'Dhu'l-Qarnayn, Gog and Magog are ruining this land. Will you build a barrier between them and us?' (Sura 18:93-94) They offered to pay him for this service, but he answered that 'the power my Lord has given me' was already greater than any payment; that all he wanted was their labour; and then he built a great wall from molten metals, which Gog and Magog could not scale and which their arrows could not penetrate; afterwards he prophesied that, at the end of days, the wall would be torn down, as God would not need it as he finally eradicated Gog and Magog and all the disbelievers.

The strange thing is that the name Dhu'l-Qarnayn means 'the one with two horns'. There is a satanic image here. Many think that this figure is in fact Alexander the Great, absorbed into Islamic tradition and made a messenger of God. Even the Devil, perhaps, may be converted – or perhaps the name refers to the two extended jaw protectors of the Macedonian helmet. Certainly there is some ambivalence about Alexander, as we shall see. Even so, artists in the Islamic nations would paint Alexander building this wall. By now, he has become fully absorbed and is dressed like a Meccan prince with beard and turban. On the other side of his great wall, the followers of Gog and Magog, invaders from where the sun rose in the east, are appropriately bestial – and probably Mongols or Chinese. Alexander was absorbed into almost all the cultures he came across. There is a lovely Indian Mughal (therefore Islamic) painting from 1595, showing Alexander experimenting with a submarine. The scientific education he had received lingered as part of his reputation as much as the greatness of his conquests.

Despite this, Alexander was absorbed but never completely assimilated. He was a figure always slightly apart. His efforts to dress the part, marry the locals, pay respect to their temples, outwardly conform to their customs, were all signs of the world's first great multiculturalist. In his very short life, he went further in his personal habits than Cyrus in Persia, although he was certainly influenced by the sheer scale of multiculturalism in the Persian Empire. But he remained forever the disciple of Aristotle, the scientific and rational person, the believer in secular reason, and the protagonist of a symbiosis between reality's form and the ideal form – where heaven was an emanation from earth, not the other way around.

Even so, when in *The Parliament of the Birds* the poet writes of the contrast between the 'thought of Alexander' and the luminous transcendent Sufi attachment to God, he is not writing of a contrast between something within and something outside local culture. Both were *within*. The 'thought of Alexander' had come originally from without, but it had found its place and achieved some value in the intellectual and other debates of the Islamic world. It had been absorbed as a key strand of thought – all scholars knew it and were influenced by it – but it had not been assimilated into the everyday teachings of religion. Except that, even within religious debate, the question mark over what constitutes a free action by a free agent, as opposed to a contingent action by a creature of God – unable to do anything, even have free will, except by God's will – was a feature of much elevated Islamic theological/philosophical work. The writings of the famous twelfth-century scholar Muhammad b. 'Abd al-Karim al-Shahrastani are a case in point – where entire chapters are devoted basically to this question.[10] However, the key aspect of al-Shahrastani's work is that it was a refutation of Avicenna's. The great Persian philosopher Avicenna believed

---

10. *Struggling with the Philosopher* (the *Kitab al-Milal wa'l-nihal*), ed. and trans. Wilferd Madelung and Toby Mayer, London: I.B. Tauris, 2001.

that the absoluteness of God could be compromised by independent human action. At its simplest, Avicenna's work held that a human being didn't *have* to do what God wanted; at its most complex, it was a hugely complex metaphysics. But he and many others owed greatly to Aristotelian and neoplatonic debate. They in fact *preserved* what is now assumed to be the Western intellectual heritage, when it was almost lost in the medieval West. Some flavour of this was caught in Umberto Eco's novel *The Name of the Rose* – and even in the appalling film of the book, starring Sean Connery – where a demented monk discovers the hidden book of Aristotle, but would rather see it burn than have its forgotten and unseen treatise on laughter revealed to his gloomy world. To the 'thought of Alexander', as an integral part of Islamic scholarly and theological debate, the West is indebted – one of those detours of history that describe yet another crooked path with unintended intersections. But, even outside debate, Alexander was an influence simply in poetry. The eleventh-century poet and thinker Nasir Khusraw – very much a proponent of free will in his somewhat tumultuous and gypsy life – wrote a lovely poem in which flowers were metaphors of heavenly virtues. What the following metaphor means is an interesting question:

> See how the new-sprung daffodils, shining silver and gold,
> Resemble the colours of Alexander's crown![11]

Khusraw suggested that all things should fulfil their highest purposes in life – achieve their essence (a neoplatonic suggestion) – and that, for human beings, one of the highest purposes was to attain the highest learning. And this was, not only for the colours of a daffodil, but for the attainment of ideal human heights,

11. Quoted in Alice C. Hunsberger, *Nasir Khusraw: The Ruby of Badakhshan*, London: I.B. Tauris, 2000, p. 40.

something wrapped up in the name of Alexander. It is a consummate pity that a current Western generation has the debauched impression that Alexander was like Colin Farrell in the thunderingly poor film directed by Oliver Stone – even Brad Pitt managed marginally better as an excruciating Achilles – although, to be fair to Farrell, Richard Burton wasn't much better in the 1950s' version. From the Persian empire's point of view, Alexander became a devil-made-good, a complex addition, complexly and somewhat crookedly inserted into an already rich multiculture.

Devils may cry

It seems that only monotheistic religions develop a true Satanic figure, as if the weight of all creation was conceptually too much for humans to ascribe to a single being. Although religions with pantheons of deities have malign or duplicitous members – Loki in the Norse pantheon being a case in point, paralleled by 'trickster' deities in West African pantheons[12] – the grinding responsibility of monotheistic perfection and infallibility requires a figure of antithesis, a figure of imperfection who wreaks further imperfection. From the time of Milton, however, the value of such a creature was questioned. Might there not be something heroic in having to bear the weight of all imperfection? The antithesis of God became an anti-hero in the face of God. With the advent of plural visions of Satan came also a plurality among his demons. There has not been much rehabilitation for Gog and Magog but, in the contemporary technological imagination, the world of devils has undergone a huge expansion in its complex sociology, class systems and value structures. The electronic game *Devil May Cry* is a case in point. Dante, its hero,

---

12. Robert D. Pelton, *The Trickster in West Africa: A Study of Mythic Irony and Sacred Delight*, Berkeley: University of California Press, 1980.

is himself half-devil. He wears the costume of the cool Byronic punk demi-monde – a long red coat, black clothing underneath, black boots; they set off white hair which, depending on which of the so-far four instalments is loaded, is teased with hair putty, or left to billow in the wind; he packs two pistols on his hips and carries a magic sword on his back. He is surrounded by duplicity. He seems to love Trish, but she is in the pay of the Master Devil and is apt to betray him. Dante's mission is to wipe out bad demons – he's part of an internal ethnic self-cleansing – and, here's the rub, the player of the game can magnify his powers, distort Dante as himself, give him choices as to whether he should run or fight. The game has sold more than 4 million copies; on consoles around the world, an electronic parallel to the comic series *Tien Ha* is coaxing youngsters into action and identification with a brooding creature of *good* darkness. It's a long way from Doré and Delville and the notion of heroic rebellion. Now the rebellion is shooting its way towards a Constitution and Bill of Rights for all creatures – devils and humans.

Dante is probably not based on the Italian Renaissance writer who had his characters approach the lower levels of hell. The name is probably appropriated from a self-promoted and self-inflated New York martial artist of the early 1970s who called himself 'Count Dante', and headed the Green Dragon Society, promising his students, even by mail order, rights to the 'death touch' and other arcane and implicitly evil skills. Count Dante made himself a comic-book figure who postured in real life, but his students swore he was in fact genuinely skilled. That kind of aura of ambivalence is carried over into *Devil May Cry* for, after all, Dante in the electronic game is still half-devil, and something brooding and smouldering inside him may yet emerge in future editions of the game. Games technology being what it is, players may in future be able to choose how good or how evil

Dante will be. He will never lose his evil side completely. He even has a twin brother who seems destined to convert from evil to good and back again forever. Dante survives in his world of evil because he *understands* it. He understands it because it is part of him. It is part of his genetic drive. But he makes decisions in his life – rather, the players of the game can decide for him – as to what drives him most, a moral vision or a base, devilish autarky. The way he goes around ruthlessly slaying hordes of his half-cousins, I'd say the equation that makes up Dante is a set of sliding numbers and hypothetical values. For Dante, evil and good are an algebra. They are not absolutes.

And angels may cry too

So it is not as simple as saying 'there is good in everybody', but is more to do with complex investigations and calculations as to how best to intersect. But even Jesus, after his death, went to visit the fallen angels in Tartarus (the underground dominions to which they had been exiled). No Gospel recounts why he did this or what was discussed there. Perhaps he had friends in Tartarus. Perhaps it was to do with the recognition of a new era, on the part of the fallen angels, and a new balance in the affairs of humanity now that Jesus had come and died. As in the account of Job, there is an interaction, an intercourse between heaven and the domains of Satan. Perhaps the earth, and all who live on it, are the intersection – and we are all made into crooked timber as we are twisted and bent one way then another.

The earth, humanity and humanity's health are certainly the intersection of the quarrels between values, and they are increasingly labelled confessional or religious values. On one side, Western strategists rant about 'fundamentalist Moslem hordes', and the response on the other side can be the great un-nuancing of the 'Great Satan'. But there is required a series of more subtle and escalating intersections before we get to humanity's health or humanity's fate. Enough intersections *before* an eschatological point, before competing doctrines of apocalyptic last days, and we might be able to talk instead of humanity's hope.

The first step might be an abandonment of heroic virtue – even the appropriation of heroism for one's 'side'. If we take the great Homeric epic the *Iliad*, who there is the hero? The poem is effectively subtitled 'the anger of Achilles' – but is Achilles the hero? Or is his anger a warning, a moral fable against over-weening pride and anger? By today's political geography, Troy is in Turkey (so, too, are Constantinople/Byzantium, Ephesus, and any number of biblical cities). Does it make it easier to see Achilles as a hero if the Trojans are Turks? Even on the Greek side, is it Patroclus – insisting upon going out to fight for his hard-pressed Greek brethren despite the anger of his best friend and commander Achilles – who is the hero, or is it Achilles? Is it the Trojan Hector, a family man simply doing his duty, who is brave or foolhardy enough to go out and face the demi-god Achilles, while impudent or imprudent enough to do so while wearing Achilles' own armour looted from Patroclus – or is it Achilles? Is it the Trojan king Priam, who goes out unarmed and alone to reclaim Hector's body by kissing Achilles' hand – 'forgive me, Lord Achilles, for I have kissed the hand of the man who killed my son' – or is it Achilles? In so many ways, Achilles is the least sympathetic person in the entire *Iliad*. In fact, he is a complete and vain bastard. He makes a good Brad Pitt.

If there is complex value in all sides, even those casually and lazily labelled 'devilish'; if there is heroism on all sides; if there are intersections and parallels within easy sight (easy enough sight to sling a bridge between – to create an intersection), then that is the end of the sort of two-actor game theory that was the hallmark of cold war strategising. There are so many more than Western and Eastern cold war blocs today, so many intangible things to balance among so many actors in so many different countries that the neoconservative and hawkish doctrine still emanating from some quarters in Washington – of taking out one country, one actor, at a time: Afghanistan, then Iraq, then Iran, then... – is an impossible naivety. It is also a lazy naivety, because these hawks have refused to abandon the cold war logics of strategic behaviour. They are not expert in the new applied algebras of competition and similarity, so cling to the basic pure geometry of old, content to imperil the world as they do so.

But if a balance of faiths is impossible, and the balance of power is antique, what is to be done? This book thus far has, by using as much imagination as possible, drained away some of the easiness of our concepts of the world. It has tried to make them more complex and problematic. It has tried to advance an argument by illustration from a wide range of literatures, beliefs, philosophies and religions. It has tried to be sympathetic to almost all of them or something in all of them. It has proposed the need to find intersections and make them into fusions. But they can't be fused solid. They need to be seen as energy points that mix energies and take the body forward. Sometimes the body even has to accept temporary harm, behave deontologically, for the sake of a greater eventual health. Even those wedded to a single history must appreciate how that history was influenced by so many others. Globalisation has been around for a long time. Our memories of our histories, our memories of ourselves, need to be crooked. We must imagine ourselves crookedly in order to have a memory to take forward into a true future of a true internationalism. The remainder of this book looks at some of the questions raised in a somewhat harder manner, and tries to construct signposts and a map. But, for a signature to the imaginative part of this book, and since this chapter has had an angelic – even if fallen angelic – theme, let us remember that it is possible even for the purest of angels to fall a little in love with something strange and supposedly outside his nature. Gabriel is a rare angel in that he plays a major role in both the Bible and the Quran. In the biblical tradition – that is, in the folklore surrounding the Bible – he stands on the left hand of God (Michael stands on the right) and is thus one of the highest of the archangels. He is God's messenger and is trusted always to get the message right, to deliver it correctly. Nothing deflects him from his missions. *The Parliament of the Birds*, however, in a brief passage, leaves a very different vision of a humanised and captivated Gabriel.

A certain king of wide dominion had a beautiful daughter 'like the moon in his palace'. She 'was the envy of fairies', had a dimpled chin, and

> Her curls kept a hundred hearts wounded.
> Each of her tresses held a jugular vein in spirited animation.

Her eyebrows were shaped like bows, her eye-lashes fluttered like thorns piercing a man's gaze, and

> Of her two ruby-lips, that were food for the soul,
> The Archangel Gabriel was forever in awe.[13]

I imagine Gabriel on a mission, carrying a sacred message, suddenly distracted, looking away from his cosmic satnav and breathing a huge wistful sigh at these ruby lips. If we cannot intersect and fuse, let us at least appreciate the imaginative and poetic beauty of those who comb their curly tresses on another crooked line.

---

13. Faridu'd-Din 'Attar, *The Speech of the Birds* (*Mantiqu't-Tair*), trans. Peter Avery Cambridge: Islamic Texts Society, 1998, pp. 341-2. I prefer its other translated title: *The Parliament of the Birds*.

7

Buying loyalty

In 2007 a somewhat over-hyped and not fully successful addition appeared on the world's electronic games market. Called *Assassin's Creed*, it was set in the Middle East of 1191, the time of the Third Crusade when Richard the Lionheart and Saladin were battling each other for control of Jerusalem. In a way it was a pity it did not garner more success as a game, but its storyline was probably too esoteric. In a twenty-first century where the West and Middle East are increasingly at loggerheads, the concept of a cabal of assassins – not taking sides, but working to kill corrupt leaders on both sides, especially those leaders seeking to prolong the war because of their financial gain – slaughtered at least half the game's potential market in the United States. The barely nuanced critique of Vice President Dick Cheney and his links with Halliburton was one thing; the implication that he should be killed something else entirely. Even so, no expense was spared in creating the game. Jerusalem and Damascus are rendered as accurately as archaeologists could advise, and the lead assassin, Altair, is programmed with 1,000 fighting moves and 6,000 acrobatic moves. In a way, the choices are too complex, even for today's game players; but Altair is very much a figure drawn from today's streets. His acrobatics are a form of *parkeur*, the building leaps pioneered in the working-class districts of French cities; he wears a hood very much like the much-criticised young 'hoodies' of British shopping centres; and he kills with daggers, like any street fighter in today's tempestuous world. Altair is not amoral. Curiously, he is very moral. He fights a global capitalism which unites treacherous political elites on both sides, to end a war between civilisations that would otherwise stigmatise and divide us all for generations to come. It is game as critique – but such games, no matter how many embedded thrills, do not sell.

It is not the first time that images have been crafted of the antagonists in the Third Crusade. Karen Armstrong has uncovered a fourteenth-century Christian illumination of Richard the Lionheart in hand-to-hand combat with Saladin.[1] Richard is winning, but his triumph is not reflected in his face as it is covered by his helmet. Saladin's helmet, by contrast, is in the process of flying off his head, and his face is a rictus of blue-skinned anguish and anger. Armstrong is incorrect in claiming that Saladin's shield bears the device of a black demon. It is the head simply of a black man. But the conjoint image – Saladin as blue veering to black, and his symbol of blackness – was enough to suggest a force of darkness. By contrast, Gustav Doré's much later engraving of Saladin in triumph over the Christian armies is reminiscent of his images of Satan. This is a mounted warrior in armour and flowing battle robes, a crescent moon atop his helmet, arms raised in victory, and with a shaven jawline as square as any Hollywood hero's. Dead and dying bodies litter

---

1. Karen Armstrong, *Holy War: The Crusades and Their Impact on Today's World*, London: Macmillan, 1988, p. 112c.

his path, but his stallion picks a considerate path between them. Saladin does not trample his fallen foe.

Outside Parliament in Westminster, a statue of Lionheart sits astride his horse in similar pose, sword upraised. An Englishman could not be depicted more nobly. No doubt Middle Eastern storytellers of his time devised tales of him as fearsomely ugly, devilish, perfidious and loathsome. There is nothing that illustrates either Lionheart or Saladin as somewhere in between triumphantly handsome and hellishly ugly; somewhere between the symbolic representations of virtue and evil. There is no fatally flawed person wrestling with his doubts, no enigmas of conscience and guilt, no stuttering unhandsome, uncourtly but deadly complex and determined person – full of complexly reasoned justifications for his determination. There is no fusion of opposite, at least contradictory, qualities of the sort that compose almost every person on earth. There are, instead, caricatures. Even Altair is in this line – so, technology apart, we have not made much progress.

It is surprising, nonetheless, that in the intellectual ferment that is Washington – and outsiders do not always recognise this – a ferment that mirrors, parallels, is inspired by, and serves the political ferment, caricatures should form part of carefully framed discourses. However, these carefully framed discourses depend often on caricature. The discourses themselves are painstakingly rendered in often enormous, and enormously researched, books; though the painfully slim volume has also featured. Apart from France, no other Western society sees such a close relationship and frisson between policy and published thought.

Not only that, but the actual human traffic back and forth between the groves of academe and the corridors of power is considerable, with the huge array of think-tanks being a halfway house. Cabinet members retire to visiting chairs at universities, bringing with them an insider knowledge, but also a 'name' that might attract students anxious to learn how the inside works; but academics aspire, consciously and assiduously, to be summoned to second-echelon positions – assistant secretary is not an ambition too far – and some have become members of the first echelon, secretaries of state, national security advisers, or UN ambassadors. Henry Kissinger is a prime example; Zbigniew Brzezinski, Madeleine Albright, Jeane Kirkpatrick and Condoleezza Rice are an almost seamless genealogy. What it takes is a sacrifice of theory and philosophy in the first instance, and a concentration on the analysis of the 'real' world, on actual international relations – from which, in the voluminous array of books, an applied theory or philosophy might arise. But analysis comes first – analysis relevant and attractive to an incoming administration being foremost – with theory and philosophy important but second-order questions. It is an inversion of normal academic practice, but the justification is couched in the sense of urgency that says the world is perilous, the US position tenuous, and better policy is needed now. There is the additional, if unspoken, justification of personal ambition. Every four years there is the possibility of a wholesale repopulation of Washington's administrative and advisory elite. This very cycle fosters ambition within the starkness and regularity of its possibility. Noam Chomsky warned of this. He criticised the cult of those wanting to become the priests of power – those originally dedicated to truth who become a clergy who mediate the 'truth' that speaks from power, and that maintains power; those who, with their intellectual authority, convince the public that what is morally bad is politically good and desirable, and, in those terms, 'truthful' to the American cause and its interests.[2]

---

2. Noam Chomsky, *American Power and the New Mandarins*, New York: Pantheon, 1969.

Chomsky overgilds his argument, but it is a cautionary tale he tells. In any case, not everyone seeks power, but many do seek *influence*: the capacity to remain in their academic groves but be listened to in Washington; to be sought for advice; to be flattered by senior people; to have a photograph taken with the president. The dissident public intellectuals – people such as Chomsky and Edward Said – do not get invitations to cocktail parties at the White House.

Even so, the priests of power only rise so far. They do not, as in France, become prime minister like Dominique de Villepin. They cannot alternate being thorns in the sides of governments and cabinet ministers in government like Bernard Kouchner. They cannot, like Régis Debray, have histories of imprisonment for being, literally, fellow travellers of Che Guevara in his last guerrilla campaign. And the books they write are all concentrated on the politics of the international. They do not write books of poetry and about poets, like Villepin; nor books of theology, like Debray.[3] But the books of influence are typically grand affairs. One stands out as portentous but deeply researched; others less so.

The great master work that set the Washington salons alight was Paul Kennedy's *The Rise and Fall of the Great Powers*.[4] It had 82 large pages of small-print footnotes alone, containing a much greater word count than a book by Robert Kagan (103 small pages of large print) which will be discussed later. Kennedy's was a work of history, but also one which took the rise and fall of great powers into the future – until 2000. It seemed a modest soothsaying, but the book was published in 1988, a year before

3. Régis Debray, *Dieu, un itinéraire: Matériaux pour l'histoire de l'Éternel en Occident*, Paris: Odile Jacob, 2002.
4. Paul Kennedy, *The Rise and Fall of the Great Powers: Economic Change and Military Conflict from 1500 to 2000*, London: Unwin Hyman, 1988.

the beginning of the end for both Communism and the Soviet Union. Kennedy did not foresee this fall, but what filled the Washington salons was what was taken as his inflection that the United States was a great power also bearing the warning signs of fall, and Japan seemed on the verge of an eclipsing rise. In the early 2000s, of course, the gossip and Washington alarm are about the rise of China; but in 1988 the United States appeared vulnerable in a world that had not yet been turned upside down. The rapid fall of Communism and victory in the first Gulf War, in a swift sequence, changed all that.

It is difficult now to recall the huge euphoria that greeted the fall of the Berlin Wall in 1989, not just in Berlin itself and in Eastern Europe, but in the United States. It was Communism, not capitalism, that had collapsed under the weight of its own contradictions. It was as if the West did not lift a finger – and the beast fell. No one had dared hope and academics had not predicted this would happen, let alone imminently. Then, in 1990, when Saddam Hussein marched into Kuwait and the United States led a great Western and Arabic military coalition to force his exit, the readiness of disparate states to contribute their forces (even Syria sent thousands of troops), and the ease of their victory, enraptured the US sense of itself as the newly achieved pre-eminent global leader that could cut through opposing forces like a scimitar cuts through butter. (Even if it must be said that different states saw their roles as pre-eminent: the British advanced into Iraq as the flying flank of the US forces, but the French moved even more swiftly as the flying flank of the British; on French television, the French tanks were of course decisive and their crews and commanders heroes.)

Even before the first Gulf War, but when the USA was already basking in the fall of the Berlin Wall, Francis Fukuyama published a short article which, though (or because) it was imbued with references to Hegel, was seized upon as the philo-sophical mood-music of triumphalism.[5] Fukuyama suggested that the Hegelian moment of history's apotheosis, of history's self-consummation, had arrived, because history could never produce anything better. All its strivings over thousands of years had now led to the final aim of history, the perfect outcome of human agency: a resplendently unchallenged liberal democracy which was the most powerful paradigm on earth. It was as if Washington needed this philosophical endorsement, and a quite slight article became celebrated.

When, three years later, Fukuyama had found time to digest the implications of his own writing, and produced the book of the article, his views had become buoyant but cautious – and this caution was notwithstanding the desert triumph in Kuwait and Iraq. The book had a curious title, *The End of History and the Last Man*,[6] and it is important here to recognise the intel-lectual debt Fukuyama himself owed to Kojève, and Kojève's reading of Hegel. In fact, there is no guarantee Fukuyama read Hegel himself, but read instead Kojève on Hegel.[7] The frustrat-ing thing here is that Kojève conflated certain of the motifs of Hegel and Nietzsche, but Washington polite society thought throughout it was being treated to a disquisition prompted by Hegel alone. Hegel's use of the terms 'Overlord' and 'Bonds-man', as representative of two poles, was precisely to indicate that a polar society could never be reconciled while each pole lived out only its own subjectivity. If it did that, the Bondsman would grow ever more victimised in his self-appreciation or lack of appreciation; the Overlord ever more masterly. There

5. Francis Fukuyama, 'The End of History?', *The National Interest* 16, 1989.

6. Francis Fukuyama, *The End of History and the Last Man*, London: Penguin, 1992.

7. Derrida launched a corrosive attack on Fukuyama's borrowing: Jacques Derrida, 'Spectres of Marx', *New Left Review* 205, May/June 1994.

would be no meeting place, no rendezvous, for the prospect of a communitarian future. The subsuming and socialisation of both into a properly interactive civil society was, for Hegel, the historical path forwards.[8] Nietzsche used similar terms, 'Master' and 'Slave', but for Nietzsche there was no socialisation that subsumed the two into a communitarian world. The Slave was bound to dig more and more deeply into himself and achieve a realisation of self as oppressed. Even without external oppression, the true Slave would almost revel in an internalised self-oppression, in order to sustain his sense of self. The much abused Nietzschean term 'the will to power' refers to this powerful drive towards self-realisation, even when it is completely negative. It is a moral bankruptcy. The rising of the Slaves to overcome and supplant the Masters is a clash of opposing self-realisations and moralities. Fukuyama, or Kojève through Fukuyama, then went on to link the opera of the Slaves and Masters to the fate of both 'First Men' and 'Last Men'. At the end of history, the Last Men of history might be *too* triumphantly self-satisfied; they might continue to exhibit desire and reason, but lose *thymos*, the craving for recognition, since recognition had been granted. By contrast, lurking in the shadows there might well be the First Men of a new history, or those wishing to start history anew on their own terms. These First Men of the new history would have no desire and reason – they would thus be uncivilised, bestial – but they would be consumed by *thymos*. They would be as Slaves, rising against their Masters. None of this is properly Hegelian, or even properly Nietzschean, but it is quite powerful stuff. Suddenly, amidst the triumphalism and euphoric self-satisfaction of the self-realised Masters of the Universe, there was a note of pessimism as to what lurked in the shadows of the

---

8. Mervyn Frost, *Towards A Normative Theory of International Relations*, Cambridge: Cambridge University Press, 1986.

future. Fukuyama's prophetic tome was published after the first Gulf War and well before 9/11 – when the First Men struck New York. But when they did, the 'bestial' tag stuck.

Well before the First Men wounded New York there were already disquiets growing about the uncontrollability and un-predictability of Middle Eastern and Islamic radical forces. These disquiets were crystallised in Samuel Huntington's startling 1993 article asking if there was a pending 'clash of civilizations'.[9] In many ways this brief article was a necessary and valuable provocation. The 1996 book of the article stretched Huntington's material thin.[10] There were 29 pages of footnotes (in slightly larger type than those of Kennedy), but the striking thing was how Western-originated almost all these footnotes were. In a book about 'civilizations', there were very few materials cited from or authored within non-Western 'civilizations'. To be fair to Huntington, he tried later to redress this by convening symposia to which scholars were invited from far and wide; but his key text on the issue of moment, the USA with the West in tow versus the emergent hostile challenges of a strange world, remained without revision. The other striking aspect of the book was the maps. The font of Western civilisation, Greece, is omitted from the Western world of 1920, on the grounds it was not then 'ruled' by the West as a colony, nor a mainstream part of independent Europe. It is a clear part of the West during the cold war years of the 1960s. Then it is a member of the 'free world', alongside Turkey, apartheid South Africa, colonial Angola, Mozambique and Namibia, the Shah's Iran and South Vietnam. And, in the post-1990 'world of civilizations', Greece is again no longer part

9. Samuel P. Huntington, 'The Clash of Civilizations?', *Foreign Affairs* 72, Summer 1993.
10. Samuel P. Huntington, *The Clash of Civilizations and the Remaking of World Order*, New York: Simon & Schuster, 1996.

of the West; nor are large chunks of what is now the enlarged European Union; and nor is majority-ruled South Africa. Papua New Guinea is, however, firmly Western.[11] It is a peculiarly United States-centric set of maps – states that support US interests – but curiously drawn. Israel is left out of the West in the post-1990 world. This is because of the book's division of the world into 'civilizations', wherein Israel is depicted as part of an Islamic 'civilization'. These are not maps of nuance, nor do they reflect contestation. They do not reflect fusions. What I have sought to argue and illustrate in the previous chapters is that fusion constitutes, or can be seen to constitute, a very great deal. There is no such thing as a separated and hermetically sealed 'civilization' – and Edward Said criticised Huntington on this basis.[12] Even so, the impact on Washington's chattering classes was established on what was seen as Huntington's proposition to pull back to 'civilizational' boundaries; to retreat to (quite large) enclosures with one's like-minded friends; to enter an age of confessionally circumscribed splendid isolation.

But, having so recently established its self-view as the triumphant paradigm of the world, the United States was in no mood to retreat. And, in 1996, as Huntington's book was being discussed on the cocktail circuit, the Taliban were storming Kabul and, with a certain Osama bin Laden as ideologue-in-residence, were transforming Afghanistan. The 9/11 attack on the Twin Towers meant that the option of splendid isolation was lost. The United States had not withdrawn from the world. Now the world, in its lucid fury, was coming to the United States. But, when it did, the attack seemed both bestial and as evidence that 'civilisation' was being assaulted by uncivilised values, and that a world of difference was asserting itself. The response was to assert right

11. Maps 1.1 to 1.3, pp. 22-7.
12. Edward W. Said, *Reflections on Exile*, London: Granta, 2000, ch. 46.

back, and the legacy of Huntington, compounded by the attack, was the end of dialogue and the refusal to complete the work of fusion among 'civilisations'.

In the furious response, and what is now bedding down as a long, fractious and diffuse war, Osama bin Laden has become in Western depictions the twenty-first-century equivalent of Karen Armstrong's fourteenth-century illumination of Saladin. The ambition is to topple him, just as Lionheart is toppling Saladin from his horse; to cause a rictus of anguish and anger on his swarthy features; to wipe the smile from the faces of all the dark-skinned peoples who parade upon his shield. Huntington, in retrospect, was the author only of a contemporary cartoon – but a deadly one that must carry much weight in a deadlier and much more complex world than Washington imagined.

To the world of intellectual cartoons was added a short, and slight, book by Robert Kagan.[13] This appeared in 2003 and was received as the contemplation that justified the reckless rush into Iraq earlier that year. It was, in many ways, a seminal neo-conservative text. Like many of the animating thinkers among the 'neocons', Kagan has since moderated his harsher stripes. His more recent book on United States history contains more reflection.[14] By that is meant that the United States is portrayed as a creature of constant and consistent morality. Others have depicted this as yet more neoconservative propaganda, giving, for the first time, an Idealpolitik for US policy, full of 'pure idealism and hatred' for militarism, fascism and communism.[15] But this is precisely the point: it is an advance, of sorts, over the rather crude Realpolitik of the 2003 book. Both are somewhat

---

13. Robert Kagan, *Of Paradise and Power: America and Europe in the New World Order*, London: Atlantic, 2003.

14. Robert Kagan, *Dangerous Nation: America's Place in the World from its Earliest Days to the Dawn of the Twentieth Century*, New York: Random House, 2006.

15. Michael Lind, 'Dangerous History', *Prospect*, November 2007, pp. 29–30.

one-dimensional, and Kagan's earlier book implied strongly
in any case that the use of power was in the cause of an ideal,
whereas in the later book the author makes this clear. Kagan
lives in Belgium now, electronically eavesdropping upon Washington, and contributing to its debates. And it must be said
that his articles at the end of 2007 were moderations of the
original neoconservative agenda, as applied to specific cases.
President Musharraf, far from being a truly valuable bulwark
against terrorism, was discerned as using terrorism as a front
to maintain US support for his continuing ambitions to rule
Pakistan.[16] Following the release of the CIA report that admitted
Iran had long ceased its nuclear weapons project, it was now
important to enter talks with Tehran.[17] Through it all, however,
the unifying theme of Kagan's writing is the weighty centrality
and importance of the United States. It has a mission and it has
power. In the 2003 book, it was power that was stressed. Power
was something to be brandished like a sword, and used like a
sword; and used even though the cavilling European allies had
a paradisical belief in negotiations, international organisations,
and international law. Kagan dropped some philosophical names,
using them in a crudely generalised manner – Hobbes (the USA
should adopt his 'nature red in tooth and claw' depiction of the
world) and Kant (upon whose notions of universal justice and
norms the Europeans fawned) – but the key thrust of his argument was the need for Europe to come onside with the United
States' historically developed determination to apply power and,
at this critical moment of history, to crush the Islamic terrorists
of the 9/11 epoch.

---

16. Robert Kagan, 'Musharraf and the Con Game', *Washington Post*, 22 November
2007.

17. Robert Kagan, 'Time to Talk to Iran', *Washington Post*, 5 December 2007.

In 2003, Kagan also became US Vice President Dick Cheney's foreign policy adviser. It was a family affair: his wife, Victoria Nuland, became Cheney's deputy national security adviser in the same year. From 2003 to 2005, in those early years of the occupation of Iraq, the intellectual coherence of the Bush/Cheney/US policy did not deviate from its core message: the invasion had been the exercise of power to save international democracy; the ongoing application of power was to defeat the international forces that sought to sabotage the emerging domestic version of democracy in Iraq. Here was a combination of US-centric idealism and power. But, some short years later, when it is clear democracy has not emerged well in Iraq, there is only the hard-edged use of power. And this is as core-Kagan as it is thought to be core-Cheney. The USA, in being true to itself, is being true to its power – is exercising its vocation as power. Within the USA it is still depicted as a moral and idealistic mission, even though the result is an amoral crucible of manoeuvrings, opportunisms and corruptions in Iraq itself (in which US corporations have played a mighty role). And all the pettifogging devilish details like equitable laws, equitable law enforcement, respect for constitutional protection of religious beliefs – things that interest only weakened Europeans – keep getting in the way. But they have not stopped a ransack that also passes as a reconstruction of the country. Iraqi engineers talk of bridges that should have cost $$x$ million to reconstruct costing several times that amount when built by US firms awarded the contracts. The daily Doonesbury comic strips in American and international newspapers poked continual fun at Dick Cheney's association with such firms. Doonesbury's favourite rogue character, Duke, a morality-free zone of toxic opportunism, met even his match at the hands of these firms. And the admixture of projected power, political and administrative chaos, and massive profiteering, was what inspired the creation of *Assassin's Creed*, with its avenging eagle (Altair is Arabic for 'flying') swooping upon the profit-lords with his daggers like talons. Even without the critiques of comic strips and electronic games, there are many with much to answer; and they include many of the priests and intellectual courtiers of Washington.

There is, however, another side to the Washington coin of academic service and powerful employment. Here, the writings and the career of Joseph Nye are instructive. He was Bill Clinton's first preference for national security adviser, before the political horse-trading diminished his chances. Even so, he served sporadically in considerably higher positions than Robert Kagan. Nye was twice a deputy undersecretary and once an assistant secretary, all with portfolios to do with international security. He was also once dean at the Kennedy School at Harvard, where he remains; the actual running of a university, or part of one, is sufficient training to inure any person against surprise at the petty treacheries, naked manoeuvrings and myopia of a capital city. Nye was, with Robert Keohane, the founder of the 'neoliberal' approach to the academic study of international relations. However, this approach had significant repercussions far beyond the cloisters of the academy. The shorthand for characterising his contribution is to call him 'the father of complex interdependence'; this contribution was spelt out in a significant work of 1977, *Power and Interdependence*.[18] This book did not become the subject of Washington salon talk; it was not on the lips of that city's intellectual fashionistas. Its influence percolated through over the years, and it is a book that still sells steadily thirty years after its first publication.

---

18. Robert O. Keohane and Joseph S. Nye, *Power and Interdependence*, Boston MA: Little, Brown, 1977.

What *Power and Interdependence* argues seems obvious today: that the world is interdependent, but that this interdependence is not symmetrical – that is, some states are more dependent than they are able to contribute fully to an international interdependence. But none of this is simple, for even when dependent, no state is fully so, but contributes something to the outer world; so that there is an asymmetrical and complex interdependence. The neoliberal approach is therefore to stress the role of international institutions in fostering principles, protocols, procedures and even standards of interdependence – even when this approach veers into the territory of its rival school, neorealism, which stresses the hegemonic nature of certain states, particularly the United States. To Keohane and Nye, a hegemon in an international neoliberal regime is simply part of the asymmetry – and, in so far as the hegemon might be the United States, their American readers would usually find this desirable.

Even so, it is almost impossible to stress what a breakthrough this was in Washington's conception of itself as the head of the United States. It meant that, even if asymmetrically, the USA had something to *receive*, something to gain from what was 'out there'. Even the USA was part of an interdependence. There was benefit from 'out there'; the implication was that what was received by the USA could also change it.

To be sure, the United States remained in a key position to change all other states. The asymmetry meant that the 'out there' was on the receiving end far more than not. However, it was at this point that Nye made his second major contribution: his encapsulation of the practice and desirability of 'soft power'. He was not, like the neoconservatives who took over Washington in the era of George Bush the Younger, an advocate of hard, militarised power alone. His soft-power approach had been rehearsed for many years, but its latest expression was in his 2004 book, naturally entitled *Soft Power*.[19] It is important to note that Nye is not against hard power, but stresses that it is best used sparingly and, preferably, with international support and with the active participation of allies. And, if there is enough soft power deployed, hard power will seldom be necessary. The usual instruments of 'softness' are those that simultaneously benefit a target group, and make the United States seem both generous and attractive. Foreign aid and financial help can literally buy affiliation to the US world posture; but the real trick is to obtain buy in to the benefits of the American way, to infiltrate taste and thought. So, for Nye, cultural projects and sponsorships are important.

This much is well known about Nye's soft power project – and it *is* a project. He has been assiduous in promoting it in the public sphere. A prolific writer of op-eds, he has criticised reliance on military power alone; decried mere propaganda as not being itself soft power; and criticised the George W. Bush administration in the policy journals for traducing the reach and effects of soft power.[20] But all this has tended to cloud his most astute diagnosis of how power, of any sort, is played like a chess game. For Nye, this is a game of three-dimensional chess. On the top board, military power can be played out, and the United States has a unipolar capacity to dominate the world militarily. Having said that, key powerful players, such as Russia and China, can put a check on US military outreach within their own regions. On the second board, economic interests are deployed. Here,

19. Joseph S. Nye, *Soft Power: The Means to Success in World Politics*, New York: Public Affairs, 2004.

20. Joseph S. Nye, 'Why Military Power is No Longer Enough', *Observer*, 31 March 2002; 'Propaganda Isn't the Way: Soft Power', *International Herald Tribune*, 10 January 2003; 'The Decline of America's Soft Power', *Foreign Affairs*, vol. 83 no. 3, May/June 2004.

power is multipolar. The European Union, Russia, China and Japan can all deploy economic power. And on the last board, the chess pieces are to do with issues such as terrorism, international crime and climate change. Here, there are no readily ascertainable poles of power. Here, power is chaotically distributed. The critique must be, therefore, that the administration of George Bush the Younger, and of Vice President Dick Cheney, and the regime of the neoconservatives, badly confused how power can be played on these three levels. They sought to exercise what they thought was unipolar military power against the problem of terrorism, where power is chaotically distributed. US power found no counterpart coherent power it could effectively attack, and nothing it could crush. Moreover, on the second board, the rise of China, the slow but growing coherence of the European Union, and the renaissance of Russia, mean that the USA has far more to lose now than at any time in its history. Finally, if a country like China is able, one day soon, to compete on all three boards – or at least obstruct the United States on all three boards – the world will have become complexly multipolar and, at last, three-dimensional. For Joseph Nye, the project of persuading Washington to take soft power seriously, and to apply it with gusto and without remission, is a project of ambition far beyond what a cloistered life in an old university should have led him to do.

Even so, this is a project of a distinct sort. It has two key characteristics. The first is that it does not repudiate hard power. It would wish to subordinate it. However, its premiss is that hard power exists, and is well maintained, as preferably a secondary if not tertiary resource. When it is finally applied, it is applied in a nuanced way. This power is nevertheless content to anchor powerful influence in a complex and multidimensional world. What Nye has provided is an extensive menu for a pragmatism of power. So far as it goes, it would certainly make the world a better and safer place than under the court and courtiers of George Bush the Younger. The second key characteristic, however, is that it would be a safer place under US leadership, and it would be a better place in the US image – and preferably with its cultural and economic habits increasingly embedded. Nye, after all, held senior government positions and was within a whisker of achieving a first-echelon post under Bill Clinton. He is necessarily US-centric. And that is precisely the point. Even the most liberal, or neoliberal, of the priests of Washington remain just that – the priests of Washington and not just the mediators of truth to the American people; Nye proposes that the United States, with people such as him in key positions, should spread this truth to the entire world. It is the advocacy of a foreign policy that is already, to an extent, under way. The world has long been seduced by huge chunks of the glamour and the habits emanating from the United States. For years, young Iranians smuggled back into their country CDs and DVDs of Madonna. There was more than just reading *Lolita*. High, low, and classy low culture all reached out with their appeal. But Madonna lived for years in the United Kingdom, and her stylistics and musical motifs, even in Iran, have been appropriated and fused with local influences and musical histories. There is nothing wrong with spreading influence. There is something presumptuous in expecting it to be naturally hegemonic, as if the world were a blank slate for the very young USA approach to taste, thought and expression. We shall see, in the following chapters, how other thinkers have approached the question of international fusion, accepting for their intrinsic – though not dominating – value what the West and the United States have had to offer.

There is, however, a final comment to make about an aspect of Nye's soft power, and that is the extensive and generous use of foreign aid. I have discussed aid earlier in this book – and it is something that, as an interim mercy, is greatly welcomed. But there is something a little naive and certainly, from many perspectives, malevolent about the use of aid to rebuild a country one has first destroyed – and to have one's corporations profit greatly from it. It is not unlike the darker readings of the biblical book of Job. God restores to Job double that which, on a wager, on a game, he has caused Job to lose. As if loved ones – wives, children – could be replaced; as if the clones from God could compensate mere human grief. There is something about grief that policymakers seldom see up close. They should get out and try to see it more often: not in armoured convoys, but face to face, without intermediaries, bodyguards and a battalion of interested 'helpers' to mediate the truthfulness of what those who suffer would like great men and women to see and, momentarily at least, feel.

This chapter began with a description of the electronic game *Assassin's Creed*. Its lead character Altair flies, as his Arabic name implies, like an eagle. But, away from the borrowings of the game, Altair is also a white star. It can be seen at night, and is seventeen light years away. This star features in many mythologies in many cultures. It is a star in the same constellation as Vega. Throughout almost all of each year, these stars remain apart. They cannot touch, yet they are kindred stars in their light and beauty. Oriental legend says they are husband and wife. Their story is still celebrated in Japan where, every year, on the seventh day of the seventh month of the lunisolar calendar, on the occasion of the *Tanabata* festival, it is as if the heavens have moved – as if the gods had relented – and, once a year on that day, Altair and Vega, husband and wife, are able to touch and embrace and become one.

This might be the truer vocation of Altair: not to kill, but to embrace. What writers outside the United States have said about ways of embracing, of fusing, is discussed later. In the next chapter there will be a disquisition about how laws and constitutions allow people to move towards, if not embracing, then the freedom to recognise the possibilities of embracing.

8

Writing politics

One of the key features of ancient Greek drama, quite apart from the relationship between humanity and the gods, was a meditation on the justiciability of that relationship. We all know that Oedipus is unfairly treated by the gods. His fate is determined by his ignorance, and the knowledge of those in the heavens. In many ways it was not in the Athenian *agora*, the public debates, that concepts of justice were determined, but in the Athenian theatre. There the gods receded as the full force of human effort and tragedy was enacted. The gods became baleful, and the often futile efforts of men and women noble. The plays became a celebration of human agency, despite the judgements and edicts of heaven. Even so, the plays also suggested that human agency itself required arbitration. The debate between Antigone and Creon is about the lines of intersection and division between an impulse – frenzied or not – on behalf of one's conscience, and a duty to one's state which, after all, as Creon stressed, stood for a common good. That debate has continued to this day, but has found its fullest expression in modern times. When the youthful Hegel declared he had seen the future of Europe and it was on horseback – referring to Napoleon's dashing conquests – he might also have noted that everywhere Napoleon went he planted constitutions. If not between gods and human beings, then, for the first time on a panoramic scale, the intersections and divisions between state and individual were spelt out: not as questions in a theatre, but as binding guidelines to modern, increasingly technologised and literate life.

Hegel himself never attempted to specify what a model constitution should provide, but his fellow German thinker Immanuel Kant did. The problem is that there have been many translations of *Perpetual Peace*, in which Kant outlined his political vision, and many of these differ in conveying precisely what Kant meant.[1] There is a vexed question as to the extent Kant relied upon the possibility of the fully moral citizen, and the final need for a coercive state.[2] Some of this devolves into a question of translation in which either wicked citizens renege on treaties agreed between states, or states themselves behave in bad faith. In a way, therefore, *Perpetual Peace* continues the tension in Kant's philosophical work, in which the moral autonomy and moral possibility of an individual is both an achievement of his or her freedom and an expression of a 'categorical imperative' to do with an overarching universal justice. Even so, Kant's little political book offers two key prescriptive elements: one which defines the content of a domestic constitution, and the other which looks towards a form of international constitution that embraces many states. It is amazing that so much of his thinking,

---

1. As partially enumerated by Kenneth W. Thompson, *Fathers of International Thought: The Legacy of Political Theory*, Baton Rouge: Louisiana State University Press, 1994, p. 107.

2. As discussed by Janna Thompson, *Justice and World Order: A Philosophical Enquiry*, London: Routledge, 1992, ch. 2.

albeit in generalised, almost soundbite form, has found its way into the basic political assumptions of Western policy.

First, he proposed the necessity of republican governments, each with a constitution which accorded citizens the right to consent to government and government policies, particularly those to do with waging war. The government was itself to be as representative as possible – though not democratic – with a clear distinction between executive and legislature. Kant's appreciation of democracy was of course conditioned by its early manifestations, but his caution here has made many think that he had in mind a benign and constitutionally responsive executive dictator – as, in a clear way, Napoleon finally became. Nevertheless, the idea of a separation of powers, and the idea of citizen consent, were radical in his time. Second, such 'free' states should jointly protect their rights, and freedom from war, by forming an international federation. Only constitutional republics could join this federation. This proposal by Kant has mutated over time to the oft-repeated mantra that democracies do not wage war against other democracies – although, given Kant's caution about democracies, this is a view of which he might not have approved.

There was, however radical, also something curiously conservative about Kant's political vision. He decried colonial projects since they disregarded the rights of the native inhabitants of other countries. He had the American settlers and their depredations against the Indians principally in mind here. He also advocated that all republics should extend hospitality to visiting foreign strangers. But all this was premised on the essential foundation that states, even republics, do not themselves change and evolve – that is, they do not accord rights to foreign strangers, only hospitality; they may become part of a federation, but do not become part of a union. The citizens of a republic are the citizens of that republic in which they are born and which contains their aspirations, and in which they are represented. Even a nation of natives is a form of state, and the natives should be left to themselves. The fragmentary state of Germany was, for Kant, an *a priori* political condition; it should change from principalities and duchies to representative republics, but their plurality should remain. Kant was radical within a curious status quo. His world was to be reformed in its political condition, but left unchanged in its political geography. Even so, he was a rare philosopher who saw that, moral philosophy aside, his moral person had also to be a citizen, and this proposed practical problems which Kant tried to address. The key to his efforts was the necessity of constitutions, and in this he has had a legion of disparate descendants, who are curiously united in seeing the need for a constitutional foundation to their state projects, or their hopes for a federation.

It is interesting, for instance, to observe how, in underdeveloped countries or those in turmoil, the quest for a precise (if not always benign) constitution looms large. Throughout recent African contemporary political history it has been the nature of constitutional provision that has exercised the public imagination and engagement, as much as efforts at democracy. The advent of a nationally organised opposition party in Zimbabwe in 1999 facilitated the first electoral defeat Robert Mugabe had ever experienced, when his efforts in 2000 to win a referendum, giving him constitutionally increased presidential powers, was defeated. To a large extent, the struggle in Zimbabwe ever since has been over the extent of constitutional power wielded by the president, and Mugabe's exercises in electoral rigging since 2000 have always been to ensure he commands a sufficient majority in parliament to change the constitution at (his) will. Even with the advent of a coalition government in September

2008, the question mark over the arrangement was the extent of constitutional power accorded to either the president or the prime minister. In neighbouring Zambia, throughout the recent period but with a maturity and restraint absent from Zimbabwe, there has been a complex and highly informed debate about constitutional reform – precisely again to ensure there are limits on presidential power. In a way, there is something clearly Kantian in both cases, with opposition, church and civic action groups urging that the executive should be separated from, and responsive to, the legislature, which should itself be freely and fairly representative.

To a large extent, the inspiration for such struggle, each with a clear constitutional vision, came not from Westminster, Napoleon or the United States – nor even the new constitutions of an emerging post-Communist Europe – but from the accomplishments of the South African constitution that accompanied elected majority rule in 1994. Until recently, even the national anthems of Zambia, Zimbabwe and South Africa had the same tune, though with different words. There is an intimacy of co-habitation in the region that has defied even the chaos and meltdown in Robert Mugabe's post-2000 Zimbabwe (though it is Zimbabwe that has now adopted a new national anthem), and this extends to a recognition among jurists, church and civic action groups, if not always government politicians, that the South African constitution is the most progressive not only in the region, but probably in the world.[3]

First, the thirty-three constitutional principles are without parallel in the comprehensiveness of their coverage and the pointedness of their demarcations of rights of citizens and limitations of government. Separation of powers is emphatically

---

3. Rob Amato, *Understanding the New Constitution*, Cape Town: Struik, 1994.

stressed, but the truly expansive list of Fundamental Rights is what took the international juristic world by surprise. Given the country's apartheid history, everyone expected special mention of racial equality. That is certainly there, but, in twenty-four separate articles of the constitution, rights of all types, *for* all types, were laid out. Rights to do with equality were therefore accorded to people regardless of race, but also regardless of gender, sex, ethnic or social origin, colour, sexual orientation, age, disability, religion, conscience, belief, culture or language. An interpretation of this provision, which separates gender, sex and sexual orientation, suggests just how comprehensive the provision of equality is. 'Sex' presumably applies to biological sex; but 'gender' would apply to intermediate forms of sexual identity, not biologically apparent, but felt in the avocation of transvestitism and transsexualism; and 'sexual orientation' would apply to homosexual as well as heterosexual identities – although, presumably, claims could be made for constitutional protection for practising bestialists (provided they could demonstrate a consenting partner). The constitution, in leaving itself open to mild satire, in fact establishes its progressive and inclusive intent. The categories of 'race' and 'colour' cover permutations evident only in a country emerging from the perversities of apartheid; but 'religion', 'conscience', 'belief' and 'culture' form a considerable range of affiliations to which equal rights are addressed. The constitution specifically includes 'academic freedom' under 'belief and opinion', and this means it is the only constitution in the world to guarantee the original vocation of universities – that is, to speak truth, even if it is truth to power.

If the South African constitution, for all its exemplary characteristics, has not yet been emulated in surrounding countries, there has been a curious carrying forward of its essential sense of concern – that is, at the heart of the constitution is its sense of universal provision. The second of the foundational constitutional principles made it clear that 'everyone shall enjoy all universally accepted fundamental rights, freedoms and civil liberties, which shall be provided for and protected by entrenched and justiciable provisions.' Government was to be made subject to the constitution and its justiciable provisions. Its justiciability meant people could take government to court, be heard by a constitutionally independent judiciary, and government could not resist such process. This concern for universal rights, universally distributed, and of benefit to all people in the first instance – not government – remarkably found its way into the charter of the new African Union (AU), established in 2001 as the successor to the Organization of African Unity (OAU), the original effort to establish continental political cooperation among the newly decolonised African states.[4] The OAU, however, despite the hopes of its founders – that it might one day pave the way to a political union, or some form of closer federation of independent states, was an amazingly timid organisation. One of its best-known principles, enshrined in its charter but used repeatedly to justify inaction, was the principle of 'non-intervention' in the affairs of members who were independent states. It was as if the African experience of metropolitan European intervention had been so traumatic that it was a prerequisite of painfully achieved independence to seal the borders of each new and often inchoate state. Not even the OAU could intervene without the state's permission. This was, in fact, the repetition of an international norm. The world system made a virtue – even if it was often transgressed – of non-intervention. But, in Africa, non-intervention became a default justification of inaction in

---

4. Zdenek Cervenka, *The Unfinished Quest for Unity: Africa and the OAU*, London: Julian Friedmann, 1977.

the face of slaughters, dictatorships, ethnic cleansings and rank inequalities. The African Union surprisingly abandoned outright non-intervention. In its charter, in Article 4h, the AU assumed the right to intervene in a member state in grave circumstances, these being circumstances requiring humanitarian action – the humanitarian needs of people being greater than the inviolability of governmental authority and its default appeal to state sovereignty. The AU may agree to intervene *without* the consent of the affected state, and even without the participation of that state in the deliberations leading to intervention. A somewhat watered-down effort to accomplish just this has seen the deployment of AU peacekeeping forces in Darfur, Sudan. This became the 'hybrid' AU/UN force at the end of 2007 – the AU, for all its imperfections, moving more swiftly and effectively than the UN as a world body; and establishing at least a fledgling norm of intervention, based on 'non-indifference', ahead of the rest of the world.

Of course, the effectiveness of any constitution of any state, or any charter of any potential federation, lies in its enforcement. In the early days of the AU, enforcement is weak, slow, painfully cautious and bureaucratised. The institutions of the AU have yet to be caught up by a true pan-African 'culture of norms' that are committed to what the AU stands for in its constitutional documents.[5] And the same should be said of projects for constitutional change within individual African states, or former East European ones for that matter – one of the fundamental obstacles Croatia could not overcome, in futilely seeking to join the European Union in 2007, was to assure Europe of the integrity, independence and initiative of its judiciary. The capacity and

---

5. Paul D. Williams, 'From Non-Intervention to Non-Indifference: The Origins and Development of the African Union's Security Culture', *African Affairs*, vol. 106, no. 423, 2007.

independence of the judiciary in enforcing constitutional law are everything. In a clear way, they are even more important than democracy, as even freely elected governments have sought to tamper with the courts. The partisan appointment of Supreme Court justices in the United States is a flagrant example of this in the world's supposedly greatest democracy. In this sense, Kant was right. Government must be representative, but government must be subject to the separation of powers. In the Kantian political universe, the represented people ensured this would be the case. In the Kantian moral philosophical universe, an overarching *recht*, a great supervening moral law, ensured that people were moral in the first place. Perhaps it is time in this chapter to move on from Africa, and the perhaps surprising constitutional progress there, to ask a hitherto unasked question: how Kantian is the constitution of Iran?

A brief first note, however, to the effect that surprising constitutional provisions exist in even the most troubled, or seemingly troublesome, groupings. I refer here to Hamas, the embattled and controversial resistance movement that in 2006 became the democratically elected government of the Palestinian Authority. Even Edward Said, twelve years earlier in 1994, was startlingly unimpressed by Hamas. He dismissed it as 'a protest movement against the Israeli occupation'; its ideas about statehood, even Islamic statehood, he observed, were 'inchoate and completely unconvincing to anybody who lives there', as were its ideas on economics, power stations and housing.[6] This was an uninformed judgement, given the Hamas record, even then, in social provision; but the organisation's ideas about statehood were also evidently sufficient for a detailed study of them to be published,

6. Tariq Ali, *Conversations with Edward Said*, Oxford: Seagull, 2006, pp. 90-91.

in Arabic, in 1996.[7] To be fair to Said, Hamas was only formed in 1987, and its defining charter only in August 1988. However, it was a surprisingly nuanced charter. It was not an Islamic 'fundamentalist' document. It was radical; in some ways it was unremitting; but it deserved much more analysis than came its way. Certainly it had a key concern with promoting jihad – in its violent and obligatory sense – as the means of liberation (Article 15). It rejected international peace initiatives (Article 13), and its most 'fundamentalist'-seeming aspect was couched in a chilling Article 8:

> God is its goal;
> The messenger is its leader.
> The Quran is its Constitution.
> Jihad is its methodology, and
> Death for the sake of God is its most coveted desire.

Nevertheless, once past the rhetorical phraseology, it is clear that this is a nationalist charter first and foremost, and a religious one secondarily (Article 12). Not only that, but the cause of nationalism is sufficient to overcome and supersede Islamic custom and practice. 'A woman may go fight without her husband's permission (Article 12).' A number of female Hamas MPs were elected in 2006, some expressing clear principles recognisable in the West as feminist, to do with a woman's right to choose marriage, to exercise her own agency, and so on.[8] Since its foundation charter, Hamas has released a stream of ameliorating documents, which, finally, limit the Palestinian

---

7. Khaled Hroub, *Hamas: Al-Fekr wal-mamarasa al-siyasiyya*, Beirut: Institute for Palestine Studies, 1996; the English edition was *Hamas: Political Thought and Practice*, Washington DC: Institute for Palestine Studies, 2000. I took an interest in this early work on the deep detail of Hamas thought, since Hroub was my postgraduate student in the 1990s and researched his dissertation on this topic. See also Khaled Hroub, *Hamas: A Beginner's Guide*, London: Pluto, 2006.

8. Huda Naeem, quoted in the *Guardian*, 18 February 2006.

struggle to the occupied territories, rather than commit to the eradication of Israel; these even included a 1996 code of combat, honoured perhaps in the breach, that limited armed confrontation to action against military units.[9] The thing is that, alongside the obvious community following developed by Hamas, based as much on service and development as resistance, there has always been enough within the Hamas self-enunciation to allow an engagement with the West – if ever the West had wanted it. Certainly the allowance within the Hamas charter, for women to identify and practise their own agency, is a 'constitutional' provision seldom matched in the Middle East.

It was clearly surpassed in the early repudiation of constitutional and other state provisions by Colonel Qaddafi's Libya. In Qaddafi's much-ridiculed *Green Book*, almost universally caricatured as a banal equivalent to Chairman Mao's 'Little Red Book', there is a description of what Qaddafi called 'the third universal way'. This objected to states on the grounds that they are necessarily representative; this means a ceding of personal and individual sovereignty to a representative and group of representatives. His alternative system of government, in its outline, was almost like a multiplicity of Athenian *agoras* – even if corrupted in its practice by a paranoid attention to security and conformity – and involved small, local, autonomous units of government in which an individual could come as close to self-government as possible. The individual was not distanced from his or her own oversight, by virtue of being directly involved in formulating it, without the need for representatives. Libya was divided into 46 districts and 170 sub-districts, the smallest of which had 2,600 inhabitants. Within that number, any person

---

9. An Important Memorandum from the Islamic Resistance Movement (Hamas) to the Kings, Presidents and Ministers Meeting at Sharm al-Sheikh, 13 March 1996.

could make his or her voice felt directly.[10] It was, essentially, an effort to allow a tribal apparatus to function within a modern state, and reflected Qaddafi's own fierce sense of individualism – the desert warrior writ as ruler – which the world, for both good reasons and intolerant ones, took as an unwelcome eccentricity within international relations. However, the idea of free agency marked Qaddafi as conspicuously non-mainstream Islamic, as much as it marked him out as non-mainstream anything else. There was none of the contingent agency – with true free agency held only by God – that had characterised even the most liberal of the Islamic schools of thought. It was Qaddafi almost as the quintessential desert dweller, alone under the open skies and stars, described to the point of romanticism by T.E. Lawrence. It was Qaddafi as non-Kantian in the constitutional sense – against Kant's idea of representative government – but curiously Kantian in the determined insistence upon the individual as the repository of a moral responsibility that linked him to a wider universe and to his destiny. It was almost adolescent in its sense of purity – before its corruption and the development of intolerance of any individual vision other than Qaddafi's – and it certainly became quixotic in its increasingly dangerous tilting at Western windmills; but, like Hamas later, there was more to understand than first met the eye. And certainly Qaddafi was Kantian in his constant desire for a federation of all Arab states, and also a federation of all Africa. But what was to be understood in Qaddafi contrasted with the Iranian sense of constitutional rule, which again the West did not interrogate, concentrating instead upon the maverick manoeuvres of a radical clergy, which, all the same, still had to govern a complex state with competence as well as Islamic rigour.

---

10. John Davis, *Libyan Politics: Tribe and Revolution*, London: I.B. Tauris, 1987, especially chs 2 and 5.

It was precisely because the triumphant clerical faction, after the 1979 revolution, inherited a middle-class country of high per capita income – and had accomplished the revolution in any case, in concert originally with liberal intellectuals, by utilising developed media and communication systems[11] – that the efforts at constitutional provision had to accommodate modernity while seeking to be theologically correct. Despite this, the rhetoric of the regime was taken at face value, and the idea of a theologically led revolution giving rise to a theologically led government, governing under a tightly conservative theological constitution, became a commonplace Western perception. The arrangement seemed as un-Kantian as possible – with neither free moral autonomy for individuals, nor proper representation and proper separation of powers in government, the spectre of the Ayatollah Khomeini looming over all.

In fact, as noted earlier in this book, a traditional Islamic document cannot be the sole source from which law is drawn. The requirements of modernity and even reluctant participation in globalisation mean the invention of law and constitutional principles that could not have been envisaged in any epoch in the formation of sharia. The constitution is full of exceptional clauses that, literally, give exception to an 'Islamic' way of doing things.[12] The constant tension in the constitution is directly represented in its provision of a multitude of governing bodies, some seemingly secular and some obviously intended to be theocratic; but even the supreme Ayatollah has a body over him that, should it wish, can circumscribe and perhaps 'impeach' him. The fact that the elected parliament can be

---

11. Annabelle Sreberny-Mohammadi and Ali Mohammadi, *Small Media, Big Revolution: Communication, Culture, and the Iranian Revolution*, Minneapolis: University of Minnesota Press, 1994.

12. Asghar Schirazi, *The Constitution of Iran: Politics and the State in the Islamic Republic*, London: I.B. Tauris, 1998.

effectively shorn of powers – by virtue of its powers being circumscribable and supersedable by other organs of government – does not mean that it is powerless. In fact, the very necessity of other organs to monitor and supersede parliament means a constant game of gambits and power-plays. The clerically dominated organs have to be as vigilant and careful as secular politicians; and the clerics, in any case, have their own factions, each of which seeks to dominate the balance of power even within a single organ of government, which, in fact, can be superseded by yet another. When looked at in this manner, Iranian government, both in its constitutional outline and in practice, is a particularly dynamic game of checks and balances. There are many separations of power, but none is reliably fully separated from another. It is a separation of powers in which the parameters of separation constantly morph, and can be made to morph, by political agency and political reaction. The fundamental struggle lies between those who advocate the necessity of secular law and progress, and those who advocate the fullest content possible of sharia in all transactions of government and within the principles of governance; and the secularists seem to be winning.

This is precisely seen in the stand-off, in the early 2000s, between Iran and the West, particularly the United States, over the Iranian nuclear power programme. It is perfectly possible that, during the cold war, the Shah's Iran hosted US nuclear capacity within its borders. There were Iranian nuclear scientists in the Shah's time, and so the only surprise is that it took so long for nuclear capacity to become a major project after the revolution. But the technological and scientific requirements of a nuclear programme were never envisaged within sharia, and even the strident affirmations of an entitlement to nuclear power on the part of the Iranian leadership cloak a necessarily close observation of protocols and procedures that are secular. Finally, whether for power-stations or armaments, the nuclear programme is a *nationalist* project. It is an affirmation of Iran's coming not merely of modern age, but of high modern age. It is only secondarily likely to be a planned 'Islamic bomb'. The two ingredients are tied, symbiotically so, but it is the negotiated tension between the two that, as with Hamas, actually allows individual systems of responsibility to triumph over Islamic rhetoric. Even the most radical Iranian leader would be fearful of a very one-sided nuclear war, and all the rhetorical sabre-rattling will stop well short of any even proto-military deployment – for whatever cause, Islamic or otherwise. In fact, if there ever was, or is to be in the future, a military nuclear programme, its goal would be to establish a proper balance of power with a nuclear-armed Israel. In this, the ambition is remarkably antique in strategic terms, properly conservative in terms of its military cautiousness and diplomatic care, and entirely secular.

If the nuclear programme is seen as a prime example of the constantly evolving system of checks, balances, compromises and rhetorical statements that cloak manoeuvres behind the scenes, then it is possible to read much if not all of Iranian politics as such a system. It is not finally that there is meant to be a Supreme Leader – although, technically, the Assembly of Leadership Experts stand over him, and the Assessment Council sometimes rivals him – but that the various organs contest what Kant called the *Recht*, the question of what might be the universal law by which all of us, through 'categorical imperative', should live our lives. In his assessment almost two decades after the Iranian Revolution, Asghar Schirazi proposed that the advocates of sharia were losing, that the demands of modern secularism were such that even jurisprudential provisions originally intended as Islamic wind up looking remarkably similar to their secular counterparts.[13] Since Schirazi wrote, the entire contretemps over nuclear capacity has only served to deepen the secular fabric of Iran – so that there is certainly a radicalism at the core of modern Iran, especially in its seeking a peculiar place in international relations, but it is not necessarily an Islamic radicalism. The 'Islamic Republic' of Iran is a title that contains two parts, and the demands of republicanism perhaps, finally, dominate the Iranian *Recht*. What we all live under in the twenty-first century are the demands of modernity, the demands of capital and oil, the demands of global transactions, and the demands of running governments to satisfy increasingly middle-class voters. Having said that, Iran is an example of simultaneously a curious anti-Kantian and Kantian constitutional government. It is not representative, and certainly not truly democratic, in that even a freely elected parliament and president must take their place amidst much powerbroking, which, increasingly, is a basic requirement for the unrepresentative clerical class to remain in power, as opposed to its dominating all other classes with sharia. Precisely because there is an inescapable condition of powerbroking and shifting parameters as to which organ of government can, at any time, do what, there is a separation of powers of the sort not envisaged by Kant – that is, there is no Germanic stability and exactitude to the separation of powers – but a separation of key powers is required for there to be a contestation in the first place. It is a separation of powers with changing limits of all powers. It is, in this sense, organically Kantian, contestedly Kantian. There is enough within it for the West to achieve engagements way beyond the frontiers it has drawn, just as much as strident Iranian leaders can. There is a curious fusion under way in Iran, albeit sometimes expressing

---

13. Schirazi, *The Constitution of Iran*, pp. 301–2.

itself in violence and repression. But Ahmadinejad as president is no Xerxes with the ridiculous absolutism painted in the film *300*.

The clerical faction still dreams, however, not so much of a federation of Shia believers internationally, but certainly of a Shia zone of influence in the Middle East – but this precisely limits the Iranian ambition to those areas of Shia population – which constitute only a minority part of the geography of the Middle East and Transcaucasia. Again, there is an antique cold-warism about this. The Shia in both Iraq and the fringes of Afghanistan become the buffer zones to Western outreach, and to the outreach of Western Sunni allies. The support for Hezbollah in Lebanon takes its place within the Iranian sense of a balance of power with Israel. This is a political project as much as one of confessional unity reaching across state borders. It is also a curiously materialist one. Iran, with its projects of modernity, and its huge poetic and philosophical history (of poets celebrating, metaphorically, if not literally, the pleasures of the senses) has no place for the austere Wahhabism that has begun to seep out of Saudi Arabia into the wider Sunni Islamic world. Curiously, it is Iran that could have been a great ally of the West in its war against Osama bin Laden as the personification of terror. For that to have taken place there should have been an engagement many long years ago.

If the exercise in matching a theological impulse to a republican constitution proved harder than first met the eye, then the effort in crafting a religious declaration, uniting the representatives of many religions behind coherent human ethics and responsibilities – ethics loosely thought as common to almost all religions – was almost balefully insufferable for at least one of the instigators of the project. The idea was to establish an ecumenical charter, a constitution of mutual and common ethics that could act as a unified guide in today's world; and a separate but complementary charter of responsibilities of sufficient weight to take its place alongside the Universal Declaration of Human Rights. The first would have the advantage not only of being ecumenical but of having been forged ecumenically. There was nothing naive about the instigators of this project. They were Helmut Schmidt, the former German chancellor, who as a young man was worldly enough to write one of the first proposals for tactical nuclear warfare (as opposed to the universal destruction caused by 'strategic' mass usage of nuclear weapons); and Hans Kung, the outstanding theologian who had been threatened with excommunication by the Vatican for his arguments against papal infallibility.[14] Kung had been through the 'wars',[15] and readers can catch a glimpse of how the 'hounds of God', the Vatican's enforcers, work in a best-selling Morris West novel in which one of the leading characters, a theologian from the University of Tübingen, is modelled on Kung (who was at the University of Tübingen).[16] Of the two, the more ambitious partner was Kung, who had published a series of outstanding works on comparative religion and ecumenical possibility.[17] Their collaboration was to compile two declarations, one on a global ethic, and one on global responsibilities. In 1993, Hans Kung assembled a Parliament of the World's Religions to contemplate the drafting of a global ethic.

Helmut Schmidt's work with the InterAction Council on a Universal Declaration of Human Responsibility was completed

14. Hans Kung, *Infallible? An Enquiry*, New York: Doubleday, 1971; see also Hans Kung and Leonard Swidler, *Church in Anguish: Has the Vatican Betrayed the Council?*, San Francisco: Harper, 1987.

15. Hans Kung, *My Struggle for Freedom: A Memoir*, London: Continuum, 2004.

16. Morris West, *The Clowns of God*, London: Toby Press, 2003.

17. E.g. Hans Kung, *Christianity and the World Religions*, New York: Fount, 1987.

in 1997.[18] This was a deliberate effort to enable the Universal Declaration of Human Rights: that is, to advance its agenda by recognising that all had responsibilities to observe standards of behaviour and action that encouraged the possibility, observation and propagation of rights. Rights were not abstract. It was a curiously non-Kantian formulation. They were not *a priori*, but had to be 'acted' into place. Schmidt's Council comprised several retired statesmen – the former heads of government of Australia, Thailand, Costa Rica, the United Kingdom, Mexico, Switzerland, France, Spain, the Soviet Union, Zambia, Singapore, Japan, Columbia, Israel, Portugal, Brazil, Korea, Finland, Canada, Sweden, Cyprus and Austria – all contemporaries in office with Schmidt (and comprising no women, so that the rights and responsibilities on display were not able to be illustrated by the participation of women who had reached the most responsible positions). As in all such assemblies of the retired – themselves now shorn of state responsibilities – the language is august, the sentiments noble, but the commitment of state and international resources to 'make the thing work' negligible. It was, however, an exercise in good faith (or good guilt) and hoped it would benefit from the good offices of the participants (one of whom died before agreement was reached).

Hans Kung's parliament comprised a mass of representatives from inter alia the Bahai, four strands of Buddhism, three strands of non-Catholic Christianity, Catholic Christianity, various 'native' religions, Hinduism, two strands of Judaism, Sunni as well as Shia Islam, 'neo-pagans', Sikhs, Taoists, a Theosophist and Zoroastrians. It was almost like a scholarly compendium of the religions of the world assembled for reference purposes as well as purposes of dialogue and agreement. Because it was a

18. Hans Kung and Helmut Schmidt, eds, *A Global Ethic and Global Responsibilities: Two Declarations*, London: SCM, 1998.

typically generalised statement reminiscent of grand treaties, all members of the InterAction Council signed their declaration. The Parliament of the World's Religions mustered only a majority of its members to act as signatories – and that following a protracted debate, *after* agreement had been reached on the contents of the declaration, on whether there was a God or not. This might have seemed a perverse debate on the part of religions, but the Islamic representatives had proposed that the completed agreement should be reverentially prefaced by the words 'in the Name of God' – an innocent suggestion on their part – only to be met by staunch opposition from the Buddhists, on the grounds that there was no God. By that the Buddhists meant that the spiritual universe did not centre upon a single creator deity (although full-blown atheism is in fact possible in Buddhism) but their objections staggered the Parliament, and the publication of its agreement was much delayed.

Having said all that, the two declarations are something of a triumphant example of how universality, if declared, must be generalised (the Schmidt declaration); but that commonality might be all that can be aspired towards, even if expressed fractiously among religions, rather than any generalised theological universality – for example, that there is a God (the Kung declaration). In these two declarations there is no Kantian universe. There is a Kantian *wish*, but the labours and the working assumptions behind them were always to the effect that human agency was required to create the just universe. The universe did not, under a supernatural operation of *Recht*, require and ensure the creation and behaviour of the just human. It is an irony that the most aspirational of constitutional efforts should be so non-Kantian, but that even those of controversial states and organisations should have a discernibly Kantian impulse within them.

It is down to human agency, therefore, to make constitutions just and to render them justiciable. In this effort, God or the gods do not intrude, except as background assumptions and not as foregrounded and reliably active agents in their own right. The Kantian stipulation of a separation of powers is something that can, in practice, be constantly renegotiated, as in Iran; and there is no such thing as a genuinely representative government, even if it is government within the smallest possible units – but those units never challenged or sought, for instance, to depose Qaddafi in Libya. But the effort to make constitutions just must also define all people as equal – as in the South African constitution. And the long list of our differences that must then be spelt out only serves to indicate what a pluralistic species we are, but able all the same to be brought together by governing documents that, finally, recognise us and unite us, pell-mell, gender-confused but understood, into a commonality of citizenship.

9

Transcendence and power

Wahhabism might never have emerged from the deserts had it not been for the corruption, opulence and crass indulgence of the House of Saud. The purity and asceticism of the Wahhabi message contrasted so markedly with the consumption and materialism of the Saudi princes that the poor of Mecca seized upon it as both an alternative and an antidote to the moral despoilation of the holiest city on earth. It was not hard to depict the House of Saud as a sacrilege.

It is not only the Shia who have a messianic creature – the hidden Imam who will come again to bring a new history of just men. The Sunni also have a hope that the Mahdi, the redeemer, will come and rid the world of evil and injustice. In both strands of Islam, it is the thirst for justice – and this has come to encompass an agenda of international justice, a desire for the equality of all states, the poorest on a par with the richest and most oppressive – that demarcates the late twentieth and early twenty-first centuries. It is religion become an ideology of resistance and change. As we shall see, religion and ideology were not always coterminous. But in Mecca in 1979, a young imam called Juhayman al-Utaybi rose up. His followers were convinced he was the Mahdi; with several hundred of them, on the first day of what in the Islamic calendar was the new millennium, he stormed the Grand Mosque and held 100,000 worshippers hostage – demanding the resignation of the House of Saud.

The Saudi armed forces were poorly trained and, in any case, sympathetic to al-Utaybi. The CIA was called in but botched the operation to seize back the complex. Finally, two weeks after the occupation began, the French Foreign Legion gassed its way in and took the rebels – all of whom, including al-Utaybi, were afterwards beheaded in public.[1] But the House of Saud knew that, notwithstanding the bloody public spectacle of its retribution, there was no choice but to appease at least the clerical animation of Wahhabism in the kingdom. An unholy pact was agreed between the opulent princes and the stern Imams, the price of which was that, whatever it said in public, the House of Saud either directly or indirectly would finance Wahhabi militants around the world. This is why Osama bin Laden can simultaneously be disgusted with the continuing hypocrisy of the Saudi ruling class and benefit from its financial support. The city may indeed encroach upon the isolation and asceticisms of the desert; it may ameliorate these asceticisms; but the city cannot host their exact polar opposites. But, because of the deal done with its clerics, and like the Pakistani military and intelligence services that play both sides of the Western and Taliban stand-off, the House of Saud works hard to be the darling of the West's 'war on terror' while bankrolling much of the terror. In a curious and ironic way, the West, the United States in particular, has chosen the wrong ally. It has chosen one

---

1. Yaroslav Trofimov, *The Siege of Mecca: The Forgotten Uprising in Islam's Holiest Shrine and the Birth of Al-Qaeda*, London: Allen Lane, 2008.

that has committed a conspicuously bald act of bad faith, one of the most naked in recent politico-religious history. Yet the United States has taken to reviling the thought that animated and still animates the Iranian Revolution. The task of this chapter is to ask whether in both recent Iranian Shia and Sunni political thought, there is evidence of efforts to transact the world radically – a banner of change and resistance flying – but with equal efforts at thoughtfulness, nuance, and the fusion of Western and Islamic ideas and practices.

At the end of his life, Edward Said wrote a book, *On Late Style*, in which he – entering lateness himself – suggested that the characteristic quality of late style in the works of great artists was an almost contented rebellion *against* the idea of having to reconcile everything in life. Let criticism live beyond death.[2] But perhaps Said had no choice but to die thinking that. For him, his great political cause, the freedom of the Palestinians, would remain betrayed and unfulfilled for years after his death; and, for him, the great follower of Adorno, as a perpetual, restless and creative critic, the lack of reconciliation was an article of faith. For others, however, hopes for the grandest of reconciliations are almost the leitmotif of later life and late style. The great Indian economist and humanist Amartya Sen, whose work on entitlement to food amidst famine *and* politics is a corrective to every international aid programme – or at least a rendering of such efforts to the category of partial and interim mercies – in his seventy-fourth year published a book that called for the ultimate reconciliation: that of the entire human race.[3] It

2. Edward W. Said, *On Late Style*, London: Bloomsbury, 2006.
3. Amartya Sen, *Identity and Violence: The Illusion of Destiny*, London: Allen Lane, 2006.

is typically witty, self-deprecating, clever and idealistic. It is a statement against division, particularly between West and East, and even more so between Islamic and other thought. Sen argues that one's outlook on life should not be demarcated by a horizon line that cuts our view in two. Despite our differences, which can be celebrated, our commonalities should be celebrated even more. It is a clarion call, but unfortunately the book also tends towards shallowness. My argument here is that, in the contemporary quarrel between Islam and the West, it is Islam that has made the greater intellectual efforts to utilise commonalities – even though these efforts have been banalised into hatreds by simple-minded Imams. But the opposition to simple-mindedness cannot itself take the form of simple depictions and descriptions. Some of Sen's descriptions of one-half of the view divided by the horizon are simple. The thinkers I explore below, however, did not have reconciliation in mind. They had revolution, or at least major realignments of society, in mind. They realised they had ongoing projects that could be viewed as the mobilisation of agency to influence the dynamism of history that would live long after them.

The advent of Paris

It is sometimes forgotten that the spiritual instigator of the Iranian Revolution, Ayatollah Khomeini, spent some years in exile in Paris – where, from Palestinian exiles, he was exposed to Marxist visions of the way forward for the Middle East and his own country; doctrines of Third Worldism derived from Fanon; and a staunch anti-imperialism which rendered the world almost into two Manichaean halves, oppressor and oppressed, locked in struggle, to which Khomeini added the struggle between the impure and the pure, with a true Islam championing the pure. For him there was indeed a horizon line.[4] Khomeini never became a Marxist, but he would at least have understood the enthusiasm many of his revolutionaries showed for the work of Ali Shari'ati, a towering intellectual figure who died in 1977, only two years before the revolution, and who had as much claim to being the progenitor of that revolution as Khomeini did. However, despite the two men often being conflated into a single genealogy, Shari'ati had very different ideas to those of Khomeini, and these have never died – despite the post-revolutionary hegemony of the clerics. But this hegemony had to make room – even after the 'reign of terror' unleashed by the clerics as they triumphed over moderates, liberals and communists – for an array of fierce factions within the corridors of Iranian power. To this day, under President Ahmadinejad, the factions contend, and part of Ahmadinejad's fiery rhetoric is as much to bolster his own support within Iran as to inflame the West.[5]

Ali Shari'ati was a student in Paris in the late 1950s and early 1960s. He called it the 'city of all beauties and all freedoms', not because he wanted to be a Parisian, a Frenchman, but because he could savour the huge debates that were taking place – the arguments of Sartre and Camus, Sartre and Merleau-Ponty, Sartre and Aron, Sartre against the whole world. It was possible in Paris to challenge the whole world; to learn everything; to reject everything; to fuse everything. He was a latecomer compared to Senghor, who had come to Paris just before the 1930s, and Fanon, who came to France ten years later. But, like them, he forged the intellectual foundations of a peculiar nationalism. And, just as Senghor, in composing his *négritude*, had been

4. Nikki R. Keddie, 'Iranian Revolutions in Comparative Perspective', in Albert Hourani, Philip S. Khoury and Mary C. Wilson, eds, *The Modern Middle East: A Reader*, Berkeley: University of California Press, 1993, p. 618.

5. Ray Takeyh, *Hidden Iran: Paradox and Power in the Islamic Republic*, New York: Times Books, 2006.

deeply influenced by the existentialist, surrealist and symbolist movements to which his friends belonged; just as Fanon was a contemporary of Camus and had cited Lacan and Hegel in his early works, seeking to posit a way out of racism; so Shari'ati mobilised Parisian currents of thought, particularly Marxism, to his developing ideas of an Iranian nationalism that was also a Shia nationalism. The combination of Shia with nationalism was the foundation for making Islam into not only a religion but a political ideology.

Curiously, after his initial shock at the 'decadence' of Parisian life, especially among the young, Shari'ati became impressed by the Catholic Church for its moral sense and far-reaching organisational penetration of society. Compared to that, Iranian religious capacity and organisation were 'archaic and stupid'.[6] Although Shari'ati had been sent to Paris to write his doctorate (which he almost grudgingly did), he obtained his true education by attending a large number of courses that caught his attention. Having been politically active in Iran, he entered the world of diaspora Iranian radical politics in Paris. He published a translation of Jean-Paul Sartre on poetry, and an article on the Chinese nationalist leader Sun Yat Sen; so that his Parisian formation ranged widely and included exposure to religious organisation, aesthetics and comparative nationalism. He also, like Qaddafi after him, flirted with the idea of Athenian-style democracy, in which all had a say and none was represented by another. But, like all students drawn to Paris at that time, he also came under the spell of Sartre's existentialism, of Fanon's

---

6. The collected works of Shari'ati, in Farsi, comprises thirty-five volumes: Ali Shari'ati, *Rahnama-ye Khorasan*, Tehran: Entesharat-e Alefba, dated according to the Iranian and Islamic calendars as 1363. I have relied on various secondary sources, notably Ali Rahnema, *An Islamic Utopian: A Political Biography of Ali Shari'ati*, London: I.B. Tauris, 2000. Rahnema, like Shari'ati before him, lives in Paris, and has researched his letters from this period as well as all thirty-five of the above volumes.

attack on colonialism, and Marxism. For Shari'ati, the project was, somehow, to fuse these influences with his own somewhat mystical approaches to Islam, to think through how to revive Iran as independent and free, how to reconnect Iran to its history, and how this history had no choice but to be configured as synonymous with the history of the Shia. The revival of the Shia would infuse the revival of Iran itself, but it also demanded that the country be organised as a force in the modern world. All this constituted a formidable intellectual project, and to accomplish it Shari'ati had to utilise Western intellectual tools.

Shari'ati also utilised exactly the same fictive device as Bernard-Henri Lévy, but for reasons of mystical methodology. Like Lévy, he put himself into the minds of the thinkers who inspired him and added to their thoughts his own – but attributing his thoughts to the other. Thus Lévy, in his imaginary conversations, *became* Sartre or Benny Lévy, or whoever he placed within his fictive dialogues. For Shari'ati, the origin of his technique was born in tragedy, part real and part imagined. He had experienced a brief love affair with a Catholic woman, Solange. She died, but Shari'ati re-created her death as a drowning in the English Channel. He swam repeatedly (whether physically or metaphorically it is not clear) in the Channel trying to claim her back from the waters. But the episode came at a time when, as a result of his Western exposure, he had developed grave doubts about whether his project was supportable from faith. He had developed doubts in his belief. The rationality of the Western philosophical project was threatening to drown him as the sea came to drown Solange. It took years but gradually, in an almost Sufi manner, he came to appreciate that the sea – into whose depths he would peer, seeking his beloved – was in fact a vast representation of the sea of heaven and heavenly love. Solange had been embraced by heaven, had achieved an ecstatic union with God – of the sort, as we shall see later in this chapter, that was celebrated by the Sufi poets and saints. By seeking his own closeness to God, Shari'ati would be able to come close once again to Solange. This might have remained a personal mysticism for Shari'ati, but he applied the methodology of creating a fiction to redress a tragedy by attributing his own verses to those of ancient writers, allowing them to be used as entry points to a commentary on modern politics. From the sea of God's history emerged a bridge towards the future. Shari'ati had rediscovered faith, and he married the means he had used to regain faith to a means of practising politics back in Iran. This methodology also meant that the future of Iran depended on a past that was capable of reinvention towards modernity. No matter how Islamically radical Shari'ati's message became, it was always part of a project of modernity for his country and for his religion – so that it could stop being 'archaic and stupid'.

In the end, after much vacillation, effort and care to fend off the strongest expressions of persecution, Shari'ati's important work was expressed in his lectures at Ershad, an 'alternative' religious college, established to provide a theological voice other than that of the mosques. By now, it was the late 1960s and early 1970s; Marxist guerrillas had begun an armed campaign against the Shah's regime, and this distracted official attention away from Shari'ati's increasingly radical lectures. The first set of these lectures was to look at Islam through the comparative perspective of other religions. The lectures were a call for Islamic renewal, torn from the claws of 'Islamic civilization, culture and sciences', by which he meant the legalists and dogmatists; an appreciation of Christianity, by this time Protestantism rather than Catholicism, precisely because Protestantism had renewed Christianity by transforming it from what it had become under Catholic jurisdiction; the argument that there was an implicit condition of contradiction and dialectical process in all religions so that they were, thereby, dynamic; a reinterpretation of the concept of *entezar* or 'longing', which had been previously propagated as a patient, long suffering until the return of the Hidden Imam and his new history of justice – in Shari'ati's lectures, 'longing' became an ongoing search for the ideal and a preparation, by activism, for this ideal; an argument that the prophets of the great religions of China, India, and Iran had been revolutionaries, and even Buddha had been such; a claim that all modern societies needed both religious teaching and programmes of material provision and renewal – in short, that socio-economic justice was as important as faith – and that the great prophets of Taoism, Hinduism and Sufism were, in a sense, 'class warriors' for having given up comfortable lives to live among the poor; the construction of a parallel between the Sufi desire to unite in the great splendour of God and the revolutionary's desire to become one with the masses; and an analysis of Zoroastrianism as, in its original form, a pure religion that had become falsified over time – just as, later, Islam had been corrupted. Shari'ati argued that for a religion to be successfully monotheistic, there had to be a socio-economic definition of monotheism. His message was a direct indictment of the clerical class for having institutionalised itself as an adjunct of the ruling class. Although he used some Marxist vocabulary, it was not a purely Marxist message. He sympathised with the more orthodox Marxist guerrillas, but was not hopeful of their success, yet he came to endorse their courage and, after capture and execution, their 'martyrdom'.

Shari'ati had, as outlined above, given a revisionist history of religions to his students, aimed at establishing a critique of Islam as it had become. Before going on to talk about martyrdom, he gave a second set of themed lectures concerned with what, in his view, a true and modern Islam should look like. It is in these lectures that Shari'ati's religion became Shari'ati's ideology, and – to an alarming but real extent – the ideology that has been appropriated but traduced in order to confront the world. To an extent, a similar ideology had already been put into the Iranian situation. The guerrilla uprising was Marxist but, in Shari'ati's view, reductionist. Just because the material conditions for a moment of historical change were present did not mean that change would come. People would not rise up if they lacked deep understanding as to why they should. To that extent, Shari'ati was talking not simply about ideology, but about ideologisation. This placed a huge but necessary burden upon intellectuals, who had no choice but to lead the process. At Ershad, Shari'ati led it by plays and enactments as well as lectures. He insisted he was drawing from existing Islam only what was 'of some use to us today'. He sought a harmonious blend of philosophy, religion, ethics and scientific methodologies leading to value judgements and clear, dynamic goals. There had to be credal foundation for his (in Marxist vocabulary) 'base', and his 'superstructure' was the thoughts and actions emanating from credal foundations.

As time passed, Shari'ati became more orthodoxly Marxist, but in those Ershad days he sought to give anthropological, sociological and historical foundations to philosophy, religion and ethics. It was a questioning of what the individual was and could become. It was an effort to compose a foundation for human agency, and it was this agency, by virtue of its being a role model, that could instigate a proper class identification and eventual mobilisation. But, because of its centrality, ideal individualism also came to represent a theological critique. For Shari'ati, the dichotomies of body and soul, material and spiritual, rationality and intuition were swept away by a 'monotheism' that was, in fact, mono-dynamic. The individual was not a divisible creature, capable of alienation; the individual helped create social force that united all dichotomies in action. However, although not a divisible creature, the individual was a dialectical one, constantly struggling to reconcile himself with God and achieve union with Him. Thus united, and armed with justice, the individual would participate in the great historical drama that began with Cain's murder of his brother, Abel. Shari'ati proposed that the spiritual heirs of Abel would rise to overthrow the status quo that had descended from Cain. It was a dialectic not drawn simply from a view of Quranic (and Biblical) history, from Hegel and Marx, but also from Arnold Toynbee's non-linear life cycle of civilisations (which perhaps was the true progenitor of Paul Kennedy's work mentioned earlier in this book[7]). For someone so devoted to the renaissance of Islam and the rejuvenation of Shia, Shari'ati was amazingly eclectic.

But it was more than eclecticism. In many ways Shari'ati's methodology could be seen as an extension and development of his post-Parisian thinking, whereby the great ocean of end-product which Shari'ati had in mind allowed a confluence of currents which, in any rigorous system, could not have flowed together. His Ershad postulation of a 'monotheism' was also a statement of faith in his methodology. There was no dichotomy if everything was allowed. His discussions of Islam were depictions of his Islam, his renewal of Islam. Onto a religion he inflected his sense of modernity, composed from his sense of methodology, arraigned against the world on the basis of his mystical side-stepping of dichotomy, contradiction and inconsistency. His students loved it. It was something startling and new. But his call for the ideal individual to go forth, to be a role model, to ideologise the people, and to seek the overthrow of the descendants of Cain,

7. Paul Kennedy, *The Rise and Fall of the Great Powers*, London: Unwin Hyman, 1988.

meant that there had to be a template of action; and the only truly dynamic action was being undertaken by the Marxist guerrillas, with whom Shari'ati shared some vocabulary and a concern for the socio-economic importance of everything (in Shari'ati's case, of religion too). But if Shari'ati drew back from advocating violence, his young students could not be easily constrained. Finally, with revolutionary fervour rising in the country, even Shari'ati could not hold back. In 1972 he declared 'this is the time to make one's move ... there is not much more time left.'

At the end of February 1972, Shari'ati gave a lecture on martyrdom. It was a response to the death sentence passed on one of the captured insurrectionists. He gave another on the same theme in March, after the execution of several Marxist guerrillas; and one in September of that year, following yet another execution. Simultaneously, Shari'ati stepped up his reinterpretation of Shia Islam, and his rewriting of doctrine – both to accord to his view of what modernity required, and to redress the loss of Shia authenticity caused by a stultified clerical class. He attacked the clerics as quietist, complacent, timid and fearful; as supporters of the ruling class and impediments to both a new nationalism and a reauthenticated Islam which was the key to the new nationalism. Shari'ati had already reinterpreted the concept of *entezar*, or longing; now, he reinterpreted *jihad*, and called for insurrection. He sympathised with the secular Marxist guerrillas, declared they were dearer to God than the quietist believers, but wanted above all a Shia uprising that would replace the work of the Marxists. On 10 November, Shari'ati gave his last lecture at Ershad (on existentialism). On 17 November, Ershad was surrounded by police. Shari'ati went into hiding but was arrested in September 1973. In the meantime, it turned out that the police excuse for closing Ershad was a letter signed by twenty clerics, accusing Shari'ati of being, of all things, a Wahhabist. There was, however, a logic in that. If Shari'ati was not a Marxist, and claimed to teach a purer Islam, then he had to be a member of the purist Wahhabi sect Al-Masjit al-Haram, which six years later would attack Mecca.

Shari'ati was unexpectedly released in early 1975, and there is much dispute as to whether he secured this release by penning two books in prison, denouncing the Marxists and repudiating any possible linkages between Marxism and Islam; books which were effectively a revisionist take on his entire Ershad period. In May 1977, his part in his project broken, he fled Iran for exile in Britain, settling in Southampton. Just three weeks later, he died of a heart attack.

For a man of such fire in his teachings, Shari'ati might have surprised even himself by how easily he was broken in prison. The Shah's jailers and interrogators had, in any case, sophisticated methods. Despite this, Shari'ati's teachings had a growing influence. The notion of a Shia able to participate in the confrontations and challenges of rapid social change, and to meet the demand for socio-economic justice at home and, implicitly, abroad – enabling Iran to be seen not only in Shia but in global terms – was irresistible to the young and disaffected. Ayubi credits Shari'ati with providing Khomeini, then still in exile, with the idea that action was possible.[8] Piscatori has written that Khomeini had no choice but to acknowledge Shari'ati's influence, even if he had to do so reluctantly; the idea of revolution and Shia heroism had become an idea indelibly associated with Shari'ati.[9] Halliday says that Khomeini had to depend on Shari'ati's teachings even after the clerical faction had seized the revolution.

---

8. Nazih Ayubi, *Political Islam: Religion and Politics in the Arab World*, London: Routledge, 1991, p. 147.
9. James P. Piscatori, *Islam in a World of Nation-States*, Cambridge: Cambridge University Press, 1988, pp. 19, 35.

When war with Iraq broke out, Khomeini had to lay great stress on nationalist themes of the sort propounded by Shari'ati.[10] That, unfortunately, is precisely the point: Khomeini's clerical faction seized the revolution and suppressed, ruthlessly, secular modernisers, Marxists, and lay teachers of Islam – of whom Shari'ati had been one. It was not these people, however much they might have been inspired by Shari'ati to participate in the revolution, who carried forward his legacy after the revolution. It was the clerical party that did that. In the process, Shari'ati's legacy was made as much an instrument of reaction as one of revolution. Even now, in President Ahmadinejad's rhetoric and defiance, there is an echo of Shari'ati. The Shia heroism in the face of US, Israeli, and Sunni attempts to impose hegemony in Iraq is still apparent. But the clerical faction, rather than abetting the status quo as once it did in Shari'ati's denunciation, is now the status quo itself, and has excised the dynamism and the inspiration drawn from international intellectual influences that were the foundation for Shari'ati's appeal, albeit that the threads of his arguments were sometimes disconnected and not fully reconciled. That, however, is the key point of Shari'ati's long appearance in this book: he was an imperfect moment of fusion. Fusion can be done better perhaps, but it was a fusion all the same that underlay what became the Iranian Revolution and that has residue even now in its more conservative aftermath. But Shari'ati was not the only one to attempt a fusion for the sake of Iranian nationalism.

The advent of Popper, and the bypassing of Popper

The London of the 1970s was different to Paris in the late 1950s and early 1960s. Instead of the glistening cafés of the Left Bank

---

10. Fred Halliday, *Islam and the Myth of Confrontation: Religion and Politics in the Middle East*, London: I.B. Tauris, 1995, p. 63.

and the existentialism of Sartre, Abdolkarim Soroush, an Iranian science student at Chelsea College, found only that outlandish punks had appropriated the King's Road, Margaret Thatcher had commenced the degeneration of British political thought, and the apotheosis of a student's intellectual quest lay in the work of Karl Popper. In a very clear way, however, Soroush represented the next chronological and intellectual generation after Shar'ati, returning to Iran just after the revolution, rather than dying just before it, and representing yet another stream of cosmopolitan intellectual influence. What has been called 'Islamic intellectualism' has been formed from a wide variety of sources. The common demarcator is the attempt to utilise these sources to establish something both peculiarly Islamic and modern. But there is also something powerfully idealistic about the effort, and sometimes this idealism can be naive. Even Foucault, the French philosopher who wrote so cogently about how power constructs knowledge through the 'officialisation' of discourse, saw in the early days of the Iranian Revolution 'something new' and something of the spirit. Within this sort of idealism, Soroush returned to Iran and was appointed to a state committee established at Khomeini's behest to restructure the syllabuses of all the nation's universities. To his credit, he resigned this post in 1983 and has accepted no other state appointment. In the 1990s, he began a sustained critique of the Iranian clergy and by 1998 began, in turn, to undergo sustained persecution from them. Soroush left Iran, and since 2000 has been a visiting professor at Harvard.

Soroush's work is widely accessible in English,[11] he has his own website and Wikipedia entry, and he makes himself available for

---

11. E.g. Abdolkarim Soroush, *Reason, Freedom and Democracy in Iran*, New York: Oxford University Press, 2002.

international lectures and interviews.[12] And, unlike Shari'ati in his own time, Soroush's ongoing project is the subject of international academic comment, praise and criticism. I can think of no more succinct a summary of Soroush's work than that provided by Ali Paya, one of his (sympathetic) critics:

> 'How can one make "Islam" compatible with modernity?' Soroush's main contribution to this debate has been 'critical rationalism' – the view that 'reason' should assess all epistemic claims, including those based on revelation, and that the claims of reason itself must always be critically scrutinized – an approach he learned from Karl Popper and that he has tried to graft onto Islamic doctrines. As a Muslim critical rationalist, Soroush has urged fellow Muslims to distinguish conceptually between 'Islam' and one's understanding of 'Islam'; 'essential' and 'accidental' aspects of 'Islam'; minimal and maximal interpretations of 'Islam'; values and norms internal and external to 'Islam'; religious 'faith' (belief in the most basic elements of a religion but not necessarily in its more formal aspects and ritualistic dimensions) and religious belief (in the official body of doctrines that constitute the orthodoxy of a religion or sect); and Islam as a faith and belief system and Islam as an ideology.[13]

What Shari'ati sought to conflate into a 'monotheism', shorn of antique obfuscations, and present as an actionable ideology, Soroush has broken into key component historical, sociological, and normative parts. Even so, there is a peculiar conservatism in his work. There is no room for full-blown democracy in his reasoning, as that cannot be derived from Islamic sources – although the *procedures* of democracy can be. What this means is that, as of now, Soroush's project is incomplete: he is searching

---

12. E.g. 'The Beauty of Justice', interview with Abdolkarim Saroush, *The Centre for the Study of Democracy Bulletin*, vol. 14, nos 1 and 2, 2007.
13. Ali Paya, 'The Hesitant Rationalist', *The Centre for the Study of Democracy Bulletin*, vol. 15, no. 1, 2007–8, p. 19.

for an Islamic model of democracy, one able to be derived from Islamic sources, but which is not available – except in a manner curiously reminiscent of Khomeini, and that is a *guided* democracy, with the guides being a peculiarly qualified elite.

There is no way in which such a formulation can withstand the application of a Popperian critique. The Karl Popper who both advocated that every conjecture be subjected to refutation, and wrote that historical 'laws' should not be used to predetermine the direction and conduct of human society, would have been horrified.[14] But, although reminiscent of Khomeini, Soroush does not have in mind a clerical class acting as beneficent guides. It is at this point that Ali Paya accuses Soroush of mysticism, because – again in a most un-Popperian manner – Soroush makes a logical leap through a reliance on the insights of poets like Rumi. Paya says that Soroush 'sees a world of mysteries that only those individuals endowed with cognitive faculties not available to ordinary people can understand. These individuals, of which the Prophets ... are the prime example, produce true wisdom. Soroush maintains that genuine intellectuals are in the same league as the Prophets and the mystics.'[15] A league of philosopher-kings, proceeding democratically among themselves, might be the Soroushian vision. But, to an extent, Paya is being unfair. It may not be Popperian, but the mystical side of much historical Shia, its ancestral links to Zoroastrianism and affinities to Sufi transcendental belief and practice make it illogical – irrefutable as conjectures – but are also evidence of an ecumenicalism. It is simultaneously exclusive (only the wise can practice government) and inclusive (of different 'wise' approaches to government).

---

14. Karl Popper, *Conjectures and Refutations*, London: Routledge & Kegan Paul, 1963; *The Poverty of Historicism*, London: Routledge, 1957; *The Open Society and Its Enemies*, 2 vols, London: Routledge & Kegan Paul, 1945.

15. Ali Paya, 'The Hesitant Rationalist', p. 20.

Rumi himself was always on the cusp of an outlaw existence. His life was not always safe and he was capable of what, under Khomeini's regime, would be deemed sacrilege. He was a rebel, uncaring of public and official orthodoxies, and – even if he might have excused them as metaphorical if confronted by the censors – wrote celebrations of carnal love, drunkenness, and an almost heretical condemnation of what, in Soroush's terms, might be described as accidental and ritualistic Islam, preferring the direct possibility of a worshipful linkage between individual and God, without the mediation of clergy and mosque.[16] It was, to be sure, a wisdom acquired by revelation – against which Soroush argued as being non-Popperian – but Rumi's accounts of how revelation came to him was exactly rendered as accounts of intoxication. He was delirious with the joy of communion with God. But communion is not communication. Personal ecstasy is not the wisdom of government, and the person who claims access to divine edicts as to how to govern others is not only undemocratic but easily delirious with the power this can give him over others. Even so, Soroush is, in his work, basically advocating the omission of the clerical class – as a class – in the institutions of government. His government might be elite, but it would contain a greater pluralism than clerics of themselves could muster. In the end, his methodology, although commencing with the work of Karl Popper, contained not a little of the method of Paul Feyerabend: an anti-method, in which all was permitted provided it had its own coherence.[17] Sometimes described as

16. Jelaluddin Rumi, *Forbidden Rumi: The Suppressed Poems of Rumi on Love, Heresy, and Intoxication*, trans. Ergin Nevit and Will Johnson, Rochester NY: Inner Traditions, 2006. This was meant to be the 24th volume of Nevit's monumental 23-volume translation of the *Divan-I-Kebir*, the complete works of Rumi. This project had been supported and enabled by the Turkish government, which baulked at the prospect of this volume and its sacrilegious themes. It was therefore published separately in the USA, hence its sensational title.

17. Paul Feyerabend, *Against Method: Outline of an Anarchist Theory of Knowledge*, London: Verso, 1993.

'anything goes', Feyerabend's work is more properly described as 'everything can be included'. How to put it all together is the trick. In the end, this much of Soroush was not unlike the grand elisions of Ali Shari'ati.

The brotherhood (and sisterhood) who came to stay

For a tall and lean person, dressed in designer suits, fashionably – though also in the Iranian style – without a tie, and who likes rap music, Tariq Ramadan cuts a dashing figure unlike someone descended from the troubled backstreets and mosques of Cairo. As someone from the Sunni strand of Islam, he does not carry the Shia mystical weight of Shari'ati and Soroush, but has made of himself, or has been made, into the first 'celebrity Islamic intellectual' of the West. Barred by the US government from assuming a chair at Notre Dame University, he has been sought after by the British government for his advice (although little of it would seem to have been heeded); and his newspaper articles, constantly updated website, broadcasts, international lectures and prolific industry in writing books have won him a wide audience, which, all the same, has frequently misunderstood him.

Ramadan lives in England and took his university education in Geneva. He has not lived in Egypt since his youth. But his father and grandfather were not only citizens and residents of Egypt; the grandfather, Hassan al Banna, was the founder of the Muslim Brotherhood in that country, and the father, Said Ramadan, was a prominent member. This Brotherhood was an extremely controversial and radical grouping, accused of violence and of being a threat to the state, and was eventually banned and persecuted by the Egyptian authorities. In a very clear sense, the Brotherhood was the immediate precursor of contemporary religious subversion within the world's Islamic nations – from the Middle East to Indonesia. Tariq Ramadan was tarred by this brush and, particularly as a young scholar, was given to inflammatory statements. Even now he is accused of changing his message according to the group he is addressing, with a militant version of his message reserved for militant audiences. This is almost certainly untrue, or no longer true, but this doesn't mean he is not radical. Holding academic appointments in both the United Kingdom and Netherlands, he is a European fixture, refers to Islam as a 'European religion', calls equally for a 'European Islam' and is the voice of 'intellectual Islam' in Europe and much of the West.

The difference between Ramadan and Shari'ati and Soroush is that, while the last two were concerned for an Islamic re-authentication in terms of modern nationalism, and its reverse process of a nationalism authenticated by a modern Islam, and both located these processes in Iran, Ramadan locates his project in modern Europe.[18] It is a Europe both of nationalisms and integrations, of traditions and modernities, of a European identity and its composition by a mass of pluralities. There are entry points here for Islam, and Ramadan's complaint is that, all too often, Islamic communities have not taken advantage of them. But, while many see the Ramadan project as one to do with the modernisation and Europeanisation of Islam, there is a reverse side to what he is saying. For all this to work, not just in Europe but as an example for the rest of the world, Europe also has to become a little more Islamic.[19] This is a largely implied argument, and explains why Ramadan has been hailed by many as

---

18. Tariq Ramadan, *Western Muslims and the Future of Islam*, Oxford: Oxford University Press, 2003; *To Be a European Muslim*, Leicester: Islamic Foundation, 1998.
19. Tariq Ramadan, *Islam, the West and the Challenge of Modernity*, Leicester: Islamic Foundation, 2000.

an acceptable face of Islam. On the surface he is not threatening any change to the received European lifestyle – which is, in all its variants, a homogenisation of many styles – but advocating an Islamic adaptation to it. His suggestions seem pragmatic, they are certainly non-violent, and they make distinctions in a believer's practice of Islam. The distinction between core faith and ritualistic faith, as with Soroush, is apparent in Ramadan; although the latter is more likely to suggest a pragmatic practice of ritual, rather than downgrade it as a historically derived manifestation, rather than core attribute, of faith. The pragmatism Ramadan advocates is in fact an agenda of quite conservative modernisation: a 'keep what you have but let it adapt, though not to the point of historical change' agenda. Ramadan is not, in his European Islam, advocating a new epoch of Islam. Rather, the epoch at stake is the modern one, and it is to this that Islam in Europe must adapt. Ramadan makes the clear point that, in the tolerant societies of modern Europe, there is no force applied to make Muslims change their habits; for example, no one is forced to eat pork. In the absence of force, Muslims have no need to apply countervailing force.

But there is more than a balance of forcelessness in Ramadan's projection. When he writes that Islam is a European religion he is, of course, historically correct. All of southern Spain was once Islamic, and the beautiful Alhambra palace in Granada is a legacy; Bosnia is very pragmatically Islamic – so pragmatically that even Ramadan might not approve; and, in contemporary history, the waves of migration have meant that, in every Western European country and, increasingly, spreading into all corners of the European Union, Islam is apparent. If Turkey finally joins the Union, or is given special status as its associate, the completed Europe will have rejoined its own legacy and its historical permutations beginning with the spread of Hellenic civilisation and, later, the Christian church (Ephesus being an example of both); moving on to Constantinople's hosting the rump of the Roman Empire; leading on to the Christian splendours of Byzantium; and going forward with the beautiful palaces and mosques of Istanbul. But the visibility of Islam is not sustained by a balance of forcelessness. It depends upon interpenetrations. If Ramadan wants Islam to be pragmatic, the same has to be the case with Europe. It can't join in with a festival or two and claim thereby to be multicultural. Islam has to be given a place alongside the Christian religions, not in a tolerantly ecumenical fashion, but in the full-scale argumentative fashion that preoccupied Hans Kung in his Parliament of the World's Religions. Eventually, Europe must become inflected with Islam and when, in this manner, Muslims feel 'at home', it will have been a triumph of bipartisan pragmatisms and adaptations; when Muslims thus feel 'at home' Europe will have achieved its best guarantee against the violence of crude forms of jihad.

What Ramadan would like, but does not explicitly say, is that Islam should be to European thought what the 'thought of Alexander' was to the renditions of Middle Eastern thought with its Neoplatonic and neo-Aristotelian debates – in what was the medieval period of Europe, while Islam was experiencing the equivalent of a great scientific, philosophical and literary renaissance – with its expression of how the different modes of thought coexisted and influenced each other in the great poem *The Parliament of the Birds*, discussed earlier in this book. That represented a maturity of intellectual interaction which today's modern Europe has not yet reached. Because Ramadan wants Europe to reach it, his message can be read as one certainly of modernity. Islam does not change its epoch. Europe, in the next stage of its modern epoch, is changed by Islam.

Something more

This is a radically pragmatic vision. It is not, however, transcendent in the sense that Shari'ati sought as illumination in his thinking. He sought his beloved, undiscoverable in the arms of God, in the depths of the ocean. This great ocean, in which truth was apparent, but wherein the logic of truth constantly changed with the currents, was an invitation to immersion. Shari'ati was here influenced by the Sufi thinkers of what is now Turkey, and their own influence in centuries past on what are now the borders of Iran. It is the transcendent vision of being lost in God, intoxicated by union with God, that Rumi celebrated with images and metaphors of debauchery. Perhaps Rumi really did drink the alcohol that was proscribed by the behavioural and ritual prohibitions of Islam in his day; but his real crime, and the grounds for the very real persecutions he faced, was that he was prepared to reject the very need for ritual and prohibition in the first place – whether or not the manifestations of rejection were to do with wine, women or what, in today's writing back of contemporary taste, would be called the homoerotic relationship he shared with his own spiritual mentor. It was not just indulgence on Rumi's part. Rejection was a practice that ran parallel to the exercise of his fierce intellect and his capacity for immersion in God's ocean without intellectual questions asked. He was the poet who both celebrated flowers as aspects of the crown of Alexander and wallowed in the intoxication of God. Rumi, like Ramadan, was well versed and trained in Sunni doctrine, in the legal tradition of Islam, and was both a jurist and scholar in his younger days. This, however, is what makes the contemporary industry of 'Rumi-lite' such a fragmentary experience. To know *why* Rumi rejects something, the reader must first know *what* he rejects. He would perhaps have looked upon Tariq Ramadan as an earnest young man not unlike the first edition of himself. He would perhaps have invited Ramadan to have a glass of wine. In refusing, at least Ramadan would have offered to play some rap music to accompany Rumi's intoxication. There are, finally, many different forms of movement – and perhaps movement is what we need and all we can bear for now.

Whereas Rumi is well known in the West, Yunus Emre, another Sufi poet, is less known, although he is celebrated in Turkey. Both he and Rumi have claims to the propagation of Dervish dance as a means of bypassing giddiness to attain a mindless state in which access to God becomes possible. Emre lived in the thirteenth century. Unlike Rumi, who greatly influenced him, Emre did not write in the Persian that was then a mark of education and high culture, but in the Anatolian vernacular. He thus became a 'folk saint', rather than a paradigm of both thought and transcendence. The huge and beautifully bound commemorative volume published in a limited edition by the Turkish Ministry of Culture for Emre's 700th anniversary contains an extensively elegant commentary by Talat Sait Halman, who was also the translator. I wish here to cite two of the translated poems, one short and one longer. The short one summarises, with somewhat less stridency than some of Rumi's work, the relationship between the ocean and the little instruments by which humanity navigates it.

> Listen to my Comment
> on the strictures of the canon;
> Orthodox faith is a ship,
> its sea is Reality.
>
> No matter how impregnable
> are the planks of the ship,
> They are bound to crack and shatter
> when waves rage in that sea.

Listen, my beloved one,
let me give you a fact beyond this:
The rebel against Truth
is the saint of orthodoxy.

We yearn for knowledge and science,
we read the book of love,
God is our professor
and love is our academy.[20]

The point here, apart from the succinctness of his expression, is that Emre does not reject knowledge and science. He contextualises their meaning and import in terms of a wider academy of spiritual achievement and good human relationships. But all these things, which enter his poem only in the last verse, make minimal and illustrate the limitations of stricture and orthodoxy. Emre's huge popularity among the rural poor of Anatolia resides in part in the fact that he proposed the lifting of at least some of their burdens. If life is hard enough already, why freight it with a further raft of strictures? And why impersonate piety when you are simply sinking at sea?

The last stanza quoted above, however, gives rise to very many other considerations. What is this 'knowledge and science' which is contextualised by God and love? Emre's answer is a vast ecumenicalism and inclusiveness.

We have dashed into Truth in its mansion,
Viewing all beings in adoration,
The Visions and spectacles of both worlds –
We have found these in all of Creation.

These skies which revolve in endless races
And all these subterranean places
And the seventy thousand disgraces –
We have found these in all of Creation.

20. *Yunus Emre: Selected Poems*, trans. Talat Sait Halman, Ankara: Ministry of Culture, 1990, p. 133.

The seven layers of earth and the skies,
All the hills and mountains and the seas,
The Hell of damnation and Paradise –
We have found these in all of Creation.

The darkest nights and the glittering days,
The seven stars of heaven with bright rays,
The tablet where the Word forever stays –
We have found these in all of Creation.

Mount Sinai where Moses ascended high,
The sacred mansion built up in the sky,
The trumpet which sounded Israel's cry –
We have found these in all of Creation.

The Old Testament, the New Testament,
The Koran and the Psalms; all their intent,
And the truth embedded in their content –
We have found these in all of Creation.[21]

There is some embedded humour in this poem. The sky revolving in endless races is probably a reference to dervish dancing – where the beginner has difficulty in transacting the movement beyond giddiness into serenity, and fears falling over instead as the sky spins around him. But the poem is overall a paean to the cohabitation – there doesn't have to be a resolution – of all contradictions. But, despite the contradictions of creation, all scripture has the same intent and been essentially the same truth. Emre foregrounds the Old and New Testaments. Only after them does he mention the book of his own faith; and then immediately follows that up by including the Psalms. The confidence he displays in this ordering illustrates his belief that their intent is the same. No doctrinal differentiation is required; no differing navigation systems for what are only ships at sea. And, in any case, Emre's knowing mention of the Psalms is to inflect a

---

21. *Yunus Emre: Selected Poems*, p. 129.

view that his own poems would not, in any case, be out of place in the Psalms. Finally, and that is why mention of the Psalms comes last, they are all songs that praise and desire God.

The key aspect of Sufi transcendence, and the dervish practice of spinning typifies this, is that each individual achieves his or her own union with God. No one can spin for another. By the same token, no one can dictate to another exactly where the point of crossover between giddiness and balanced serenity will come. Everyone has to break through his or her own physical limitations to step, or spin, over the line. This is the curious point where the practice of transcendence and the practice of pragmatism coincide. It is also a point of compassion for the efforts of others. There is nothing funnier than watching beginner dervishes. But the smiles of those more practised are to do with an understanding of how hard it is to learn how to cope with the endless racing revolutions of heaven. What I wish to say in the next part of this book is that this recognition, this understanding, this prelude to compassion, is what finally allows an interim mercy to become an actual mercy in the fraught difficulties of today's world.

10

What is to be done?

God is blind by birth.
With one flap of its wings
A bird you had never fondled would create
The sky for you again.
In a leafless tree, you were going to find Paradise.

In dreams you never had, thrones were going to topple:
No more brothers' blood, no more torture or tyranny.
From the wishing wells you never bent down to look into
The sun was going to rise...
A religion with no love for sacrifice, a state without
        scimitars.

A fruit you never bit into was going to give you
All the tastes of love, forbidden and sacred.
Perhaps you'd find a fountain in the palm of your hands
When you held the withered roots for a moment,
And a rainbow
Lurching in the caterpillar you never chased.

Talat Sait Halman[1]

1. In his collection *A Last Lullaby*, Merrick NY: Cross-Cultural Communications, 1990.

T alat Sait Halman was a cosmopolitan man, a man of fusions: Turkey's first minister of culture and the translator of Yunus Emre, he was also ambassador to the United Kingdom and a professor at Columbia, Princeton and New York universities. He made his name in Turkey as the translator into Turkish of many great American authors, and for his work on the poetry of ancient cultures and civilisations. He would have been the first to say that this book, of which this is the last chapter, has lurched. But I hope he would have also agreed that it has lurched in the chase for a caterpillar of many exotic stripes, trying hard to induce it to become a rainbow butterfly that would ask states to live without scimitars.

The book has also tried to emulate those great Sufi poems which interweave their themes in the barely perceptible order of a sustained meditation; it has been an essay written like a novel, where the characters crop up again when the reader has forgotten them – and they then offer a staging post for the next part of the meditation or novel. It has tried, like a circus, to show off some of the modes of thinking of diverse cultures, but has always made the point that each mode of thought has integrated within it much that was borrowed and variously absorbed from others. And it has made a point of showcasing some Persian and Iranian thought as, in today's international relations, a taste of fruit that is forbidden.

The book is not a typically anglophone work. A reader of an early draft remarked that it read like a French book translated into English. I was flattered by that, being clearly a Francophile, but would rather he had said that it read like a book of magical realism from Latin America – a novel that lost its way and became a long essay that fountained from its pages. Not the typical sort of magical realist novel written by Gabriel García Márquez – with lyrical tales of unending love, melancholy whores and pubescent lovers – but something lyrical and rough, tough, was what I had in mind. I am not sure I have succeeded in this, but I wanted a book of imagination with a capacity to induce sobriety. We live in a world of terrible wars and flocks of Jehovah's Witnesses, outriders of the Horsemen of the Apocalypse, saying that they portend the end of the world. I had in mind something like Mario Vargas Llosa's *The War of the End of the World*,[2] in which long ago, in some dusty outcrop of the southern American continent, two communities and two ways of thinking collide. In a very certain way this novel, with its ruthless military commander, on the one hand, and spiritual rebels, on the other, could be easily transposed into a contemporary tale of massive US technological and military force brought to bear upon ayatollahs with fierce expressions and desert fighters with wrapped faces. The counterpoints would be almost exact. At the end of Llosa's book, however, the military commander enquires as to whether one of the rebel leaders had died or escaped. But a wizened old woman tells him that, instead of his dying or escaping, 'Archangels took him up to heaven.' The book ends exactly there, and we can only imagine that the ruthless and bloody Colonel Macedo must have been left, even if momentarily, wondering whether he had fought on the wrong side. And, if not the wrong side, realising with utmost reluctance that his enemies too had, just as he thought he himself had, spiritual validation and a mission of justice from heaven.

But neither Colonel Macedo's battles, nor those told from the view of the rebels, are clean. They are fettered by brutalities, suffering and slaughter. They are wearied and harried by it. They were not promised, nor did they receive, the absolution of destiny moving with conscience and justice that Krishna promised

2. Mario Vargas Llosa, *The War of the End of the World*, London: Faber & Faber, 1985.

Arjuna. Nor, in fact, did Arjuna receive absolution, but had to
spend time in hell to recompense his atrocities and depredations
on the battlefield of Kuruskshetra. The driving force of having to
live outside of hell, but still burdened by guilt – or unable to cast
off the shackles of professionally trained capacity for hatred and
murder – is brilliantly caught in two Zimbabwean novels.

The novel about being burdened, crippled, by guilt is Alexander Kanengoni's *Echoing Silences*.[3] Although Kanengoni
has lately been criticised as an apologist for Robert Mugabe's
land seizures, there is no doubt that he both was committed to
the original cause of liberation – viewing the seizures as their
extension – and recognises the awfulness of guerrilla discipline.
Forced to commit atrocity in the name of liberation, the lead
character, Munashe, is haunted by guilt that, in Shona cosmology, is personified in the form of a vengeful spirit requiring
requital. This spirit possesses Munashe and drives him towards
his death as expiation. Only in death does he find a world free of
corruption and terror, and a world of forgiveness and reconciliation. It is a literal heaven, but to attain it Munashe had to live
in an earthly hell. Although the novel depicts Munashe and the
spirit as person and personification, what Kanengoni unveils is
in fact a deep psychological disjunction and malaise within his
lead character. Pamela Reynolds has written about the psychological conditions such accounts personify.[4] However, looked
at not as metaphor but as graphic account of experiental terror
of what is carried within, Munashe represents something truly
chilling: a guilt so powerful and dislocating that no external
compensation can suffice, and the person who sacrificed others
must finally sacrifice himself or never know peace.

3. Alexander Kanengoni, *Echoing Silences*, Harare: Baobab, 1997.
4. Pamela Reynolds, *Traditional Healers and Childhood in Zimbabwe*, Athens OH:
Ohio University Press, 1996.

Yvonne Vera's work is better known in the West. Had she not died an early death from HIV/AIDS, she would surely have become a major international literary figure.[5] Her last complete novel is a plangently elegiac account of trauma[6] and, unlike Kanengoni's treatment of Munashe, the possibility of recovery. Not everyone can recover, however. For Sibaso, the former freedom fighter, for whom trauma has mutated into perpetual stalking and killing – someone inhabited by the vengeful spirits of the land – there can never be recovery. But he kills with a coolness and lucidity that is breathtaking. It takes several readings before the realisation dawns that, during his tango with Thenjiwe, Sibaso slices off her head with one hand, while cradling her in the dance with his other. He also rapes Thenjiwe's sister, Nonceba, who is left speechless both from her ordeal and from witnessing the death of her sister. Again, it is only afterwards that we realise Sibaso has mutilated Nonceba by slicing off her lips. She cannot speak both because of trauma and because her mouth has been symbolically cut away. Vera's understatement is so elegant that we are ourselves shocked into silence after our discovery of what she has depicted. The book ends on a highly conditional but hopeful note. Thenjiwe's lover adopts Nonceba as his object of devotion and project of healing. She is given skin grafts and he builds what is like a nest for her. The private nest mirrors his public project, which is to construct a replica of King Lobengula's throne, overthrown as the first depredation of colonialism. This is described on the last page of the book: 'To recreate the manner in which the tenderest branches bend, meet, and dry, the way grass folds over this frame and weaves a nest, the way it protects the cool livable places within; deliverance.'

---

5. See the critical account of her work in Ranka Primorac, *The Place of Tears: The Novel and Politics in Zimbabwe*, London: I.B. Tauris, 2006.
6. Yvonne Vera, *The Stone Virgins*, Harare: Weaver, 2002.

There are three points to note about these novels. The first, from the Vera novel, is that recovery and healing have both private and public dimensions. The second, from both novels, is that – unlike the story of God and Satan conducting cosmic wagers over Job and his family; unlike the Greek gods and their choreography of entrapment for the otherwise guiltless Oedipus – the Zimbabwean spirits are not *external* characters who act upon the human victim from a lofty perch in Heaven. They possess the person and, upon entering, become part of him or her. The struggle is then an *internal* one and, although it can be lost, as in the cases of Munashe and Sibaso, it can be won by care directed inwards as well as a care than emanates outwards to the community in which the injured person is situated. The third is that spirit madness – the madness that becomes part of a personality – can be either frenzied (as in the case of Munashe, who is driven, almost hurtling, to his death) or so calm and coolly lucid (as in the case of Sibaso) that it takes the breath away.

But the cool and lucid sense of frenzy – possible with killers in novels and suicide bombers in real life – may also be the property of those who want to save life. The Prix Goncourt-winning novel by Romain Gary, *Les Racines du ciel*,[7] depicts such a character. Morel is driven to protect the elephants of Africa (although the 1958 John Huston film of the book does poor service to the original) and is almost a prototype of remorseless contemplation of a mission in life, as well as the executor of that mission. What Bernard-Henri Lévy had in mind, however, when envying the 'freedom of Romain Gary', was the utter carelessness with which he displayed his courage fighting for the Free French forces in World War II. As a fighter pilot he flew twenty-five offensive sorties and earned an array of decorations. Afterwards

---

7. In English translation: Romain Gary, *The Roots of Heaven*, London: White Lion, 1973.

he became a senior diplomat and finally married the amazing actress Jean Seberg. In a way, Lévy has an archetype in mind: Malraux carelessly tossing bombs out of an antique aircraft window in a quixotic but necessary attempt to slow Franco's advance in Spain;[8] Gary, who took off into the blue as if the sky meant freedom and not the possibility of his own death. But, for Gary himself, that aerial carelessness was compensated by what he was trying to express in *Les Racines du ciel*. There are roots of Heaven that, once embedded in a person's heart, can never be tugged out – and those roots are the call to fight for justice. It is an almost Kantian vision: a heavenly call for justice to all, a universal justice for universal benefit, whether for humanity or elephants. It is almost a Buddhistic vision, in that there is no differentiation between people and elephants. All are, in the Buddhist cosmology, 'sentient beings'. For Gary, however, as for Morel, the point of transaction between the careless skies and the embedded roots of heaven is that cool and lucid sense of frenzy, fully under control but indisputably unavoidable in one's conduct, by which one goes about the struggle for justice. Being able to conduct that transaction and not feel fettered by it, doing it as a thing done, is probably the freedom Lévy sought to describe, if not actually envied.

But the great limitation of Morel is not his acceptance of his own remorselessness but his inability and lack of any desire to become more African. He remains unambiguously a white man in Africa. He does not even become more 'elephant', more empathetic to the object of his desire. He is *sympathetic*, but the elephants to him are objects to be rendered salvation. In one of his early novels, to a large extent modelled on his own adventures as a young looter of antiquities, Malraux depicted Perken, the

---

8. Lévy greatly admired Malraux: Bernard-Henri Lévy, *Adventures on the Freedom Road: The French Intellectuals in the 20th Century*, London: Harvill, 1995, pp. 211-14.

misanthropic would-be king of the Cambodian jungle, in exactly the same way.[9] He integrates with no other person, not even his young interlocutor, the idealistic Claude; neither does he go 'native' by becoming more like the inhabitants of the jungle. In fact, the only person to have been nativised is so because he is their captive and slave and has no choice. Although, as I mentioned earlier, Malraux is able to portray a range of people with different cultural backgrounds, particularly the Chinese rebels in his account of the doomed 1927 Communist uprising in Shanghai, the Chinese stay Chinese; the European characters stay European.[10] The internationalist cast is as much a collection of nationalities as anything internationalist in the sense of cultural fusion for which this book has argued. They are miscegenated to the solidarity, right up to and including the point of death where they exhibit great gallantry, but they do so as backgrounded figures. Their background cultures are never fused in the novel's foreground, in its sense of possibility.

Perhaps that is why Bernard-Henri Lévy tried so hard in his (imagined as much as investigated) account of the death of the US journalist Daniel Pearl, executed by Pakistani Islamic militants (decapitated in exactly the same way as Sibaso decapitates Thejiwe in Vera's novel), to see inside the minds of the Islamic militants.[11] But his is a startlingly limited book. Lévy doesn't even make it as an American. He is always the cool habitué of Parisian salons, trying hard to be rough. This is unfair on him. He has seen a large degree of bloodshed as he has tried to live out what he sees as the intellectual's role to bear witness and express outrage and foster mobilisation against the crimes of the world. But he probably wished very hard to be more like Ahmed Shah Massoud, the

---

9. André Malraux, *The Way of the Kings*, London: Hesperus, 2005.
10. André Malraux, *Man's Estate*, London: Penguin, 1961.
11. Bernard-Henri Lévy, *Who Killed Daniel Pearl?*, London: Duckworth, 2003.

heroic defender of Kabul before it fell to the Taliban in 1996. It was his Northern Alliance soldiers upon whom the Western allies depended when they retook Kabul as the first reprisal after 9/11 and the fall of the Twin Towers. But, at the time of the first great Taliban victory, Massoud, hopelessly outnumbered, was faced with the huge logistical operation of evacuating his 25,000 men in good order, and fighting as orderly a retreat northwards as he could. Even so, he personally went to the UN compound, where the fallen Communist president of Afghanistan, Sayid Mohammed Najibullah, had sought refuge within its space of diplomatic immunity. Massoud had never pursued Najibullah after he had defeated him in 1992. Now, he came to offer him a place on his convoys out of Kabul. It was a humane gesture of compassion, for Massoud knew what was to come. Najibullah refused, stayed behind, and was executed with the greatest humiliation by the Taliban. But Osama bin Laden felt obliged to track down and assassinate Massoud on the eve of 9/11. It was as if he felt he needed at least the uncontested space of Afghanistan when the inevitable Western reprisals came. Certainly, Lévy had been very active trying to convince the West, and France in particular, of the value of Massoud. Like Osama, Massoud travelled – even while fleeing capture – with a huge library of books, but he wore Gucci boots under his traditional dress and could transact cultures in a way that Lévy only dreamt about.

Five global public intellectuals: conditionalities and openness

The point about transacting cultures, making other cultures intimate with the sense of one's own – to the point of miscegenation and integration – is that it is hard and requires residence and immersion. It is not a frequent-flyer short and sharp excursion. Something of this sort was pulled off, briefly, by Susan Sontag. Whereas Lévy visited Sarajevo and had publicity photographs taken, Sontag went and lived and worked there at the height of the Serbian siege of the city. Famously, she chose to direct Beckett's *Waiting for Godot* in a theatre plunged into candlelight. In the process she discovered something about the fine – so fine they are transgressible with a sigh – lines that make people fight. The 'languages' of former Yugoslavia were very similar. They were not so much dialects as, to a large extent, regional variations. Now they are determinedly Croatian, Bosnian, Serbian and so on, with antique words hastily re-academised into official vocabularies, and much made of the use of the Cyrillic alphabet by the Serbs. But it is still not hard for a speaker of one 'language' to understand what is going on in a neighbouring capital.

In the Sarajevo of 1993 the only translation of Beckett's play was in what was once called Serbo-Croat (Sontag had memorised the entire Serbo-Croat script), and the Bosnian actors were comfortably using that under Sontag's direction. But, while they were rehearsing, the fighters of Bosnia were taking huge risks and casualties, in which even the actors and production staff participated. Just getting from home to theatre meant risking a sniper's bullet – even for Sontag. But what bemused her was the debate as to whether the Serbian translation should be 'retranslated' into Bosnian. Indeed, an effort was made, but the Serbian version was better and the actors stuck to it. Even they knew the artificiality of locating an entire war upon a light load of linguistic variations. But there were indeed people who fought for linguistic freedom as much as political independence, and the lines upon which people stand and fight are neither always sensible nor solid. During the siege, Lévy's old intellectual *confrère*, the equally dashing André Glucksmann, jetted in for twenty-four hours and, in the language of Baudrillard,[12] talked about wars being media events. Wars were won or lost on television. Sontag's riposte was brief and caustic: 'Try telling that to all the people here who have lost their arms and legs.'[13] Sontag was no easily long-suffering hero. Her account afterwards about being able to take a bath, flush a toilet, and stop at a traffic light in Zagreb (only an hour's flight from Sarajevo) was only too human.[14] Nevertheless, the experience ingrained upon her a harsh, Spartan code:

> A good rule before one goes marching or signing anything: Whatever the tug of sympathy, you have no right to a public opinion unless you've been there, experienced firsthand and on the ground and for some considerable time the country, war, injustice, whatever, you are talking about. In the absence of such firsthand knowledge and experience: silence.[15]

But the rigour in this code is insurmountable for the majority of the world. We are trapped in space and, even if mobile, trapped in culture. Sontag, a Jewish-American New York Europhile, worked hard in Sarajevo to become a wearied, war-torn, black-humoured, moderate Sunni Muslim Central European. Whether she managed this in the weeks she was in Sarajevo is uncertain – even with the compression that comes with siege and the proximity of death. What of those with families, more fixed jobs than her own? Are there not places for the contribution of empathy that comes from the work of research and the harder

---

12. Jean Baudrillard, a French philosopher famous for his statement that the Gulf War never took place, except as able to be appreciated in the media. In fact this abiding memory of him is unfair, as he has something serious to say about the fragmentations and impersonations of 'real' life. And his (in)famous statement was only ever intended to be a single newspaper article: Jean Baudrillard, 'The Reality Gulf', *Guardian*, 11 January 1991.

13. Susan Sontag, *Where the Stress Falls*, London: Jonathan Cape, 2002, p. 319.

14. Ibid., p. 323.

15. Ibid., p. 298.

work of imagination – the imagination of self as another? Is there not great merit in this effort? Is there not something to be learnt from Sontag's own last book, *Regarding the Pain of Others*,[16] in which an image – after all, able to be dismissed as only an image, only perhaps a war on television – can be powerful and rendered an instrument of power to convey pain? But there is a final limitation, Sontag wrote in the last words on the last page of the last book. The limitation of experience is that the viewer of the image cannot imagine *entering* the image; cannot imagine fusion with the reality it represents; it is, like Lévy, dodging fake bullets to create an image of his own. We all know the justice of this critique. We have all asked the question: 'With what moral authority did George W. Bush, Donald Rumsfeld and Tony Blair, all men who never experienced war, send young men and women out to endure and commit the horrors of war?' Sontag requests of us that we justify the moral authority by which we dissent from the Blairs and Rumsfelds. But, if this is the case, what can anyone do?

Let us look at some other intellectuals who have fulfilled, or not, the rigours of Sontag – but who have done more, and have done it variously. After all, as a latecomer to the rigours of immersion and participation, privation and risk of death, location and siege, Sontag could be accused of preciousness. Despite her coruscating brilliance she had always, in any case, been noted – even by sympathetic fellow intellectuals – as ambitious, failing to suffer fools gladly, and wanting the Nobel Prize.[17] It took a series of encounters with cancer, the last of which killed her, to turn her gaze outwards towards the finality not only of herself but

---

16. Susan Sontag, *Regarding the Pain of Others*, London: Hamish Hamilton, 2003.
17. Edward Field, *The Man Who Would Marry Susan Sontag*, Madison: University of Wisconsin Press, 2005.

of others. But she never endured prison, exile, censorship by the leaders of those she championed, or official surveillance; and, no matter how brilliantly and bravely she immersed herself in the rigours and perils of Sarajevo, she did this for weeks; whereas the four intellectuals discussed below struggled for decade, without losing the coherence and consistency of their stands.

Even so, this is not to say that their intellectual self-justifications are always as robust as they themselves think. That is not the point. The point is that they were or are committed to changing, if not the world, then a part of it and have not deviated from this. Of all public intellectuals, Noam Chomsky is probably the best known. A 2005 *Prospect* magazine readers' poll (run jointly with *Foreign Affairs*) placed him as the foremost of 100 'global public intellectuals'.[18] Not that such 'beauty parades' of readers' choices are in any way authoritative: the top 14 in the poll all work in Europe or the United States, or write in metropolitan languages. They include Amartya Sen, who came in at 8; but, surprisingly, Abdolkarim Soroush, whose work was discussed in the last chapter of this book, polled 15th. There were no Africans or East Asians in the top 20; so, despite one or two exceptions that proved the rule, readers championed those whose intellects were most like their own. Within this northern hemispheric enclosure, seemingly unmiscegenated, Chomsky's life and work are clearly courageous and persistent. He is well known particularly for his critique of American 'empire' – imperialism by insidious and not-so-insidious means. A stream of works has prosecuted this theme, keeping pace with every new perception of outrage.[19] But, although Chomsky deals with

18. Daniel Herman, 'Global Public Intellectuals Poll Results', *Prospect*, November 2005.

19. E.g. Noam Chomsky, *Imperial Ambitions: Conversations on the Post 9/11 World*, New York: Metropolitan Books, 2005.

the world at large, it is the US influence and power over it that most excites and exacts his forensic interest. He is, as it were, the foremost anatomist of the baleful ingredients of this power. In that project he has taken with him, into the post 9/11 era, the generation that first paid attention to his work against the Vietnam war. Unlike the Sontag prescription for non-silence, Chomsky has written extensively also about Israel, Nicaragua and Haiti,[20] without living for long periods in those countries and experiencing the wars and injustices visited upon them. He was never under shellfire, for instance. In Nicaragua, under the government whose cause he had championed against the United States, he was a fêted and honoured guest. And, although of Jewish descent, he has never faced an Israeli tank in the intifada. How much has this disqualified him from speaking and writing? He never even set about *manufacturing* the simulacra of danger – fighting a cause with the fabrication of images for magazines and television (as Lévy did in Sarajevo). Chomsky has never been in any danger of this sort at all. He has been under surveillance by his own government's security agencies, to be sure, and has received his fair share of anonymous threats, but he is a Boston Brahmin who lives modestly and safely.

And yet, if he had been silent, how much poorer the world would be in its capacity for discernment and dissent – or, at least, in its personnel with whom to argue. The injustice that is germinated at home, and flowers in lands far away, must be traced from germination to bloom. Sontag never became an anatomist of the Clinton administration's foreign policy machinery dedicated to Bosnia. She only saw and experienced the results, complain-

---

20. *The Fateful Triangle: The United States, Israel and the Palestinians*, Boston MA: South End Press, 1983; *On Power and Ideology: The Managua Lectures*, Boston MA: South End Press, 1987; *Getting Haiti Right This Time: The US and the Coup*, Monroe ME: Common Courage, 2004.

ing all the while, with her actors, about 'waiting for Clinton'.
She, too, wrote from only one end of the process. Chomsky is
the great authority on how the foreign policy machinery ger-
minates or tolerates indescribable terrors, even though he has
never experienced them. The trick is surely a cohabitation, if
not a cooperation, between those who inhabit either end. But
for those who inhabit, say, the Washington end of the process,
Chomsky is merciless. His analysis and venom coalesced in what
is still probably his finest book. *American Power and the New
Mandarins* was first published in 1969.[21] It was a denunciation of
the entire foreign policy process that had led to war in Vietnam
and, as noted earlier, Chomsky reserved some of his venom for
those academics who mediated the 'truth' of what the rulers were
purveying to their subjects. These academics had become high
priests to power and were a very long way from speaking truth to
power, challenging the truthfulness of power, and challenging
power itself. But what is often un- or under-remarked in this
book is not only the need to challenge power, but the need not
to hinder the emergence of new popular power structures.

Chomsky provides an extended paean to the Spanish Republican revolution – the one finally defeated by the fascist armies
of Franco, and the one somewhat futilely defended by Malraux's
tossing of bombs out of vintage aircraft windows. Chomsky will
have none of the Malraux romance of doing something as a
substitute for doing nothing. He knows that not all intellectuals
can fight, can mobilise out of fragments an airforce, can muster
the courage to fly into the blue and possibly into oblivion. What
the intellectual should do is refuse to impose him- or herself
upon spontaneous forms of self-organisation and expression.
These should not be given shape and form by intellectuals, for

---

21. *American Power and the New Mandarins: Historical and Political Essays*, New
York: Pantheon, 1969.

fear that these will devolve rapidly into techniques of manage-
ment and control and, from these, methods of coercion. How
far the intellectual should step aside is never fully explicated by
Chomsky; for, if the intellectual is simply to march alongside the
popular revolution in solidarity, what does he or she contribute
to either the revolution or to solidarity? Books have been burned
by other revolutions, and there must be a way to incorporate
learning into the creation of new histories. Certainly Chomsky is
distrustful of, if not fully against, the idea that intellectuals can
enter government and change it for the popular betterment. The
temptation to technologise control of the 'correct' way forward
would be too great. But, then, if it is not possible (in Sontag's
rigour) to manipulate images for the good, and it is not possible
(in Chomsky's rigour) to enter government for the good, what
is the good an intellectual can do? And, if we applied Sontag's
edict of experiental knowledge accumulated over some time on
location, then even Chomsky would not be permitted to speak
and criticise as fully as he has.

Someone who seemed to make of his life a perpetual mission of criticism was Edward Said; but he did more than simply
criticise and lived his life as much more than a gentlemanly
resident of Columbia University's gentrified (and expanding)
patch of Harlem. Much has been written about Edward Said
– not least by himself – some parts of which seem now, only a
few years after his death in 2003, almost like caricature: his
comfortable 'exile' from the old Jerusalem that had been part
of Palestine, his love of bespoke suits, the '3,000 close friends'
that made up an address book of amazing reach.[22] But so much of

22. He lived in a university apartment, which overlooked the Hudson, 'with such a
clear, close view... you feel you are almost in the water' (Gaby Wood, 'The Lion of Judea',
Guardian, 13 May 1997). His dress sense was admired by Zoë Heller, even if it distracted
her. 'It would not be unfair to describe Professor Said as obsessed with clothes' ('Radical,
Chic', *Independent on Sunday*, 7 February 1993); and even close friends like Tariq

the commentary is, if not superficial, unable to see deeply into the man. Said himself set the parameters in his autobiography, in which he seemed to reveal himself almost intimately, with thoughts for instance about his cancer, but in which he kept many of his vexations hidden from view.[23] The work on Said that said most about him was one in which he did not appear, the posthumous film by Sato Makoto, *Out of Place* (2005), after the title of Said's autobiography. Even that worked only by a series of inferences and silent visual sweeps.

The 'places of exile' of Said were not refugee camps, and his dissidence has never been accompanied by physical suffering. There were psychological disjunctures, to be sure, but this was not someone who lived in conditions like the siege of Sarajevo. I am not proposing, in a short space, to unveil the 'hidden Said'. But there is one aspect of his thought and the animation behind it which has often been neglected by his admirers, and that is the sequence of lyrical poems by Goethe, the *West–Eastern Divan*.[24] I think it can be said that Said lived his life by this sequence of poems, and it establishes a template from which the public international role of the intellectual can be drawn. Although Goethe's rough contemporary Lord Byron was much given to 'oriental' tales, he always wrote them as fantasy and entertainment and, in his poem *Beppo*, even boasted of being able to invent pastiche, 'mix'd with western sentimentalism' the 'finest orientalism'. It

Ali mocked him for, uncharacteristically, not matching his towel with his swimming trunks (*Conversations with Edward Said*, Oxford: Seagull, 2006, p. 3). The '3,000 close friends' note is an affectionate mockery in Adhaf Soueif's obituary, *Guardian*, 26 September 2003.

23. Edward W. Said, *Out of Place*, London: Granta, 1999.

24. J.W. von Goethe, *West–Eastern Divan*, trans. Edgar Alfred Bowring, accessible at www.worldwideschool.org/library/books/lit/poetry/ThePoemsofGoethe/chap41. html. This provides some 60 of the 200 poems. Another translation of selected poems from the sequence, by Michael Hamburger and Christopher Middleton, may be found as 'The Parliament of West and East (1814-18)', in J.W. von Goethe, *The Sorrows of Young Werther. Elective Affinities, Italian Journey, Faust*, New York: Knof, 2000, pp. 1110-21. I have indicated in the text which translation I have used.

is from Byron's words that Said drew the title of his most famous book, *Orientalism*,[25] and the epithet by which he established his critique of most Western approaches to other cultures – pastiches, inflected if not overrun by preconceptions, misjudged exotica, and Western metropolitan values. If, however, Byron was (by his own admission) guilty of orientalism, what was there about Goethe's work that made it different? First, Goethe deliberately wrote the sequence in the Persian style. He read and studied for this and it is as if he sought to continue the legacy of someone like Rumi; whereas Byron ran with anything that scanned. Second, Goethe sought assiduously a sense of empathy.

> Who the song would understand
> Needs must seek the song's own land,
> Who the minstrel understand,
> Needs must seek the minstrel's land. (trans. Bowring)

And, third, apart from Goethe's attempts to replicate the Persian imagery and metaphors of love, the poems to do with religious praise and endorsement of Islamic culture are, even by today's standards, exceptionally free of irony or double-entendre. They simply praise both Allah and the culture of his followers.

Simultaneously, they make a clear normative point, first about an intrinsic and absolute equality:

> GOD is of the east possess'd,
> God is ruler of the west;
> North and south alike, each land
> Rests within his gentle hand. (trans. Bowring)

And, second, about how in the absence of a recognition of that equality, and the will to live as equal cultures in the world, hatred grows. Here, guilt can also be equally shared.

---

25. *Orientalism*, New York: Vintage, 1978.

THOUGH the bards whom the Orient sun hath bless'd
Are greater than we who dwell in the west,
Yet in hatred of those whom our equals we find.
In this we're not the least behind. (Bowring)

If anything, Goethe expressed an admiration of the 'East' that
surpassed what he felt about the 'West'.

North and West and South are breaking,
Thrones are bursting, kingdoms shaking;
Flee, then, to the essential East,
Where on patriarch's air you'll feast...
Pure and righteous there I'll trace
To its source the human race...
When they honoured ancestors,
To strange doctrine closed their doors. (trans. Hamburger)

And, probably the most famous poem of the sequence, 'Gingko
Biloba', expressed that sense of alternative, of compensatory
weight to the burdens imposed upon the world by the West, that
Said sought also to express.

This tree's leaf from the East
To my garden's been entrusted
Holds a secret sense, and grist
To a man intent on knowledge. (trans. Hamburger)

Yet what exile did for Said, whether comfortably or not, was
to establish in him not a sense of 'oneself as another', but a sense
of two others within his single self. The Palestinian boy with
an Egyptian and Lebanese upbringing, an American university
education and career, and a love of European literature – fluent
in English, French, and Arabic, and able to read German as well
as other languages – there may have been many more others
than merely two. Goethe's expression of that surely rang deeply
in Said:

Fitly now I can reveal
What the pondered question taught me;
In my songs do you not feel
That at once I'm one and double?

For Said, the key 'doubling' lay in the exile, however comfortable, and the sense of homelessness it contained, despite residence in New York and roots in Palestine. There was another doubling, of course, and he expressed this very well to an Israeli journalist. He was a Palestinian drawn like a moth to the critical flame of Theodor Adorno, the Jewish philosopher who, with Max Horkheimer, established the Frankfurt School of Critical Theory in exile in New York during World War II, which gave intellectual haven to a host of European and Jewish intellectuals. Why, Said might ponder, could the Israeli state not allow itself the critical freedom and creativity of Adorno?

> I'm the last Jewish intellectual. You don't know anyone else. All your other Jewish intellectuals are now suburban squires. From Amos Oz to all these people here in America. So I'm the last one. The only true follower of Adorno. Let me put it this way: I'm a Jewish-Palestinian.[26]

This 2000 endpiece (the last words in the last interview of this collection of interviews) was not gratuitous or Said being supercilious. But, for one of the great champions of the Palestinian cause, it expressed a sadness over polarisation, about the world's inability to be double – to lie on the same divan and think the same thoughts and take the same actions in the name of freedom.

---

26. Edward W. Said, 'My Right of Return', interview with Ari Shavit, in *Power, Politics and Culture: Interviews with Edward W. Said*, London: Bloomsbury, 2004, p. 458.

Some of this was more plangently caught in a very small and not-often-remarked book. It wasn't really even a book, just the hardbound text of a lecture. But *Freud and the Non-European* was a wonderful digression into the impossibility of 'pure' identity and, as ever, but more tellingly within such a small text, Said cheekily worked over the point that Moses, the founder of Israel as a free nation, was in fact probably Egyptian.[27]

Apart from his work on orientalism and on behalf of understood difference, Said was the pre-eminent Palestinian spokesman in the United States. As described earlier in this book, he stood up even to Sartre regarding the Palestinians, in the sort of exchange that Bernard-Henri Lévy could never imagine (Sartre being a sort of hero for him). But he stood up also to Yasser Arafat, the doyen and overlong-serving head of the Palestine Liberation Organisation. His writings were for a time banned in the sketchy territory of the Palestinian Administration, and Arafat's spokesman – not knowing Said had coined the contemporary use of the Byronic term – accused Said of orientalism towards the Palestinians. But, before the falling out, Said had served on the Palestine National Council (the parliament in exile) from 1977 to 1991; he was used as an intermediary between the USA and the PLO in 1988 by Ronald Reagan's secretary of state, George Shultz; and his office at Columbia University was fire-bombed. During his later years at Columbia there was a special campus police facility detailed to respond with urgency to any call from Said (just as Chomsky continues to need such a facility at Massachusetts Institute of Technology). Said could be wrong in his judgements – earlier in this book there is an example of his misjudgement of the capacity of Hamas – but he never deviated from the basic themes of his academic and political work. When

---

27. Edward W. Said, *Freud and the Non-European*, London: Verso, 2003.

he was dying, he laboured with Daniel Barenboim to establish the West–Eastern Divan Orchestra, composed of young Israeli and Arab musicians, including many Palestinian players. It was meant to be an example of how identities can merge into a single music.

Said was not a mere enthusiast of music. He gave minor concerts with himself playing piano; he would drive Barenboim mad with requests to play duets;[28] his book on music expounded on music as a critical device as liberating as thought, using, among others, Adorno in his own musical guise;[29] and his collection of conversations with Barenboim worked hard to convince readers that, even though it had been used so easily by the Nazis, partly because his political proclivities had been so clear, the music of Wagner could still be a transcendent entry point to freedom.[30]

In a real way, the orchestra – which literally got off to a slow start (Barenboim clearly had to slow down the normal pace of Beethoven's Fifth Symphony so the young players could cope in their recorded concert in Ramallah) – was intended by Said as a legacy. Perhaps based on his own experiences trying to advise Arafat, perhaps based on his observations of successive US administrations, Said was as trenchant as Chomsky in repudiating the possibility of intellectuals being able to serve, uncompromised, in governments. Discussing the temptations that face such intellectuals, he said:

> But the only way of ever achieving [a free expression that is not hardened into an institution] is to keep reminding yourself that as an intellectual you are the one who can choose between actively representing the truth to the best of your ability, and

28. Daniel Barenboim, 'Sound and Vision', *Guardian*, 25 October 2004.

29. Edward W. Said, *Musical Elaborations*, London: Vintage, 1992.

30. Daniel Barenboim and Edward W. Said, *Parallels and Paradoxes: Explorations in Music and Society*, London: Bloomsbury, 2003.

passively allowing a patron or an authority to direct you. For the secular intellectual, *those* gods always fail.[31]

If, as concrete and performing artefact, seeking all the same to be expressive of freedom, the West–Eastern Divan Orchestra is the legacy, then Barenboim, the Israeli conductor, is the legacy's emblem. He fulfilled this role resplendently in 2008, becoming the first person to take both Israeli and Palestinian citizenship. Barenboim became double.

In the meantime, it is perhaps no surprise that the orchestra concentrates on Beethoven. Its recording of Beethoven's Ninth Symphony, with its choral call, using Schiller's poem that all people are brothers under the stars of heaven, is surprisingly good. Barenboim has been working hard on his young charges. They, like he, are double. But the doubled person must be able to express that doubling in a way that commands understanding and respect – and cuts a path through to the future.

It is this doubling, oneself as another, and beyond – oneself as two others, each of whom interrogates but completes the other – that is the answer to the dictum of Sontag. Perhaps, like Sontag, it is good to experience shellfire and siege once in one's life – but not if it is then used to make oneself even more exclusive and apart from others, elevated, and laying down the law. I shall return to the sense of doubling as, indeed, I have throughout this book. It has been in many ways the hidden theme, barely veiled, now uncovered. First, however, having made the point, it requires an immediate corrective and, if not a corrective, then an amelioration. The great Kenyan novelist Ngugi wa Thiong'o insisted upon a form not of doubling, but of *singularity* – a singular, specific base from which one could

---

31. Edward W. Said, *Representations of the Intellectual*, London: Vintage, 1994, p. 90.

develop and grow to face the world on terms of one's own. This was much more than Virginia Woolf's requirement of a room of one's own. For Ngugi, terms of one's own would decide the fate of entire nations.

Certainly, in his own nation his fate was once decided by others. In 1977 he was arrested and held at Kamiti Maximum Security Prison for writing a play, *Ngaahika Ndeenda* (I will marry when I want),[32] which was deemed to be subversive in its assertion of an individual freedom and its barely disguised critique of Kenyan political society. After his release he chose self-exile in London in 1982, where his reputation as a writer was already growing. His great novel, *Petals of Blood*,[33] had also appeared in 1977. Its account of a motley crew of outcasts, marching from their village towards Nairobi to lodge their complaints with the government, is a great narrative combining a quest for the fruits of modernity and development, stolen from the poor by the powerful, and the ancestral spirits providing a validation for the questers – people forgotten and excoriated by polite society: a former freedom fighter, a prostitute, people of low station trekking towards the high station of the land. It was this period that marked Ngugi. He never forgot his prison experiences. He published a diary of this period,[34] which coincided with the television version of the *Jail Diary of Albie Sachs*;[35] the two accounts served not only to help propel Ngugi into the public consciousness but to raise awareness about principled stands throughout Africa. However, it is the structure of *Petals of Blood*

32. London: Heinemann, 1977.

33. London: Heinemann, 1977.

34. Ngugi wa Thiong'o, *Detained: A Writer's Prison Diary*, London: Heinemann, 1981.

35. Albie Sachs was detained as a South African anti-apartheid campaigner. His *Jail Diary of Albie Sachs* (New York: McGraw-Hill, 1967) was adapted in 1978 as a play by David Edgar and performed at London's Royal Court Theatre to great acclaim, and was subsequently screened on television in 1981.

that is of great interest. Its sections are built around verses by
W.B. Yeats, so that the march towards Nairobi is likened to the
beast 'slouching towards Bethlehem'. Ngugi was much taken by
Yeats, and it would seem one passage in particular, from 'The
Fisherman', became the *leitmotif* of his subsequent statement
to the world:

> All day I'd looked in the face
> What I had hoped 'twould be
> To write for my own race.

Ngugi wrote much by way of direct political protest and critique,[36] but he has won an immense following in Africa itself by
his insistence that African culture, values, self-expression and
self-organisation can be rediscovered by re-immersion in African
languages, and his own decision to write only in one of the main
Kenyan languages, Kikuyu. (Subsequent publications in English
were translations.) This insistence was published in the book
that is best known by the non-novel-reading political classes of
Africa under the directly political title *Decolonising the Mind*.[37]
It is so well known that even the South African president of the
time, Thabo Mbeki, in a curious 2004 newsletter to his party
political colleagues, declared that Western powers should refrain
from attacking Zimbabwe's Robert Mugabe because they could
not understand his actions; and, in justifying an 'African-ness'
about both Mugabe's land seizure policies and Mbeki's own
methodology in seeking to settle the Zimbabwean issue, he
invoked the authority of *Decolonising the Mind*.[38]

---

36. E.g. Ngugi wa Thiong'o, *Writers in Politics*, London: Heinemann, 1981; and his
most recent novel, a huge and sprawling attempt at magical realism, but unambiguously a
trenchant attack on African political corruption, *Wizard of the Crow*, New York: Knopf,
2006.

37. London: Heinemann, 1986.

38. Thabo Mbeki, 'We'll Resist the Upside-down View of Africa', reprinted in *The
Post* (Lusaka, Zambia), 9 January 2004.

I am not sure this is exactly what Ngugi had in mind; although he does express an African anger against the West that is so deep and widespread it is unlikely he would repudiate such expansive uses of his work. In so far as the narrow linguistic issue is concerned, Ngugi has constantly explored the theme of speaking and writing in African languages.[39] More and more, he used the term 'pan-African intellectual', and spoke of not only Kenya but of all post- and 'neo-colonial Africa'.[40] These are terms he used at an early stage of his writing, but they are now deployed more frequently.[41] But here a problem is raised. Africa comprises fifty-three states, with two more (Western Sahara and Somaliland) posting sufficiently legitimate claims to statehood to justify much diplomatic activity and legal debate. Africa is a huge area, several times that of Europe. Susan Sontag was highly specific about Sarajevo. You had to have been there. You could not, like André Glucksmann, simply fly in and out. Being there meant living and suffering there. Yet Glucksmnan, Lévy and other French intellectuals[42] justified their concerns for Sarajevo on the grounds that it was European, just as they were also Europeans. It was an atrocity in Europe – an atrocity of their own. They had no choice, as Europeans, but to speak. Ngugi feels the same way about Africa, even though Mali is arguably more different to Kenya than Bosnia is to France. One speaks for a cause, and one speaks for an identity. The hard thing is not so much to speak for an expanded identity – Ngugi did that in order

39. E.g. in his contribution, 'Europhone or African Memory: The Challenge of the Pan-Africanist Intellectual in the Era of Globalization', in Thandika Mkandawire, ed., *African Intellectuals: Rethinking Politics, Language, Gender and Development*, Dakar: Codesria, 2005.

40. Ngugi wa Thiong'o, *Barrel of a Pen: Resistance to Oppression in Neo-colonial Africa*, Trenton NJ: Africa World Press, 1983.

41. For the sweep of his career, see Reinhard Sander and Bernth Lindfors, eds, *Ngugi wa Thiongo Speaks: Interviews*, Oxford: James Currey, 2006. This volume comprises interviews with Ngugi from 1964 to 2003.

42. Notably Alain Finkielkaut, *The Crime of Being Born*, Zagreb: CERES, 1997.

to protect what he thought was quintessentially African and which had otherwise been constantly corrupted. It is something else to speak not in protection but in an expansive mission to open out onto the world and *change* it; to speak not of binary opposites and antagonisms but to overcome the oppositions of the world by giving them a common identity; to speak on behalf of the doubled identity.

Ngugi's Nigerian contemporary, the Nobel Prize-winning Wole Soyinka, spoke of Africa protectively, but also in doubling terms. The urban myth about Soyinka is that his name is a derivative pseudonym, taken from his time in prison where he was deprived of both ink and any paper, except toilet paper. 'Soyinka' is thus a rendering of 'Shit inka', by which means, on toilet paper, he continued to write. It is an untrue story but it serves to illustrate the admiration in which he is held – an admiration devoted as much to his perseverance as to his writing. Soyinka was imprisoned in Nigeria from 1967 to 1969 because he called for a ceasefire in the civil war then ravaging the country. As with Ngugi, the experience left a mark on him and he published a book of poems about his ordeal,[43] as well as an account entitled *The Man Died*.[44] Even his famous novel, *Season of Anomy*,[45] was based on his prison thoughts; I shall return to this work later. But it had been his first novel in 1965, *The Interpreters*,[46] that had won him early fame; so the action of the Nigerian authorities in incarcerating him was both ruthless and in defiance of international opinion. *The Interpreters* is about a group of young people, all in different ways seeking a path forwards in the new Nigeria, and all confused. A brilliant post-independence

43. Wole Soyinka, *Poems from Prison*, London: Rex Collings, 1969.
44. Wole Soyinka, *The Man Died: Prison Notes*, London: Rex Collings, 1972.
45. London: Rex Collings, 1973.
46. London: Andre Deutsch, 1965.

novel, its concerns were brutally superseded by the civil war. It led Soyinka to think about Nigeria in particular, and Africa at large, in simultaneous terms of modernity and transparency, on the one hand, and mythologically, on the other. He brings the two together by calling upon the ancient gods to express their anger at the transgressions of modern tyrants.[47]

Soyinka has been excoriating in his condemnation of Nigerian and other African tyrants,[48] but he has also been full of praise for wiser leaders. As early as 1988 he wrote a book of poems directed towards Nelson Mandela,[49] and more recently he has expressed his admiration in a way that fulfils the recommendation of this book that I have been trying to write:

> I would simply name him a symbol of the culture of dialogue, backed by an unparalleled generosity of spirit ... symbol also of a futuristic cultural rainbow. He is a symbol that enshrines the principle of cultural plurality, yet advocates the necessity of synthesis or perhaps, more accurately, syncretism – a more culture-associated word for dialogue – as the optimistic face of human civilisation.[50]

It is these recent words that take us back to Soyinka's early work, *Season of Anomy*. Even while in prison Soyinka, like Mandela, never refused the possibility and desirability of fusion, of doubling. The novel, based on his prison thoughts, sets Yoruba myth alongside the Greek legend of Orpheus and Eurydice. Finally, if we all emerge from a common underworld, might we

---

47. As in his book of poems, *Ogun Abibiman*, London: Rex Collings, 1976.
48. One of whom, Sani Abacha, charged him with treason. See Soyinka's criticisms in *The Open Sore of a Continent: A Personal Narrative of the Nigerian Crisis*, New York: Oxford University Press, 1996; *The Climate of Fear: The Reith Lectures*, London: Profile, 2004.
49. *Mandela's Earth*, New York: Random House, 1988.
50. Wole Soyinka, 'Views from a Palette of the Cultural Rainbow', in Xolela Mangcu, ed., *The Meaning of Mandela: A Literary and Intellectual Celebration*, Cape Town: Human Sciences Research Council, 2006, p. 33.

not rise to a common future? To look upon the world as a site for change, to use one's culture as a means of embracing another's – is this not a greater task than simply protecting a culture against all comers?

The strictures on office

Both Chomsky and Said are agreed that, once they assume office, the intellectuals who spoke the truth – and no doubt wish to do so from within – will be controlled and, eventually, become part of the controlling apparatus. But their injunction against taking office is a stricture that, although reasonable on first expression, is as narrow as Sontag's requirement to have been sharing suffering on location. Frantz Fanon once coined an expression that now, sadly but inevitably, has been turned into a slogan on giftwrap: 'Blind idealism is reactionary.'[51] The idealist who has a vision of the world, and thinks it achievable without mess, is as much an obstacle to the gritty business of revolution as an antagonist. This, of course, is another stricture in its own right – but the Dalai Lama, despite his serene public relations, is enmeshed in extremely messy politics, both in undeclared dialogues with China and in balancing the factions within his own office. The Chomsky/Said stricture avoids a reality, where idealism is forced to deal with corrosive difficulties. If Fanon had lived until the success of the Algerian Revolution, he would no doubt have been offered a ministerial position, and he would probably have accepted, and been immediately caught up in the internecine manoeuvres that claimed the original leadership of that revolution. Malraux became minister of culture, and cleaned up Paris, while becoming an apologist for de Gaulle

---

51. On gift paper designed by Barbara Kruger and distributed to its readers for Christmas 2007 by the *Guardian*.

and the progenitor of a French love affair with the Kennedys, particularly Jackie Kennedy, and the fake Camelot of that era. Bernard Kouchner, co-founder of Médecins Sans Frontières, accepted a ministerial appointment, this time under the Sarkozy government of France, but does a modicum of good in international development. Régis Debray became Mitterrand's foreign affairs adviser in the Elysée Palace. Gilberto Gil, veteran of the Brazilian Tropicália protest in 1968, became minister of culture in 2003. John Kenneth Galbraith, Romain Gary and Mexico's Carlos Fuentes became ambassadors (although Fuentes resigned in protest); Mario Vargas Llosa and Pablo Neruda both stood for president of their countries; Léopold Senghor actually became president of his. Can intellectuals like Dominique de Villepin never accomplish any good within the machine? Are all intellectuals who enter the machine from the academy, like Joseph Nye, corrupted irretrievably? Are all the people mentioned in this paragraph fakes and reduced to being the high priests of power? They made compromises for sure – but did they avoid being blind idealists, people who kept to the truth by keeping safe, not from persecution, but from contamination? Can an intellectual be hygienic?

Is it, in short, possible for an intellectual who preaches what good government should look like, to refuse trying to be part of good government? Is this a luxury too far? Or is this a position dearly bought by persecution and suffering and the entries on the balance sheet tally on both sides? The number of intellectuals who have suffered like Ngugi and Soyinka are a minority. What do the others put into their balance sheets? And, after all, someone like Abdolkarim Soroush experienced the vicissitudes of office and emerged a better intellectual and a more effective one.

Just as it is desirable to combine the work of those who are experienced and knowledgeable from their time on location with those who are knowledgeable about the mechanics that caused devastation to that location – such that both sending and receiving ends of bad policy can be deeply presented – so it is desirable to establish a dialectical relationship between criticism and engagement. This can be engagement with the spontaneous people's groups that Chomsky advocated – but at least that is a step outside the cloisters and the library – or engagement with power. But the Madrid workers of the Spanish Republic executed people too. In any case, power of any sort is not a static unidimensional event: it corrupts, but has its own capacity to be corrupted. The trick is not to avoid power. The trick is to enter it and leave before it changes you more than you can change it. The single term, the single year, or the hundred days of office might accomplish some good, and will bring to renewed criticism on the outside a forensic sense that would amplify what the Chomskys say.

This, of course, is naive. Who ever enters and leaves so cleanly and willingly? Yet it is a stricture less self-protective than that of Chomsky and Said. And it avoids, perhaps, the dangers of indulging the stricture of Sontag beyond a certain point. Sontag inhabited a theatre and risked the shelling and sniping. She suffered a lack of candles and baths. What is the place of the person who joins the defenders of Sarajevo and, when the opportunity presents itself, shoots without mercy the Serbian attackers? This is war and, provided there is neither killing in cold blood nor atrocity, can be made to accord with the ambivalent laws of war. But all those who have fought, and who re-enter liberal and critical lives, are reluctant to talk about what they did and whom they shot and how. Everyone carries the silent guilt of a thinking person who had a normative position and seeks to regain it from ground made more slippery precisely from what was accomplished on location. For such a person, who has seen and done perhaps too much, there is not the release from silence that Sontag accorded. There is only a deeper silence.

This is to say that, in approaching the world with the responsibility of people who think, there are untold weighted difficulties upon the responsibility of speech. There are weightier difficulties heaped upon the responsibility of action. For all these weights there are no easy answers. The way forward into light might often have to be through darkness. Ernesto Cardenal, the Nicaraguan Sandinista priest and fighter, and later minister of culture, gave sermons on just cause and mercy while suffering and fighting at the front. The intellectual world, if it wishes to have a part in the world of action, must find a way to accommodate all who make an effort within and without governments, within and without liberation or resistance forces, rather than not excoriate one and romanticise the other, while staying pure in a university. This, perhaps, is another form of doubling.

The progress of this book

Whatever path is undertaken, with whatever combination of symbiotic colleagues – the insider needs the outsider, vice versa, and each must understand the fusions made by the other – there is some need to avoid the tyranny of perfection in one's judgements of others. The closing words, cited earlier, of a book by Martha Nussbaum might be reiterated here: 'Abandoning the zeal for absolute perfection as inappropriate to the life of a finite being, abandoning the thirst for punishment and self-punishment that so frequently accompanies that zeal, the education I recommend looks with mercy at the ambivalent excellence and passion of a human life.'[52] To act in mercy in the wider world might first

---

52. Martha Nussbaum, *The Therapy of Desire: Theory and Practice in Hellenistic Ethics*, Princeton: Princeton University Press, 1996, p. 510.

require a merciful view of others who seek to do the same. When educating ourselves in mercy, however, what ground has this book covered?

1. The book began with a story from the Eritrean war of liberation. It sought to establish the problematic relationships among war, love and death. In this story, we were trying to outline a basic assumption behind this book: that nothing is unambivalent or easy, but there is much, often contradictory, material in human lives and thought that should be at least appreciated. The book then sets out to render an appreciation of such material, as expressed in different cultures that are often misunderstood or regarded as in opposition to our own.

2. The first part of the book began with a chapter that looked briefly at the imagination – what was often the fiction – that went into various contemporary nationalisms. It suggested that it was possible that the same ingredients could help construct a future internationalism. The chapter then took a first look at the Persian epic the *Shahnameh*, with its multicultural reference points addressed to just behaviour by great powers.

3. However, just behaviour, ethical behaviour, whether by states or individuals is not itself unambivalent. Chapter 2 looked at various versions of the ancient Greek play *Antigone* to illustrate some of the debate on ethical behaviour. It suggested that behaviour on behalf of justice could be irrational, seemingly mad, but that this madness could have a cool lucidity embedded within it.

4. So that Chapter 3, in speculating on the agenda of Osama bin Laden – someone normally demonised in the West but here undemonised, though not validated – looked at the cool, lucid preparations of the suicide bomber. Bin Laden's spiritual philosophy of Wahhabism is described in this chapter.

5. Chapter 4, however, looked at a forebear of Osama, the sultan Saladin, someone who was victorious against one great wave of crusaders but who showed such restraint and mercy that many of his enemies suspected him of being a Christian. This chapter began a discussion of mercy, looking also at Hindu and Buddhist literature.

6. In today's industrialised world, however, mercy in any of its forms is difficult and problematic. Curiously, as Chapter 5 discussed, fantasy literature and games not only create a sense of release from reality but recreate the sense of mercy both as it once was and as it could be. The *Shahnameh* is looked at again for its ecumenical message, how state restraint provides the world with a form of mercy, and how Persian literature in many respects established antecedents to what we now regard as Western-originated values and thought.

7. But, if mercy is possible, and can be established in ecumenical thought, what about the problem of evil – a concept also established in the literatures of the world? Looking again at electronic fantasy games, as well as literature, Chapter 6 proposed that the means to examine evil is in the manner in which it intersects with good, and uses the model of the intersection of crooked lines as a path to the recognition of the fusion of human traditions, values, senses of good and mercy, and of evil.

8. That concluded the first part of the book. The second part looked a little more deeply into some key issues. The first of these was to do with the vexed question of how those in public life, or who advise those in public life, might view the world. Can it only be via the self-interest of the state? And, if so, might not the state seek its interests through soft forms of power, rather than hard? Chapter 7 also commented on how the use of hard power, acting upon advice that sees the world unidimensionally, can be disastrous. In particular, the notion that hard power can be

applied against 'fundamentalist Islamic hordes' is the harbinger of a dangerous twenty-first century.

9. Even with soft power, the notion that a state's declared system of values should be exported because 'right' is highly problematic. Chapter 8 looked at some of the world's constitutions, and at the effort by Hans Kung to compose an ecumenical charter of world ethics. There is transactionable space in the constitutions of even the world's severest states, even in the case of Iran; and the world's most progressive constitution, one of pluralism, difference, intersections and fusions, is not that of the United States or Europe, but belongs to an African state.

10. Since it is Iran and Islam that are so often and so deeply misunderstood in the West, by both policy-makers and their advisers, Chapter 9 looked at some modern Islamic thinkers, in particular two from Iran. Their drawing from antiquity as well as modernity establishes a cosmopolitan fusion that is often under-appreciated.

11. Given the possibility of fusion, the book's last and present chapter asked what it is that we, as citizens, especially as thinking citizens, can do. And what we should ask our governments to do. But few of us are global public intellectuals or policy advisers. What about ordinary scholars and, indeed, ordinary citizens who try to think about the world? What about the rest of the very different manifestations of us?

An inverse ratio of compassion to thought: a digression by way of example

Uganda is just south of Sudan, and the border has seen some crossover of violence as the conflicts of one country merge into those of another. The Ugandan political scientist Mahmood Mamdani, now at Columbia University, is concerned about Sudan because of both a neighbourliness and a deep project of seeking to explicate the complexities of gross violence. His work on Rwanda, for instance, makes the apparently simple dichotomies of Hutus versus Tutsis into a properly problematised and considered tapestry of what is required to understand the terrors that occurred in that country.[53] It's not an easy read – in more ways than one. The situation was highly complex, and it becomes no longer possible to ascribe sympathy and compassion to only one side. Lately, he has been writing on perceptions of Islam, determined again to make simple dichotomies less simple; to make the world better by first making it complexly understood.[54] In a way Mamdani is becoming Columbia University's successor to Edward Said – only with Africa and Islam, as opposed to Palestine, as his canvas. On the international lecture circuit he has been painstakingly laying out an uncomfortable equation: that the greater the horror, outrage and compassion a situation generates, the less thought it generates. The immediate recourse is to identify a simple solution with, if at all possible, a single culprit, a bad enemy to be attacked in the name of outrage and compassion. This, he argues, is what has happened in the case of Darfur – a terrible situation in Africa for which, clearly, China is to blame.[55] And, in some senses, China is to blame – in that it could do a lot more to apply pressure on the Sudanese government in Khartoum to wind down its role in supporting one side in the violence, and its atrocities. The complexity of the situation in Darfur, however, is multifaceted. Here is what a point-by-point background briefing, prepared in early 2008,

---

53. Mahmood Mamdani, *When Victims Become Killers: Colonialism, Nativism, and Genocide in Rwanda*, Princeton NJ: Princeton University Press, 2001.

54. Mahmood Mamdani, *Good Muslim, Bad Muslim: America, the Cold War, and the Roots of Terror*, New York: Random House, 2004.

55. Mahmood Mamdani, 'The Politics of Naming: Genocide, Civil War, Insurgency', *London Review of Books*, 8 March 2007.

still generalised, placed before ministers but made available to the public, should look like.

1. Darfur was, before the advent of colonial boundaries, a Sultanate in its own right, although a loosely formed one.
2. In so far as it contains a large population which might be described as of Arabic descent, this Arab lineage is different to that which populates much of the ruling elite in Khartoum.
3. However, there has been much intermarriage and other historical cooperation in the region, so that strict delineations between 'Arab' and 'African' are difficult to sustain.
4. For centuries there has been tension between nomadic pastoralist communities and settled farmers. With the advent of global warming, competition, including violent competition for dwindling natural resources, has increased.
5. This has affected not only Darfur but the entire region, the Sahel as it crosses boundaries and, in this case, Darfur in so far as it shares a boundary with Chad. Many 'African' and 'Arab' groups are 'native' to both sides of the Chad–Darfur boundary.
6. In the early 1980s, in the civil war that gripped Chad, France took the side of one faction and those who were defeated escaped, fully armed, into Darfur. These helped form what today are loosely termed the Janjaweed militias that have wreaked violence upon other communities in Chad.
7. The great famine in the Horn and north-east of Africa in 1984 has usually been depicted as centred on Ethiopia. This saw the advent of Bob Geldof and the contemporary public mobilisation of mass compassion. The same famine, however, probably had even greater impact in Darfur. The need to protect and struggle for, fight for, scarce resources was a lesson amplified by that famine.

8. Continued French involvement in supporting the present government in Chad, and the repulse of a rebel invasion of the capital city in early 2008, has helped to sustain the division of communities that is now perceived on both sides of the border.

9. When the government of Sudan was faced with its own civil strife in Darfur, it further armed groups of Janjaweed to act as its surrogate force in the region, particularly as the government remained preoccupied with the separate armed rebellion to its south. That southern conflict was settled by the Comprehensive Peace Agreement (CPA) in the early 2000s, allowing the government to turn its attention more fully to Darfur. It supported the Janjaweed with military direction and air cover. Huge atrocities were committed.

10. China has been a friend of Sudan for decades. When China was itself a pariah state in international politics, Sudan was the fourth African country to grant China recognition. The Chinese have never forgotten this and would have fought for friendly relations with Sudan even if no oil was at stake.

11. However, there is oil at stake. China buys some two-thirds of Sudanese production, is Sudan's most important trading partner, and is thus seen as able to apply political pressure upon the Sudanese government. There has been no international urging upon the purchasers of the other third to apply similar pressure.

12. However, ever since 1955, Chinese foreign policy has been strongly geared towards a principle of non-intervention and non-interference in the affairs of other states. There have been two major breaches of this principle, once in Angola and once in Vietnam, but otherwise the Chinese have adhered to it and it has become a reliable factor in the equations of those who seek to deal with China.

13. From the early 2000s, the African Union (AU) has embarked upon a policy of non-indifference and it has, itself, sought to apply greater pressure upon the government of Sudan, proposing unilaterally the insertion of an AU peacekeeping force.

14. The Chinese, between 2005 to 2007, were slowly tutored by the AU to play a part in non-indifference. As a result, on top of significant developmental assistance the Chinese were already devoting to Sudan, including in Darfur, President Hu Jintao went personally to Sudan to remonstrate (somewhat politely) with the Sudanese president; dropped its objection to a hybrid AU/United Nations peacekeeping force; and contributed its own troops to this peacekeeping force.

15. The Chinese have applied no further pressure on the Sudanese government, but nor have the southern 'African' Sudanese rebels, now with their autonomous government headquartered in Juba; and nor have Sudanese liberals in the northern capital of Khartoum. These are concerned to preserve the CPA, both because of peace with the south and because, for the first time in modern Sudanese history, there are principles to do with citizen rights that have been accepted by an otherwise fiercely conservative government (enshrined in the CPA). Both southerners and liberals fear that a sanction-ridden and internationally excoriated government in Khartoum would wreak its revenge by reneging upon the CPA. Both groups have made their cases in Beijing.

16. In essence, over the question of Darfur, the Chinese have done as much as the United States and other Western powers. The latter have spoken more, so the force of rhetoric has lightened the weight of not acting further.

17. The highly organised lobby groups in the United States, fronted and funded by celebrities, are very sophisticated

and professional machines operating on multi-million-dollar budgets, much of which is spent on a campaign against China and none of which is spent on relief within Darfur itself.

18. Meanwhile, violence continues in Darfur. However, the level of violence has decreased since 2005–06. It has not disappeared and atrocities still occur. The major problem in 2008 was not so much violence as such, but the displacement caused by violence.

19. A significant feature of the continuing violence has been its origin in the 'African' rebel groups fighting the government of Sudan. These groups seem unable to unite, indeed they proliferate, so that comprehensive peace talks have been impossible; and their disunity also renders them incapable, unlike the southern rebels, of forming an alternative government in Darfur. These groups have launched several attacks against the peacekeeping troops, in an attempt to prevent any stability being brought to Darfur. The lack of stability allows the rebel groups to press their case upon the government in Khartoum. And the rebel groups fund their purchase of armaments by looting and selling the vast shipments of international aid being sent to help the displaced in Darfur.

20. The exposure of the peacekeeping troops is precisely the factor that prevents the keeping of peace in Darfur. Neither the Chinese nor the West have contributed helicopters to the peacekeeping operation. A hundred helicopters would be sufficient to provide aerial coverage of Darfur, provide protection to the peacekeepers, and identify exactly who was breaking the ceasefire, committing atrocity and acting in bad faith. The West, despite its rhetoric, is unlikely to provide such a number of helicopters, and the Chinese will

likely not do so unless part of a provision in which the West shares.

21. There is a sentiment, however, shared even in many African countries, that the West has a long-term political interest in embarrassing the Chinese, as it would like to succeed the Chinese in being the major purchaser of Sudanese oil, but would like to do so in partnership with a different and pro-Western Sudanese government.

22. This sentiment argues that a new 'Great Game' is being enacted in Darfur, as in many other parts of the globe. In all great capitals, those who suffer are calculated as ciphers and pawns; while the rhetoric of all metropolitan players is high on compassion and finds it very useful to propose simple solutions based on those who are singled out for blame. In this process, there is an international relations not of complexity, but of deliberate reductionisms in the most sophisticated manner. It is perhaps not unlike a Hollywood scenario where beautiful American heroes and heroines ride to the rescue of benighted and helpless black natives beset by an evil yellow peril.

I trust Mamdani will not mind my turning his analyses into my own crypto-civil service memorandum, with the addition both of some new material and of an arch final sentence and my own calculation that the helicopters should number one hundred (though no military personnel to whom I have put this number, calculated from the current peacekeeping map of Darfur, has raised any dissent). The point here is Mamdani's: great compassion requires also greater thought. The Chinese are certainly as calculating and cynical as anyone else, and can do more, but so could the entire international community if it acted in concert and with an understanding of the complexities

involved. For ordinary citizens, the injunction is itself simple
– though the process requires effort – and that is, after all,
the right life propounded by the Buddhist eightfold path is one
with interconnections. Right action does, after all, require right
thought. And it is not that much of an effort. To my horror,
after having spent years researching the different countries of
Africa, I discovered that almost everything I thought I knew
about Sudan could be uncovered by a half-hour trawl of different
Wikipedia entries, courtesy of Google and the electronic age.
If both 'Arab' Janjaweed and 'African' rebel groups coordinate
their military actions by mobile phones (and they do), we can also
press some buttons to help the deployment of our own thoughts.
This is the responsibility of even the most 'ordinary' citizen of
the West. If, in electronic games, even devils and demons are
complex creatures, so are Sudanese and Chinese.

The specialists in thought: the academy

Not everyone is, can be or should be a global public intellectual;
but scholars have, all the same, special responsibilities. This is
especially true of the academic discipline called 'International
Relations' (IR). As a specialist discipline it is very young. Its
formal beginning was at the end of World War I, when an eccen-
tric Welsh millionaire, David Davies, horrified by the slaughters
of that war, endowed the Woodrow Wilson Chair at Aberystwyth[56]
– named after the US president whose advocacy of transparent
diplomacy established a benchmark which subsequent political
generations have met by manipulations and economies, spins,
of the truth. From the outset, the new discipline found itself

---

56. He also championed an international peacekeeping force. See Brian Porter,
'David Davies and the Enforcement of Peace', in David Long and Peter Wilson, eds,
Thinkers of the Twenty Years' Crisis: Inter-War Idealism Reassessed, Oxford: Clarendon
Press, 1995.

torn between two strands: one (realism) argued that war was inevitable, was the hallmark of international politics, and study had better be given to its dominant role in the world; the other (idealism or utopianism) argued that peace was desirable, achievable, and the new discipline could be applied to the discovery of how to propagate it.[57] To this day, that tension remains in IR. It is a highly Western discipline in its self-organisation and maintenance of the competing 'paradigms' of its thought.[58] In the United States, the key schools that have developed are neorealism (state interest and hegemony not necessarily through naked force but in concert with institutional influences and economic capacity) and neoliberalism (which privileges international protocols, laws, institutions and shared norms as a path towards peace). In the United Kingdom there were three main schools: Realism and its cousin neorealism; a Pluralism, which was a direct descendant of Idealism and is closely linked to neoliberalism; and Structuralism, which began life as a neo-Marxist account of economic forces in the world. More recently, the influence of those three schools has been eroded by the rise of normative theory, drawn from continental philosophy and seeking to establish a moral and philosophically sound view of the world; and the so-called 'English School', which views and revisits all international relations in their historical contexts. There is much sympathy between the normative theorists and the English School; so, to a discernible extent, there is a shared sense of a single IR in contemporary Britain – with significant

57. The foundation work in the discipline, which also expressed this tension, came out in 1939. The latest edition is E.H. Carr, *The Twenty Years' Crisis: An Introduction to the Study of International Relations*, London: Palgrave Macmillan, 2001.

58. Borrowed, not entirely accurately from Thomas Kuhn, the use of the term 'paradigms' in IR was championed by Michael Banks and A.J.R. Groom. See William C. Olson and A.J.R. Groom, *International Relations Then and Now*, London: Routledge, 1992.

influence particularly in the East Coast universities of the United States, Scandinavia and Finland, and Australasia.

Chomsky, in his criticisms of the 'high priests of truth', had in mind those realists and neorealists who translated all world events in terms of whether they affected a US state interest, and then advised the government as to its use of military or other instruments to prosecute that interest; and simultaneously assured the public that the interest at stake was valuable and the path chosen to secure it was justified, if not actually just. He would have found it slightly more difficult to castigate the neoliberals, the idealists and the structuralists – being something of a fellow-traveller of the Structuralist school. He is in sympathy with the normative theorists but does not use their theories and methodologies. However, what requires our attention here is their insistence that they do dissect what is just from the merely justified, that they speak truth to power, that they constantly debate and refine methodologies to define what can be called 'truthful', and that all this work has philosophical underpinnings, from two key eras of thought: the Enlightenment period through to the advent of Napoleon; and the post-World War II refusal ever again to allow thought to fall into the hands of dictators, the determination to make it 'critical' and therefore 'emancipatory'. I am a fellow-traveller of this school, and it is a school perfectly pitched for those who wish to add thought to compassion, but it is a school wanting.

There are three main strands to this school. The first resides in a debate ostensibly drawn from Enlightenment philosophy. On the one hand it champions Kant's view of a 'cosmopolitan' overarching and universal justice, to which each individual – as an individual – is by right and by universal law drawn, and by which he or she is governed. On the other hand, it champions Hegel's view of a communitarian society, particularly his proposition of a civil society that operates as the key socialising and normative vehicle below the level of government, and to which government is obliged to give attention, and to whose normative values government is obliged to conform.[59] This is fine as far as it goes, except that Kant and Hegel were never mutually exclusive, overlap in key parts, and reflect two sides of the same coin. The second strand resides in the determination of the Frankfurt School after World War II, reflected in the work of Horkheimer and Adorno, never again to allow philosophy and art to fall into the service of dictators, as Nietzsche and Wagner had been used to serve Hitler's Third Reich. For Horkheimer and Adorno the concentration camps cast such a heavy shadow over philosophy that philosophy henceforth had no choice but to be 'critical'.[60] However, the contemporary rendition of 'critical philosophy' has become so refined and dense that its adherents and advocates no longer speak truth to power but debate the nature of truth among themselves. They emancipate nothing and no one but replicate the medieval Parisian debate on how many angels can stand on the head of a pin. The third strand is, to an extent, drawn from the French thinker Michel Foucault – in whose Parisian flat Edward Said confronted Sartre over Palestine. For Foucault, all knowledge is constructed by power.[61] To be emancipated, therefore, requires power to be reconstructed by knowledge. All power and all knowledge thus becomes 'discursive', constructed from discourse, so that 'truth' is either that which is most politically powerful or that which is most morally powerful, and the contest between the two is fought within discourse, versions of truth, and logics of truth.

---

59. E.g. Janna Thompson, *Justice and World Order: A Philosophical Enquiry*, London: Routledge, 1992.

60. Rolf Wiggershaus, *The Frankfurt School*, Cambridge: Polity Press, 1994.

61. See, *inter alia*, Michel Foucault, *Archaeology of Knowledge*, trans. A.M. Sheridan Smith, London and New York: Routledge, 2002.

The problem here is that, within IR, all discourse is illustrated by Western examples and Western logics. The discourses of Iran, for instance, do not feature in the scholarship of IR – nor those of China, Sudan, the Hindu scriptures, the Qur'an, the Wahhabists, the Sufis, or those expressed in Ngugi's Kikuyu language. In IR, most of the world, most of the international, is omitted from its international relations.

The preoccupation of all strands of IR is to decipher one international system, one international structure, one universal set of ethics, or one epistemologically self-contained test for what might be called 'truth'. Its school of Pluralism does not admit the plurality of logics; and the search for a universalism is conducted through European and American texts, written discourse from the West, and does not admit systems of intuition, spiritual insight and transcendence. IR, having emerged from the shards of World War I, in one way or another, seeks to make the world whole. Since an entire academic profession has now arisen upon the new academic discipline, it has an interest in maintaining and guarding through means of professional recognition and esteem the professing of wholeness, of universalism, of ascertainable rationality and its contention that these are the academic paving stones that may be laid along the path to peace. IR has never tried to do what Hans Kung, with his Parliament of Religions, tried to do. IR seeks to be universal in root and branch. Kung sought a canopy of green leaves that were the foliage of universal ethics, or ethics made to seem universal by their efforts to achieve commonality; but they grew from many different roots; it was a hybrid tree; it even had parasitical creepers; it was an Amazonian extravagance that Kung heroically sought to prune into place; but it provided shade and it breathed fresh air into an atmosphere otherwise singed by the smoke of conflict and dissension.

The new tasks of the specialists in thought

There are three tasks, but they begin with a fundamental admission: the 'Other' knows the metropole better than the metropole knows the 'Other'. In *The Clash of Civilizations*, Samuel Huntington cited a meagre number of non-Western sources. An Iranian academic reply, in the form of a single article, demonstrated such a command of Western thought in its own citations, set alongside Iranian sources, that the comparison was embarrassing.[62] But Iranian thought has its own difficulties – as epitomised in the work of Abdolkarim Soroush and Ali Shari'ati. What is the nature of the point of crossover between polyglot Western sources (Shari'ati), or a central Western methodology (Popper in Soroush), and the taking forward of an argument on non-Western grounds? What is the point of crossover between something with ascertainable rationality in Western terms and the leap into intuition and faith? What is the point of transcendence in thought, and how may this point be appreciated – if not fully and rationally analysed? This is the first task for thinkers in international relations.

Epiphany is not a rational or logical device in Western thought. It is a spiritual or poetic device. It is precisely as such a device that it manifests itself in other cultures: as *satori*, the blue flash of sudden enlightenment in Zen; as the whole purpose of the Buddhist *koan* or riddle – the sudden realisation of what the answer is reminiscent of being 'tripped' into enlightenment by something seemingly unrelated. It was what Rumi and Yunus Emre tried to describe in their poems. The point is that the poetic, often metaphoric, leap is, in many non-Western systems of thought, a logical point of transition and development in an

---

62. Kaveh L. Afrasiabi, 'The Contest of Civilizations and Interreligious Dialogue', *Iranian Journal of International Affairs*, vol. 11, no. 3, 1999.

argument. In so far as it is a logical step in the work of Soroush
and others, and is what was indicated by poets like Rumi, it is a
key device in certain sorts of Islamic thought more than others:
in Shia, Sufi and Ismaili (many of whom are followers of the
Aga Khan) thought more than Sunni. Certainly more than is
contained in the thought of Wahhab.

Fafique Keshavjee tells a poignant tale of a twentieth-century
Iranian Ismaili community, in which the young are given up to
Western education for the betterment of the village.

> Their conception of human nature was pre-modern, drawing
> on Graeco-Muslim thought as it had percolated through the
> Muslim world over the centuries. Their poetry was full of
> intense religious longing and love, far from the materiality of a
> frail and inconstant daily life.... Yet out of their love poetry and
> sometimes untamed exegeses of Qu'ranic tales, these peasants
> fashioned a coherent conceptual engine for the transformation
> of their communities into modernity ... [later contrasting the
> benefits brought by their educated offspring to] that of their
> great ancestors – the poets and theological rhetoricians who
> possessed the insight to grasp mystical poetry and understand
> multiple layers of meaning.[63]

Keshavjee called this a 'paradox of world-affirming mysticism'.
The task is therefore to establish a paradox whereby a modern
world-view can also affirm mysticism. The point of affirmation
is the point of crossover, where rationality and transcendence
meet. There is a pronounced case of this in the work of the
Egyptian thinker Muhammad Husayn Haykal, whose key works
appeared in the 1920s and 1930s. He was consumed at first by
the idea that a Middle Eastern revival in thought could help
even the West, before World War I in seeming spiritual and

---

63. Rafique Keshavjee, *Mysticism and the Plurality of Meaning: The Case of the
Ismailis of Rural Iran*, London: I.B. Tauris, 1998, pp. 8-9.

philosophical decline. This revival would be conducted hand
in hand with modernisation and scientific advances. As he grew
older and understood just how hard his project could be, he came
to a four-point system of a syncretic nature: he passionately
argued for the value of ancient Pharaonic accomplishment, and
its being an achievement of both material science and spiritual
determination; he saw how Islam could provide that same spiritual foundation and determination amidst modernity; however,
he repudiated positivism in science and modernity, insisting
upon their necessity but also their relative nature alongside
spiritual life and progress; and, finally, he anchored his spiritual
system not in Islam alone but in the work of the French 1927
Nobel prizewinner Henri Bergson, whose scientific writings
came to deal among other things with the value of intuition.[64]
This illustrates an interesting proposition: that, in looking to
understand the East, there are Western thinkers who can also
be used. The new tasks of the specialists in thought need not
begin in entirely alien territories.

And it is probably not incorrect to say that, for many Middle
Eastern thinkers schooled in the West, they too found themselves
'between "otherness" and one's own country'. This phrase was
coined to describe Albert Hourani, the Manchester-born Lebanese scholar who taught at Oxford for most of his career – while
being drawn irresistibly to fashioning an understanding of the
Middle East. If we follow Al-Sudairi's perceptive summary of
Hourani's work we discern many points of crossover with familiar Western concerns. Four intellectual stages are described by
Al-Sudairi (although the analogies to Western thought given
here are largely mine). First, Hourani was concerned with the

---

64. Israel Gershoni, 'The Return of the East: Muhammad Husayn Haykal's Recanta-
tion of Positivism', in Moshe Ma'oz and Ilan Pappe, eds, *Middle Eastern Politics and
Ideas: A History from Within*, London: I.B. Tauris, 1997.

nature and role of the Islamic city and its sense of jurisdiction, political organisation and public order. The link between ruler and marketplace is reminiscent of Aristotle's concern for the *polis* as both urban centre and political unit. Second, Hourani was concerned with what Max Weber called the 'patriciate', the elders and notables who led urban society. Third, he was concerned with explicating the dynamism of the Ottoman Empire, especially at the level of urban guilds and street-level and mosque-level organisation. This is not unlike the interests of people such as the French thinker Henri Lefebvre, and his idea of urban life as dynamic and rhythmic. Fourth, he was concerned with Arab nationalism, showing how its origins were to a large extent established in the crossover between Christian secularists and Muslim modernists – not to mention in the equation the role of 'hard men'.[65] This equation is not unlike a tripartite view of the Iranian Revolution, with its cast of Western-educated and influenced intellectuals like Shari'ati; secular idealists, reformers and communists; and the clerical faction led by the ayatollahs who became the ascendant 'hard men'. In such sociologies, with their varied intellectual influences, there are discursive histories which facilitate the entry-point of Western scholars. The new task is not as hard as it first looks.

The second and third tasks may be expressed in summary form. Those working in international relations need to learn from their theological cousins who work in exegesis. The tools used in Biblical studies are not the same as those used in Quranic studies, but the basic aim of explicating key passages against an assumed or accepted holistic backdrop – the Bible or Quran as coherent, consistent and authoritative text (in that order) – means that the second task is the explication and pragmatic

65. Abdulaziz A. Al-Sudairi, *A Vision of the Middle East: An Intellectual Biography of Albert Hourani*, London: I.B. Tauris, 1999.

interpretation of holy writ. Tariq Ramadan is the best such pragmatic interpreter working in the West; it is a pity he has not been taken up more by scholars of international relations.

The work of Quranic exegesis is complicated by the parallel existence of sharia law. The problem with sharia is that, whereas once it was a dynamic body of evolving jurisprudence, it has now stultified and ossified – a process resulting from the fall of the Ottoman Empire and the eclipse of Islam, until very recently, as a world power simultaneously grappling with modernity. Lawrence of Arabia spent much time blowing up bridges and railway lines constructed by the Ottomans, then would watch in amazement at the speed of their reconstruction. There was much modernising capacity at work there. The redevelopment of the Islamic world is in everybody's interests. The third task is jurisprudential, and this has two subcategories: the first is to work to achieve a new dynamism in debate on sharia, and this might be a process ignited by work on constitutions that deal with modernity not by way of exceptional clauses, but as blended instruments within Islamic constitutional provision. The second subcategory is an application of doctrines of precedent and customary law, common in English law, to those jurisdictions where forms of authoritarian rule are sanctioned or excused, as has happened in several African states, by reference to 'traditional' and ancestral modes of behaviour. For want of another term, a 'jural ethnology' can help determine how much of such claims are fabrications, simplifications, or opportunisms. What is left requires to be taken seriously within international relations.

Minimalist stepping forward: citizens

The case example of Darfur, above, suggests that citizens need to avoid cheap assumptions about identity and the easy step

towards demonisation of one side and the elevation, purification
and gift-wrapping into victimhood of the other.

There are non-painful ways to begin learning about different
forms of Islam; a basic responsibility to demand transparency
before movements to war.

In the case of war in Iraq, no matter how tyrannical Saddam
Hussein was – and he was – he had no weapons of mass destruction, no conspiratorial links with al-Qaeda, and was no threat
to the West; before sanctions bit into Iraq, he had developed,
bloodily, a unified, largely peaceful secular state, elevated
the education and status of women, and provided nationwide
electricity, water, health care and schooling. He had been a
welcome proxy of the West in waging war against the Iran of
the ayatollahs and, even though mocked for his vainglory in
nearby countries such as Syria, held the admiration of much of
the Third World for his domestic accomplishments. The ease
of his demonisation – from successful, even sometimes internationally 'helpful' tyrant, to pariah, war-mongering threat to
the Western world, the Hitlerian figure of the early twenty-first
century – was accomplished only because citizens did not seek
information themselves and require their governments to square
this public information with their official constructions of strategic desirability. As it is, the mess created and what passes as a
government in Iraq can scarcely be more strategically desirable
than what was there before.

The idea is to think, and not be either led or simply *moved*
by images of distress. War and emotion require thought and
openness. And even Bob Geldof learned to think – even if not
always successfully. But the Geldof of 2005, trying to influence
the G8 summit, was very different to the Geldof of 1984. Then, an
angry young man was affronted by famine in the Horn of Africa
and moved people. In 2005, affronted by the world's structured

economic inequalities, he tried to move people and to argue with governments in the language of governments. Perhaps when Nelson Mandela, a great Russian fur hat on his head, wrapped his arm around Geldof in a freezing Trafalgar Square in 2005, he was thinking about how far the wild young man had come – and how much further he had yet to go. Imperfect, vain, contradictory and sometimes brazenly wrong, he is still an example for the commodified and easy world of how to *try*. After all, Mandela was trying too. Dressed top to toe in black that day, he was as much fashion icon as Geldof. He was working hard at being double – old and young, wise and 'with it' – and urging people to keep thinking as they kept demanding.

Minimalist stepping forward: governments

The international contests of the future should be by way of soft power. This is something which, finally, can work both ways and allow genuine interpenetrations of cultures and forms of political consciousness. From the Middle East comes Al Jazeera, and, from Iran, Press TV – both waging network wars for audience share and global impact. Into Iran under the ayatollahs, young people smuggled CDs by Madonna; in the Western CD shops, 'World Music' is sufficient of a vogue to merit large shelf space; and 'World Music' is influenced in turn by Western trends. Rap in Arabic, or in African languages, is more successful anyway than rap in French. 'Culture wars' are less bloody at least than wars with desert tanks and missiles.

But there is one very big thing that governments in Europe can do, and even that is a minimalist contribution to something bigger: admit Turkey into the European Union. There was great misgiving in the West when a moderate Islamic party won the Turkish elections. That party has been at pains to point out that it is simply the equivalent of a Western European Christian Democrat party – and this is probably true. However, its Islamic credentials have allowed it, very boldly, to establish a team of reformist scholars to rewrite sharia, to make it more fitting to the twenty-first century, to allow sharia to become something upon which Turkey can pivot, looking both East and West. In fact, what is already loosely dubbed the 'Ankara School' is being advised by experts on how Christianity evolved and mutated over the years, with particular attention to reasoning from first principles – what Islam itself calls *ijtihad* – to reconstitute Islamic principles according to changed times, environments, technologies, and more complex interactions. In some ways, it is the most important and exciting thing happening in Europe,[66] in a country that once hosted the capital of the Western world – the Roman Empire, Constantinople, Byzantium – and that produced that most cosmopolitan of men, Talat Sait Halman. What happens in Turkey with this project, which will take some years to 'bed in' after its completion, will help transform Sunni Islam around the world. And it will allow greater closeness with Turkey's other main Sufi Islamic strand, and its own links with Shia.

The lessons of the intellectuals

Earlier in this chapter we looked at the work of some well-known global public intellectuals. Although Ngugi wrote primarily on Kenya and for Kenyans, Soyinka on Nigeria and Africa, and Chomsky on the formation of US foreign policy, each sought to contextualise his concerns with a sense of transnational commonalities. No citizen of any country wants, for instance, to die senselessly. These concerns revolved around four key principles

66. This is also the view of Martin Kettle, 'The Most Interesting Country in Europe', *Guardian*, 27 February 2008.

which formed a common, transnational quest: (1) transparency; (2) lack of arbitrariness; (3) accountability; and (4) redress. To which could be added a fifth: whatever causes grief is something to be investigated compassionately. The principled person who dies in jail is not just the victim of an arbitrary, non-transparent, unaccountable and non-recompensing government, but also someone who suffered – perhaps terribly. Compassion extends throughout the context of the works of all these writers.

Few public intellectuals have achieved a complete work, but progress is evident in the writings of those discussed here:

- One's expression determines one's identity (Ngugi).
- One's god determines one's sense of good (Ramadan).
- One's restless questioning determines one's citizenship of a moral universe (Chomsky).
- One's becoming double allows the moral universe its natural, contemporary home in the world of human beings (Said).

If we can all, individually, seek to progress through these stages, then perhaps we shall become less flawed in our membership not only of a moral universe, but simply of a sad, almost failed species.

The huge effort towards lucidity amidst cool fury, and towards defeat (another story ends it)

The same lucidity and cool fury drive forward both the meticulous suicide bomber and the forensic investigations of Chomsky. The common denominator is not a madness or fanaticism. It takes a lot of thought to die – and kill. It takes a lot of thought to spend a lifetime in deeply researched denunciation. It is a case of adopting and using that same lucid cool fury on behalf of a world of commonalities, integrations and doublings. I am deeply suspicious of overuse of the term 'universalism'. It is this that, often in the name of justice, presupposes a single approach to it. I am suggesting an exploration of the many crooked paths that, eventually, lead us maze-like to a common point. I am not suggesting that we begin with a predrawn map, a preformed plan.

I am suggesting the need for, if not a doubling in our attempts to view and live the world, a far greater and more open-mindedly informed empathy towards and within the world. In the end, we really shouldn't have been whisking the Falashas off to a strange new life in Israel. We should have been working with them to restore what had been theirs in the land of their home.

The great socio-anthropologist and philosopher of religion Mircea Eliade wrote much on the 'eternal return' as a common emblem in almost all religions. Spring always comes again after winter. The entire saga of Sir Gawain and the Green Knight has the hero returning safely – if chastened by a high winter of his shortcomings – to a new spring in Camelot. There, out of solidarity with Gawain's undertaking forever to wear a green sash as a public symbol of his failures, all the knights undertake to wear a similar sash. Perhaps it was not so much solidarity as empathy. 'There but for the Grace of God' was a thought that would have passed through many of their heads, if not their hearts. The problem about the eternal return is that we do not always learn from our mistakes but commit them anew in moderated forms. The minimalist suggestion here is to be conscious of how we moderate ourselves as we journey into the future.

And, besides, humanity is not that committed to the universal return. The death and resurrection of Jesus are not always accepted as the symbolic moment of spring. Legends abound of how he survived the cross, went on to marry Mary Magdalene, while his 'feet, in ancient times, walk[ed] upon England's mountains green'. And even the death of Judas Iscariot, the betrayer of Jesus and the perpetrator of winter's last stand, may be moderated. The New Zealand novelist C.K. Stead has written the most successful of the current rash of novels and other works that depict the longevity of Judas.[67]

The maximalist suggestion of this book is to be like Alexander – who, after all, did not die at a young age in the midst of his conquests, did he? In Islamic legend he went on to become a very wise and scientific king, fully immersed not only in experiments with submarines, but in the learning that surrounded him in the lands he had conquered. Wearing his Macedonian helmet, with the twin cheek guards jutting forwards like horns, he might have looked like a devil on horseback. He was called Great because he went forth to conquer – then gave himself up to be conquered by new ideas and cultures, finally achieving a location within them where he helped form the debates that took those cultures forward.

Coolly – for me, in a frenzy of anticipation, because there is so much to learn – we need to ride out and not be afraid of defeat. Sometimes there is much mercy to be gleaned when we fuse our destinies with others.

---

67. C.K. Stead, *My Name was Judas*, London: Vintage, 2006.

Afterword

Brave new world,
with such backwardness in it

When Barack Obama was elected president of the United States, he promised much internationally. The world of instant communication and instant image allowed an instant charisma to flood from the campaign trail to the poorest slums of the Middle East, South Asia and every other part of the globe. A year later, at the beginning of December 2009, after three months of agonised consultation, procrastination and sheer indecisiveness, he announced reinforcements of 30,000 troops for the counter-insurgency effort in Afghanistan. The long wait was due in part to differences of opinion within even the US armed forces. Counter-insurgency is a doctrine being slowly and, for those on the receiving end, painfully rewritten. It is edging towards an amalgamation of soft power – hearts and minds – with overwhelming hard power in reserve. The hard power never goes away. It just gets backgrounded. Be softly conquered or die. The strategic debate within the emerging new doctrine is over precisely when soft gives way to hard and when hard withdraws for soft. In any case, hearts and minds usually means hearts and minds that feel and think the way a US heart and mind would feel and think. There's more sympathy for the hard lives of others but, as yet, no real progress towards *empathy*, the first real step towards understanding and proper negotiation – negotiating from equal *philosophical* foundations, if not economic, military and political ones. But this is, perhaps, the most pernicious form of interim mercy. The drone will not strike your wedding party today. It will strike tomorrow.

Obama set out to do too much. The sheer scale of US debt and the sheer reaction that confronted his health-care proposals were underestimated by his advisers. Foreign policy became the nice-to-have extra, and a number of 'putting out the message' initiatives were undertaken – precisely to hold the line until the president was able to think and act coherently and persistently. The 2009 Cairo speech, in which he held out the olive branch to Islam; the slightly less confrontational approach to Iran (which may yet melt away); the more obviously accommodating approach to China as an emerging equal; and the late scramble to appear engaged with climate change at the Copenhagen summit, were all holding-the-line measures throughout his first year. But, in the early months of 2010, Dubai's economic miracle is being unveiled as yet another naked emperor – with consequences for the liberal-economic globe; the credit crunch and Western recession are not yet over; the approach to Islam is being condensed into a geostrategic concern for Afghanistan and, belatedly, Pakistan; the approach to Tehran is oscillating between fresh diplomatic initiatives and updates to the 'bomb the reactors' plan; China is refusing to revalue its currency and is quietly happy with and unimpressed by the new US president. Obama has not created any real purchase over Israel and its settler colonisation of the West Bank; he has had to extend the slow-motion timetable for closing Guantánamo Bay, and placate the national desire for vengeance by allowing the trials of detainees in New York City; and the divisions in his own military are, in the case of Afghanistan – for now at least – allowing the reassertiveness of the hawks.

In a very real way, the complexities of US foreign policy and those of defence policy mean that no new approach is possible without decisive leadership that creates a new philosophical doctrine. That would have to be a doctrine of *un*-superiority; not *less* superiority since, for many years to come, the US will remain superior militarily and economically to anyone else – even if problematically so. It would have to be a doctrine where superiority does not assert itself, is not taken as the 'given', the starting point of all formulations of foreign and defence policies. Very often, the defence of US 'interests' has nothing to do with national interests as such, and everything to do with international superiority being not just maintained, but asserted. But, in that case, there is no possibility of an equal world, or even a plausible pretence of one. In that sense, the emergence of China is welcome, in that it has the capacity to dilute unchallenged US hegemony – but it is also most unwelcome in case it creates, yet again, a bipolar world around whose poles all must cluster as opponents rather than empathetic friends. My first point is that the quest for equality becomes, in the long run, a precondition of successful empathy, and empathy is the precondition for imagining and beginning to understand another's philosophy.

As for that Other's philosophy in Afghanistan, the US must first determine which part of its quarrelling military should seek to understand its declared enemy. Should it be General McChrystal's Brussels-based NATO command, or General Petraeus's Kabul-based US command, or whoever is in charge of Central Command – in the geostrategic divisions of the world that the Pentagon has constructed. None of these commands has ever seriously studied how and why the Soviet war in Afghanistan failed; and none is well equipped with Pashtun-language capacity. And, as for the civilian foreign policy establishment headquartered in the State Department, no one seems to have taken seriously the commonplace discourse in Arabian diplomatic circles: that such al-Qaeda as exists deliberately lured the US into Afghanistan, precisely to mire it in the same conflict the Soviets could not win, have it make the same mistakes the Soviets made, and retire hurt and diminished as the Soviets did. In the long cycle of Islamic assertiveness envisaged by the authors of this counter-doctrine – counter to that of US superiority – a diminished US is the precondition to a wider and more successful international Islamic renaissance. To that extent, no one in al-Qaeda wanted the US in Iraq, although they made the Western presence there as problematic as possible. In asymmetric warfare, the 'weaker' party can often fight more strongly on a number of fronts. But it is very happy with Obama's 30,000 troop surge in Afghanistan. It is in Afghanistan that al-Qaeda wants the US to be, with the snowballing collapse of neighbouring Pakistan – a US ally and nuclear power. It is convinced the US will not win. And, if Pakistan's transformation can destabilise India, then an entire constellation of Western interests would suddenly be imperilled. The Arabian imagination of what is going on may have fanciful elements and assumptions, but it shows how the US game of macro-strategy – based on state interests and alliances with other states – can be played in reverse.

What we see at the beginning of 2010 is the contest of two doctrines, both of which are hegemonic in their aspirations. It seemed appropriate therefore to rehearse once again the arguments of this book, and to make a statement as to how they relate to an Obama era which, regretfully for those who believed mere charisma would be transformational, will fail to make the world

outside the US a better place. It will fail because Washington
is not grappling with the prospect of genuine global equality, has no talent for empathy, and has no ambition to engage
philosophically. Those who have advocated soft power always
had it as a desirable alternative to, but not substitute for, hard
power. The doctrine emerging in the Obama era is where soft
power becomes not an alternative, but an instrument of hard
power. The idealistic young black man may yet wreak havoc
upon the world.

This book has made a point of proposing US soft power not
as a virtue *in itself* – and not as the reverse decor of drones and
surges – but as a means of engagement with the soft power of
others. Second, it has proposed that sustained interim mercies
need to be accelerated until philosophical foundations emerge for
a genuine global mercy towards the immiserated and deprived.
Whether it will be able to do anything for the inconsolable
– those who have lost everything because of the application of
power and misrule – is another question.

It is not, however, as if Washington were the only capital
city that needs to change itself. There, the avenues spinning off
Dupont Circle are lined with think-tanks. This is the epicentre
for Chomsky's mandarins of truth. Commissioned research from
State or Defense are best fulfilled by variations of what State and
Defense want to hear; want to apply; want to discard; want to
rank from ridiculous, to untenable, to problematic, to desirable,
to necessary, to sustainable. Philosophy makes it at least to the
realms of the untenable and problematic. This is better than
the Party-dominated think-tanks of Beijing. There, it is not just
research income that depends on providing product sympathetic
to the ambitions of the paymasters; entire careers and livelihoods
depend on it. Individual researchers find it necessary to be Party
members, and Party discipline in China is still such that dissent

is difficult, and even nuanced amelioration of a Party policy is fraught with dangers. No one gets sent to the countryside for re-education any more, but job security, promotion and the ability to travel (in chaperoned groups) for 'research' depend upon good intellectual behaviour. Each great capital has a variation of this kind of intellectual command-economy. Some are sites of greater sophistication, where rarefied forms of dissent are incorporated into rhetoric, precisely to depict the state as sophisticated, worldly and philosophical. Paris is the past master of this. But no philosopher – no matter how many state funerals and interment in the Panthéon of learned (mostly) men – has changed the modern state in France. The bold young thinkers become not so much the mandarins of truth, but dandies of dissent who dance upon the kerbstones of the Quai d'Orsay.

But in my book I proposed a number of questions, a number of scenarios, about the extent to which those who think empathetically about the world should – could – engage with the structures and systems of power. And the hundred days of power, and out, remains an attractive – if knowingly glib – aspiration. For the book is about the need for engagement, and that means forms of engagement within, as well as without, the state. The state is not wished away on behalf of the globe. So the book, with all its efforts at elegant flourish, proposes some messy and murky avenues. Susan Sontag is dead now, but if she had staged Beckett in Kigali at the time of the Rwandan genocide, or in Beijing at the time of the Tienanmen Square killings, she would have had as much chance to stop the killings as her staging Beckett in Sarajevo. A play about the absurd, staged amidst the absurdity of war, in her own formulation, gave Sontag the right to speak *afterwards*. In what ways do people achieve a right to speak *before* wars can begin? And, here, the long list of exclusion clauses advanced by intellectual classes the world over – clauses that speak of impurities and contaminations – must be examined. They are lists that caution against the possibility of becoming Chomsky's mandarins. They are lists for people who, like Sontag did after Sarajevo, need their hot baths to feel clean. I think my book has tried to propose a problematic question: who are we who are clean when the world is full of mud and blood? Valiantly and cleanly protesting may not be all there is. So I proposed the (problematic) possibility of becoming, preferably briefly, the mandarin who is *not* transformed into an intellectual monster within a ravening machine. But my hesitations are such that I retreat behind the need for brevity. There is no clear answer here. There are questions and messy possibilities.

December 2009 saw both the Copenhagen conference on climate change and Obama's acceptance of the Nobel Peace Prize in nearby Oslo. Obama behaved contritely, saying he had not deserved the prize as much as his more accomplished predecessors, but he also lectured his audience at the ceremony on just war – using historical arguments and, to an extent, referencing philosophical ones. It was not a speech for prime-time television back home or, indeed, anywhere else. It was, however, still a political speech in that he called the US and Western war in Afghanistan just. It was just war that justified his troop surge of 30,000. The reference to justice as a means of justification is of interest. The Obama argument made a direct parallel between al-Qaeda and Hitler. This is hardly a justifiable parallel, given the very different ambitions and ideologies involved, and the very different organisational templates of an amorphous, single-leader-free al-Qaeda, on the one hand, and a charismatic leader with a formal, regimented, militaristic and genocidal machine, on the other. The Obama argument also said that the non-violent philosophies and practices of Gandhi and Martin Luther King could not be used to halt al-Qaeda, just as they could not have halted Hitler. But no one has proposed they could have in either case. Both were concerned also with internal liberations, and not with external threats. Obama also briefly mentioned the limits of reason. These limits were evidence of the imperfections of mankind. This, however, is the core message of my book: there are not so much limits to reason but limits to our readiness to accommodate and engage with multiple reasons, multiple forms and systems of reasoning. And, as a simple counter-example to the ones used by Obama, there once was a president of Zambia, Kenneth Kaunda, who did try – largely successfully in terms of the security of his nation – to use Gandhi's philosophy of non-violent resistance in the face of military and economic destabilisation emanating from apartheid South Africa.

In Kaunda's formulation of the world, his case materials were drawn from Gandhi's philosophy, British social democracy and visions of a welfare state, Christian inclusiveness, and a some- what selective history of African communalism. Using these philosophical means, he united between seventy and eighty tribal groups, speaking seventy to eighty separate languages, into a single nation. It was not as seamless as a single sentence suggests, and he made huge mistakes; but the selective use of philosophical and historical examples can be used to build some- thing, or to justify something which does not necessarily build anything. There is nothing being built in Afghanistan except the avoidance of defeat for the US; the prevention of victory by the Taliban and al-Qaeda; and the maintenance of a certain view of geostrategy that would be better served by a wholesale concentration on Pakistan – including its relationship with Kashmir – and the organisational capacities within Pakistan for international 'terror', which simply do not exist in Afghanistan. History, someone might one day point out to Obama, indicts those who choose the wrong location for history's struggle.

And philosophers might want to say that a just war requires just cause beyond one superpower's sense of pride and self-interest. For finally, as noted above, if one is to believe the diplomatic gossip in Arab capitals, al-Qaeda deliberately lured the US into Afghanistan to challenge and reduce the assumption of American hegemony in all circumstances. In this scenario, the young American president fights to sustain the global rights that come with hegemony. He cannot cut his losses and retire from the fray – and al-Qaeda is very happy. Its own sense of historical struggle is served as long as the US stays in Afghanistan. In laying this trap, al-Qaeda would seem to have understood American thought – and exploited its predilections – much more than the US has ever understood, or wishes to understand, al-Qaeda. Likening it to Hitler postpones any further interrogation of what it is the US has chosen to fight.

How, then, do my real or metaphorical hundred days in positions of power and influence do anything about discourse that appears learned and considered, but that is learned and reductionist? Precisely because there was considerable debate within the US military itself, and within other quarters of the US administration, there is evidence of 'doves' who need strengthening. The way forward, however, is across a broad front. That means the coexistence and, I feel, the *cooperation* of the archetypes I personified in my last chapter. The aloof and achingly, restrictively pure, stance of Susan Sontag – but shorn of its condescension; the forensic investigations of Noam Chomsky – but less judgemental of all mandarins; the narrow exemplariness of Ngugi wa Thiong'o, insisting on the peculiar expression of a people – but widened to all peoples; and the empathetic self-personification of as many identities as one person has capacity for – as in the case of Edward Said. The fusions of Ali Shari'ati are also required. And even the mandarins like Joseph Nye are required, if only to ensure it is harder for those like Robert Kaplan. Each has a role to play, if each also knows that even the greatest effort to widen one's moral and empathetic scope can only be partial. Oneself as another is one particle that seeks to identify with another particle. And each particle is in danger of getting it wrong. The stand-offish and uncontaminated critic warns of the road ahead, but does not carve out that road.

For all President Obama's mistakes in Afghanistan, there are still signs that his might become a post-imperial presidency, in that the US might pull back a little of its interventionist frontiers and allow other voices to be heard – at least out of politeness. Some suggestion of that emerged from the badly negotiated (on all sides) and slightly theatrical climate-change talks in Copenhagen. In December 2009, at a very late moment, Obama arrived in a snowstorm and returned to the United States in another. The overall talks were a failure and, in some ways, a fiasco. But Obama went straight to a grouping of what he had identified as 'key players', and negotiated a fig-leaf accord with China, India, Brazil and South Africa. This was the US in concert with the key rising players in the G20 – and it would seem as if the G20 will play a major role across a range of issues in the years ahead. But what the US must accept in such proto-alliance as emerged in Copenhagen is the fact that China will one day be a rival; India has major problems with Pakistan and, as noted above, the Pakistani problems could well seep, if not sweep, into India; Brazil, on climate change issues at least, is deforesting faster than its will to stop it, and speaks for no one else in South America; and South Africa cannot be regarded as the sole representative of forty-eight sub-Saharan African countries. There was no space in Obama's talks for Russia, Saudi Arabia and Iran – and there will be none when it comes to other issues. And, even if there were such space, the US would seek to use it as an entry-point for its own influence and leadership. The world of equality will not be a creation of the United States of America.

Obama's will still be a neo-imperialist presidency. No great power has ever rescinded a broad swathe of its perceived interests in a single four-year term. The time to judge might be at the end of his second term, if indeed he is accorded a second term by a most conservative people. Even then, eight years is a short time in which to re-engineer a position that took decades to develop. And, even if it waits until then, the Nobel Prize was certainly far too early, just as the history and philosophy of the acceptance speech were far too rudimentary. There is an end of certainty, but the attractions of certainty will be a powerful nostalgia in a backwards-looking international relations.

Pimlico, London
January 2010

Bibliographical essay
and acknowledgements

I have tried to write this book in an unusual style. In itself it has tried to exemplify the point that there are many ways to think and express thought. There are, however, many areas where I am not expert, but have written with the enthusiasm of an amateur. Neither of these aspects of my work should disguise the fact that I have attempted, over many years, to read as deeply and widely as possible, and to think about what I read. Some of the results of reading and thought have been published in scholarly journals and collections and I indicate some of these below, as well as some of the key works that have animated one of the major projects of my academic career.

One book that I did not have as I wrote, but which reached me afterwards and which I wish very much had appeared earlier, was Talat Halman's *Rapture and Revolution: Essays on Turkish Literature*.[1] The richness of his insights into Sufi and other mysticisms in the history of Turkish literature made this a very

---

1. Syracuse: Syracuse University Press, 2007.

enjoyable book for me. There is more to Sufi expressionism than what a New Age preoccupation with Rumi can allow. Commodified Rumi, greetings-card Rumi, Rumi-lite all make of him what fortune cookies make of Confucius. The work that helped me avoid that was Franklin D. Lewis's *Rumi Past and Present, East and West: The Life, Teachings and Poetry of Jalal al-Din Rumi*.[2] I am very grateful to Talat Halman and Ali Rezania for making gifts of these two books to me. Throughout my work I cite works of Sufi and Persian poets and thinkers published in the I.B. Tauris list. I am grateful to Lester Crook and Iradj Bagherzade for allowing me, quite shamelessly, to ransack their catalogue.

Any expert reader of my book will have no trouble discerning that my readings of Islam remain inflected by Sufi, Ismaili and, to an extent, Shia writings. It didn't begin like that and, although I acknowledge his influence in the body of this book, I wish to reiterate how much Altaf Gauhar helped me as a very young man in the 1970s. His work is out of print and he himself was a controversial figure both in his Pakistan homeland and in London where he settled. Nevertheless he was extremely patient with an overly naive young man and presented me with the translations he had accomplished while Ali Bhutto's prisoner in Pakistan. His *Translations from the Quran*[3] paint an extremely humanistic Islam.

As a schoolboy I had been (an extremely bad) Classics scholar, and it was the later appreciation of how much the preservation of Greek philosophy owed to the Islamic thinkers who lived in a sort of 'parallel universe' to Europe's 'Dark Ages' that gave me a new appreciation of Alexander the Great and the meaning of his early multiculturalism. This should not have been a

2. Oxford: Oneworld, 2000.
3. London: Islamic Information Services, 1977.

surprise. The foundation work, Tarn and Griffith's *Hellenistic Civilisation*,[4] painted a hugely cosmopolitan picture, but like all schoolboys and undergraduates I never read it deeply enough; and its concluding outlook was that Hellenism paved the way not for a cosmopolitan Islam but for Christianity. That helped to achieve the somewhat lazy recourse Western speakers have to a 'seamless' historical legacy – Greek and Judeo-Christian – but it eventually occurred to me that it could have easily paved the way for a cosmopolitan Islam that, if it had survived and prospered as cosmopolitan and inclusive, might have meant a very different modern world history. I confess that some of my work in this book is probably anchored in such a 'what if?', and in a 'why not?'

The gifts of books to me over recent years by Hassan Moradi reawoke this question. In particular, he gave me a splendid richly illustrated edition of Ferdowsi's *Shahnemeh: The Epic of the Kings*.[5] It is clear from my constant references to it that I was beguiled both by the beauty of its literature and by its message of cosmopolitan tolerance. All toleration was based on understanding. The disquisition on the world's religions to the Roman Caesar bespeaks a cosmopolitan understanding and toleration which touched me deeply.

Such understanding as I have of Hindu and Tibetan thought I confess I owe, originally, to their religious artistic expressions, and to popular literature. For systems of the spirit, as opposed to the 'Word', that might seem appropriate, but my approach was quite vulgar. I have absolutely no entry point to the Upanishads, for instance, without being able to relate the teachings to the spiritual folk stories of the Mahabharata, where the wicked wanderings and sins of Arjuna and his brothers give a human

4. London: Edward Arnold, 1927.
5. Tehran: Yassavoli, 2001.

expression to what the higher teachings mean. Even there, the stories are so extensive and repetitive that I confess I spent much time trying to enter them via Indian comics on stranded stopovers in what was then still Bombay, and in atrocious early Bollywood depictions. It was Peter Brook's theatre production of the Mahabharata, as filmed for Channel 4 television, that proved a turning point. It may be that I watched it while suffering from fever, but I thought it was a profound rendition. Brook's account of how he made it, in his *The Shifting Point: Theatre, Film, Opera 1946–1987*[6] offers, in addition, some insights into his own nuanced readings of Hindu doctrine. Even so, I confess I am not very good at depictions of Hindu thought. What I have done is to have bounced my own incomplete ideas off the better-formed ones in Ruth Cecily Katz's *Arjuna in the Mahabharata: Where Krishna Is, There Is Victory*.[7] I confess also that my appreciation of Tibetan religious thought is limited. The figurines and other religious art from Tibet are wonderful, but I have been privy to a little of the below-surface diplomatic transactions between the Dalai Lama and Beijing, and suspect very much that the Lama's acolytes express Tibetan teachings much as the sudden admirers of Rumi – idealistic and fluffy. I have nothing by way of antidote. I confess this is an area where I must apply myself more greatly.

Similarly, my study of Chinese and other oriental thought has a vexed history. Everything began by way of reaction against my upbringing. I wanted to reject everything – certainly in the way it had been taught me. I wanted, like all immigrant children, to be 'modern' and to 'fit in'. It was the Communism of Mao's China, particularly as rendered by Zhou Enlai's foreign policy, that eventually led me to 'reverse-engineer' my Chinese roots. It

6. New York: Theatre Communications, 1987.
7. Columbia: University of South Carolina Press, 1989.

really took until just over a dozen years ago for some last pennies to drop. Kuo-kang Shao's *Zhou Enlai and the Foundations of Chinese Foreign Policy*,[8] especially the early passages where he traces Zhou's influences back to Gu Yanwu (1613–82) and Wang Fuzhi (1619–92) and their repudiation of neo-Confucianism, led me to look again at the neo- and earlier Confucianism Zhou was meant to have rejected. In fact he did no such thing, but the synthesis of both a form of Confucianism and the pragmatism of Gu and Wang goes a long way to explaining, at least partly, modern Chinese political behaviour and the thought behind apparently gnomic pronouncements.

For a long time I thought I had found a degree of personal affiliation with a secular Buddhism. I now find this somewhat more problematic than I had assumed. As with the Upanishads, I cannot appreciate the various sutras. The notion of secular compassion and tolerance was simply attractive in itself. There is a link here obviously to my ambivalence regarding Tibetan Buddhism. Art was the most sympathetic entry-point for me to that, and Marylin M. Rhie and Robert A.F. Thurman's *The Sacred Art of Tibet*[9] gave very helpful commentaries and histories as well as reproductions of artworks. Similarly, the martial arts have been a means to enter Buddhism in action. Eugen Herrigel's *Zen in the Art of Archery*[10] gave a brief but articulate rendition of applied Zen, but I confess my reading has always been patchy (even if, by some counts, patchily extensive) and my teachers have had to exercise unremitting patience with me.

I want to conclude by indicating two other areas of engagement, or attempts at engagement. I have been reading the Quran for many of my adult years, but I began reading the Bible and

8. London: Macmillan, 1996.
9. London: Thames & Hudson, 1991.
10. London: Routledge & Kegan Paul, 1953.

other Christian works from childhood. I count some three times through the Bible as a whole and seven times through the New Testament. Even as a child it was easy to recognise the discrepancies in the four Gospel accounts. As a young man I readily noticed the clear distinctions between a Pauline New Testament and a Johannine New Testament. I fell very much into the camp of John. My first university teachers discovered the Gnostic Gospels in the late 1960s and early 1970s and would pass on their editions to me, but it was the publication of Elaine Pagels's *The Gnostic Gospels*[11] that gave me a truly alternative Christian view, one that tied me into Hellenic, other Middle Eastern and Zoroastrian thought. To that extent Tarn and Griffith were right: Hellenism's reach gave rise to the preconditions for Christianity. Where they were wrong was underestimating just how many strands of thought and belief in the vast Hellenic outreach wrote and thought themselves back into Hellenism, into the Roman Empire, and into a major strand of Christianity that was later suppressed in the Church's power struggles – leaving John as the sole official alternative to the fussy Pharisee-like strictures of Paul. It seemed to me that the wrong side of the Christian struggles triumphed. The openness of Gnostic thought, its likeness to its influences, its mystical cosmopolitanism and its feminism provided a brief template for another 'what if?' and 'why not?' series of questions.

In this book I have tried to give some examples of contemporary African thought. I have done this mostly by referring to the incredibly rich literary output of Africa. I have many people to thank for their encouragement and almost insistence that I should spend time investigating African literature, most recently Ranka Primorac, so I should conclude this short essay by indicating her deep study of Zimbabwean literature, *The*

11. New York: Random House, 1979.

Place of Tears.[12] I am grateful to her and to all those I have mentioned above – more so than my often surly nature might lead them to suppose.

For the readers of this book I hope I have laid out some key animations and also expressed honestly what I feel are my key limitations. They will undoubtedly uncover many others. For those I apologise. I especially apologise if some of my sweeping summations offend. All I can indicate, and they are imperfect in themselves, are some more 'academic' efforts to express myself in years gone by. These contributions have, I should note, made me a curiosity in the discipline of International Relations. 'That's Stephen at it again.' I am grateful to my colleagues for their fond scepticism. They were always helpful as well as sceptical. I hope I can make more than a debating point here, that world events which we currently find hard to understand – Iran, the rise of Islam, suicide bombings, terrorism, the flexing of Chinese muscle in unpredictable ways – do suggest that we should all have been looking at the foundations in thought of these things many years earlier. Better scholars than I might have made understanding less difficult.

I hope also that others can make such investigations 'fun'. The world does not have to be a soberly bitter place of antagonisms, thoughtful or otherwise. Moving from one certainty to a multiplicity of them can be a joyous exploration. It was men and women who sat down and thought and wrote, often with delirious smiles on their faces. In that regard let me thank Hutan Ashrafian. Our dinner colleagues have more than once looked on bemusedly as we made one ridiculous Zoroastrian joke after another. 'When will it all end?' they seemed to think, while catching the spirit and pitching in. Well, never, I hope.

---

12. London: I.B. Tauris, 2006.

Lester Crook, Michael Dwyer, Amber Older, Katy Crofton, Talat Halman and Ranka Primorac all read the manuscript of this book, or parts of it, at various stages of its preparation. My thanks to all of them for their helpful and perceptive comments. Vivienne Jabri has, throughout our parallel academic careers, supported my work even when our colleagues thought it unrelated to the concerns of International Relations. My thanks to my editor at Zed, Ellen Hallsworth, who was always enthusiastic and helpful. Only I am to blame for the finished book.

Select bibliography of Stephen Chan's related writing

'China's Foreign Policy and Africa: The Rise and Fall of China's Three Worlds Theory', *The Round Table* 296, 1985.

'Anthropological Diplomacy – A New Perspective to International Relations', *India Quarterly*, vol. 61, no. 1, 1985.

'Small Revolutions and the Study of International Relations: A Note on the Problematic of Affiliation', *Political Science*, vol. 43, no. 2, 1991.

Kaunda and Southern Africa: Image and Reality in Foreign Policy, London: I.B. Tauris, 1992.

'A Summer Polemic: Revolution, Rebellion and Romance – Some Notes Towards the Resacralisation of IR', *Paradigms*, vol. 7, no. 1, 1993.

'Culture and Absent Epistemologies in the International Relations Discipline', *Theoria* 81/2, 1993.

'Cultural and Linguistic Reductionisms and a New Historical Sociology for International Relations', *Millennium*, vol. 22, no. 3, 1993.

Renegade States: The Evolution of Revolutionary Foreign Policy, ed. with Andrew J. Williams, Manchester: Manchester University Press, 1994.

'Beyond the North-west: Africa and the East', in A.J.R. Groom and Margot Light, eds, *Contemporary International Relations: A Guide to Theory*, London: Pinter, 1994.

Towards a Multicultural Roshamon Paradigm in International Relations, Tampere: Tampere Peace Research Institute, 1996.

'Seven Types of Ambiguity in Western International Relations Theory and Painful Steps to Right Ethics', *Theoria* 89, 1997.

'Too Neat and Under-Thought a World Order: Huntington and Civilisations', exchange with Samuel P. Huntington, *Millennium*, vol. 26, no. 1, 1997.

'Redefining the Third World for a New Millennium: An Aching Towards Subjectivity', in Lloyd Pettiford and Nana Poku, eds, *Redefining the Third World*, London: Macmillan, 1998.

'A Story Beyond Telos: Redeeming the Shield of Achilles for a Realism of Rights in IR', *Millennium*, vol. 28, no. 1, 1999.

'Aspirations and Absent Methodologies in Universalism: Towards a Multicultural Normative Theory', in Jan-Stefan Fritz and Maria Lensu, eds, *Value Pluralism, Normative Theory and International Relations*, London: Macmillan, 1999.

'The Warlord and Global Order', in Paul B. Rich, ed., *Warlords in International Relations*, London: Macmillan, 1999.

'Typologies towards an Unchained Medley: Against the Gentrification of Discourse in International Relations', in Vivienne Jabri and Eleonore O'Gorman, eds, *Women, Culture and International Relations*, Boulder CO: Lynne Rienner, 1999.

'Rorty as Shadow Warrior: Hans Kung and a Global Ethic', *Review of International Studies*, vol. 25, no. 3, 1999.

'Writing Sacral IR: An Excavation Involving Kung, Eliade and Illiterate Buddhism', *Millennium*, vol. 29, no. 3, 2000.

'The Construction and Export of Culture as Artefact: The Case of Japanese Martial Arts', *Body & Society*, vol. 6, no. 1, 2000.

The Zen of International Relations, ed. with Peter Mandaville and Roland Bleiker, London: Palgrave, 2001.

Composing Africa: Civil Society and Its Discontents, Tampere: Tampere Peace Research Institute, 2002.

'The Performativity of Death: Yukio Mishima and a Fusion for International Relations', *Borderlands*, vol. 2, no. 2, 2003.

'A New Triptych for International Relations in the 21st Century: Beyond Waltz and beyond Lacan's Antigone, with a Note on the Falun Gong of China', *Global Society*, vol. 17, no. 2, 2003.

'A Problem for IR: How Shall We Narrate the Saga of Bestial Man?', *Global Society*, vol. 17, no. 4, 2003.

Robert Mugabe: A Life of Power and Violence, Ann Arbor: University of Michigan Press, 2003.

'The Imagination of Land and the Reality of Seizure: Zimbabwe and Complex Reinvention', with Ranka Primorac, *Columbia University Journal of International Affairs*, vol. 57, no. 2, 2004.

Out of Evil: New International Politics and Old Doctrines of War, Ann Arbor: University of Michigan Press, 2005.

'Trauma and the Idea of Unreconciled Citizenship in Zimbabwe: The Novels of Vera and Kanengoni', *Third World Quarterly*, vol. 26, no. 2, 2005.

'Fanon: The Octogenarian of International Revenge, and the Suicide Bomber of Today', *Cooperation and Conflict*, vol. 42, no. 2, 2008.

'After the Order to Civilization: Weightless International Relations and the Burden of Unreduced Responsibility', *Interventions*, vol. 10, no. 2, 2008.

Index